Equipping Learners with Computer Science and Technological Skills

Equipping Learners with Computer Science and Technological Skills

Edited by:
Adele Kuzmiakova

ARCLER
PRESS

www.arclerpress.com

Equipping Learners with Computer Science and Technological Skills

Adele Kuzmiakova

Arcler Press
224 Shoreacres Road
Burlington, ON L7L 2H2
Canada
www.arclerpress.com
Email: orders@arclereducation.com

ISBN: 978-1-77407-742-9 (Hardcover)

ABOUT THE EDITOR

Adele Kuzmiakova is a computational engineer focusing on solving problems in machine learning, deep learning, and computer vision. Adele attended Cornell University in New York, United States for her undergraduate studies. She studied engineering with a focus on applied math. While at Cornell, she developed close relationships with professors, which enabled her to get involved in academic research to get hands-on experience with solving computational problems. She was also selected to be Accel Roundtable on Entrepreneurship Education (REE) Fellow at Stanford University and spent 3 months working on entrepreneurship projects to get a taste of entrepreneurship and high-growth ventures in engineering and life sciences. The program culminated in giving a presentation on the startup technology and was judged by Stanford faculty and entrepreneurship experts in Silicon Valley. After graduating from Cornell, Adele worked as a data scientist at Swiss Federal Institute of Technology in Lausanne, Switzerland where she focused on developing algorithms and graphical models to analyze chemical pathways in the atmosphere. Adele also pursued graduate studies at Stanford University in the United States where she entered as a recipient of American Association of University Women International Fellowship. The Fellowship enabled her to focus on tackling important research problems in machine learning and computer vision. Some research problems she worked on at Stanford include detecting air pollution from outdoor public webcam images. Specifically, she modified and set up a variety of pre-trained architectures, such as DehazeNet, VGG, and ResNet, on public webcam images to evaluate their ability to predict air quality based on the degree of haze on pictures. Other deep learning problems Adele worked on include investigating the promise of second-order optimizers in deep learning and using neural networks to predict sequences of data in energy consumption. Adele also places an emphasis on continual education and served as a Student Leader in PyTorch scholarship challenge organized by Udacity. Her roles as the Student Leader were helping students debug their code to train neural networks with PyTorch and providing mentorship on technical and career aspects. Her hobbies include skiing, playing tennis, cooking, and meeting new people.

TABLE OF CONTENTS

LIST OF FIGURES

LIST OF ABBREVIATIONS

AMP	Adequacy of Manipulative Skills
C	Correctness
CAI	Computer-Assisted Instruction
CAL	Computer-Assisted Learning
CAS	Creation of Appropriate Situation
CB	Clearing the Board
CC	Comparing and Contrasting
CCTV	Closed Circuit Television
CGL	Computer-Guided Learning
CL	Cognitive Link
CSF	Changes in Sensory Focus
CSP	Changes in Patterns of Speech
ECP	Eye Contact with Pupils
GPS	Global Positioning System
HCI	Human-Computer Interface
HHD	Hard Disk Drive
HMP	Highlighting Main Points
ILL	Illustrations
L	Legibility
MR	Meaningful Repetition
NMS	Network Modeling and Simulation
NNVR	Nonverbal Reinforcement
OMR	Optical Mark Reading
PM	Pupil Movement
PPP	Point-To-Point Protocol
PT	People Talk
PVR	Positive Verbal Reinforcement

SA	Size and Alignment
SAL	Significant Aspects of Learning
SOP	Sequential Order of Presentation
SSD	Steady State Drive
STAG	Stanford Teacher Competency Appraisal Guide
T.G	Teacher Gesture
T.M	Teacher Movement
TAT	Thematic Apperception Test
US	Utilization of Space
W.P.A.B	Writing Pupil Answer on The Blackboard

PREFACE

With the advent of the digital computer in the latter part of the 20th century, it arrived a whole new branch of sciences, namely computer science. A program which is the set of directions that this digital computer uses is the work and sometimes playground of a computer scientist. In a sense, computer science can be broadly defined as the study of the dynamics of data interaction usually represented in the form of programs. It is one of the disciplines that fall under the general family of computing. It is safe to assume that information technology and computer science roles are growing faster than any other profession. Career opportunities are so high that with a specific type and level of skill would virtually mark you as self-employed. Two out of the top five richest people in the world forged their wealth almost solely in this vibrant arena. The almost astronomical advances in the field make computer science a difficult field to keep up with. During the 1950s, computer scientists worked either in very large corporations or in scientific computer science research laboratories. However, today, a few hundred dollars and a good understanding of a computer can virtually deem you a computer scientist. The current trends in computer science today include robotics and artificial intelligence, data analytics, computer-based education systems, bioinformatics, cybersecurity, and many more. Long-term goals in computer science research today include the invention of devices that operate using an element of human intelligence and also the reinvention of systems that can store, retrieve and transmit extremely large amounts of data.

Therefore, the process of equipping learners with computer science and technological skills is an important value, no doubt. This volume is of great value on numerous levels. These include those individuals that want to explore different fields related to computer science, those researchers that are already doing technological studies, ultimately, this volume offers important insights for different audiences. This volume was compiled with utmost scrutiny of different journals, articles, research, and a wide array of computer science and technological books. The main objective of preparing this volume was to actually offer a base knowledge in the field of computer science and technology regarding learners' competence. This volume is more informative to reach a wider public. It can be used by a wide range of readers who are directly or indirectly interested in computer science and technology, especially in teaching and learning.

The volume has 10 chapters, and each chapter discusses about a specific topic: Chapter 1 is all about a teacher's guide to teaching computer science; Chapter 2 is about the aims and objectives of teaching computer science and technology; Chapter 3 discusses about applying micro-teaching in computer science and technology; Chapter 4 discusses about methods and tactics of teaching computing and computer science aided instruction; Chapter 5 presents information about instructional aids in teaching computer science and technology; Chapter 6 discusses about latest trends in information technology; Chapter 7 offers detailed information about the use of ICT in teaching computer science; Chapter 8 offer information on evaluation of computer science; Chapter 9 discusses about computer science education in developing countries; and lastly, Chapter 10 is all about role of government in computer and technological education.

These 10 chapters were extensively prepared for the readers with more emphasis on the easiness of the content in order to make the volume clear and understandable to all readers.

It is my hope and trust that this volume will make a valuable contribution towards nurturing many to ride the wave of collaboration in equipping learners with computer science and technological skills.

Chapter 1 A Teacher's Guide to Teaching Computer Science

CONTENTS

1.1. INTRODUCTION

Due to the advancements in the education sector globally, there is a need to incorporate computer science and technology in learning. This chapter was prepared to offer vital guidelines on how to teach computer science in schools.

1.2. SIGNIFICANT ASPECTS OF LEARNING COMPUTER SCIENCE

These are themes that are comprehensive all through the learning outcomes of certain individuals. They are called outcomes and experiences. There are three main aspects of learning. These include:

- Being able to understand the world by using thinking that is computational (SAL-1) – being able to achieve this can help in the application of this information while utilizing technology and languages.
- Being able to understand and analyze technology that is used in computing (SAL-2) – so as to be able to design and build using computer science tools, it is important to understand the technology and programming languages used in computing.
- Being able to design, build, and test solutions that are used in computing (SAL-3) – this involves utilizing information that is based on technology and concepts in designing, building, and testing.

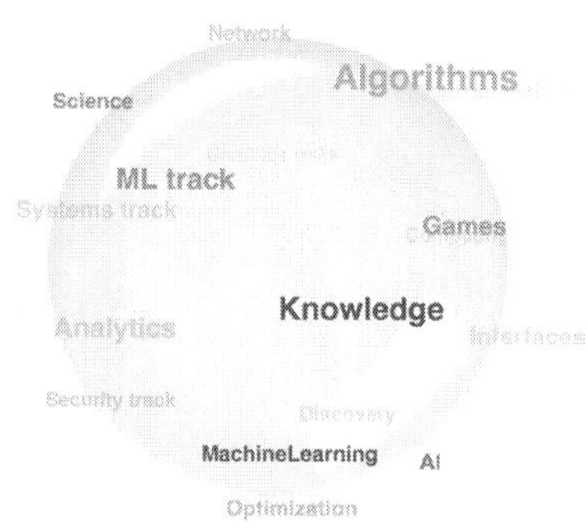

Figure 1.1. *Problem-solving is one of the most important computer skills that one must have.*

Source: https://www.cs.rutgers.edu/graduate/ms-program-in-computer-science.

These significant aspects of learning are designed in a manner that allows teachers to see the main stages of development when it comes to learning the concepts that are used in computing (Singh, 2008). This helps the instructors in the identification and correcting of misconceptions that the students may have. The significant aspects of learning don't deal mainly with the development of programs that are considered cool, in comparison to the computer science approaches that are traditional. They help in explaining the fact that before a computer can perform any functions that we desire (SAL-3), there is a requirement for the full comprehension of how the computers are told to perform certain actions (SAL-2), and also the tasks that the computer is able to perform (SAL-1).

These aspects work together. It is important to understand the definition of these aspects. Here are the definitions below:

Being able to understand the world using thinking that is computational: This is the first aspect and it deals with the theory of computer science. These computer science concepts that are theoretical involve the attributes of processing information, how information is identified, classification and also being able to see patterns. It involves being able to understand the attributes and the essence of information and processes. This can be achieved by teaching using learning tasks that are fun and active in relation to topics of computer science. These tasks should be done using a computer. It should be done while involving the students in discussions that are structured (Singh, 2008).

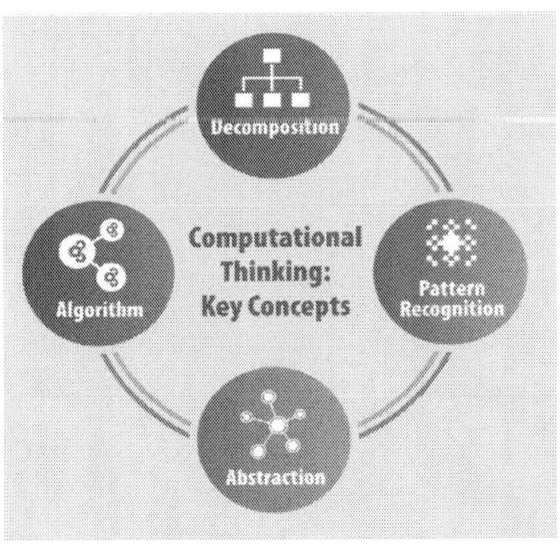

Figure 1.2. Some major aspects *of computational thinking.*

Source: https://cspathshala.org/2017/10/25/computational-thinking-curriculum/.

There is a need to focus on the recognition of computational thinking as it pertains to every-day world. An example might include calculating the fastest route from a child's home to his or her school. This enables the students to identify common patterns and steps when calculating possible options. Additionally, the students are able to evaluate different pros and cons of each computational solution. This involves being able to consider whether certain jobs can be done at the same time and compare the efficiency and complexity arguments. The students are then able to perform identification and classification of information

Being able to understand and analyze technology that is used for computing: This aspect ensures that the students have a proper understanding of the mechanisms of computers, and the programs that keep them running, that have been hidden. It promotes the exploration of certain languages that are utilized in the representation of information and processes. Some used by the users and others by the computers.

This significant aspect of learning allows the students to know how to interpret programming code and describe its behavior, as per SAL-1 outcomes. An example of this includes students being able to read certain segments of the code and make predictions on how they will function when they are put to work. The students are then able to have this learning experience as well as exploration on the many ways in which information is represented, and how this information undergoes storage and manipulation in the system if computing (Singh, 2008).

Computing systems are defined using programming languages. SAL-2 helps in explaining how systems in other computers function, also inclusive of the features of a computer, how networked computers are configured, and the software systems.

Being able to design, build and test computer solutions: This aspect involves being able to take the concepts and information that has been comprehended from the first two aspects and using them to make applications. Students are able to come up with solutions, by making designs, building and doing tests on solutions on a computer, or by being able to write a process that is computational on a piece of paper. This allows them to gain information on the process of modeling as well as information from the world as we know it today in programs, and what enables a model that is perfect to make representations or in solving certain problems. The students get to make creations of information that is represented.

Figure 1.3. *This involves creating algorithms that tell the computer what to do. Students require this skill and it is after they have learned the others that they will be able to use this.*

Source: https://www.lanner-america.com/blog/5-examples-edge-computing-solutions-use-today/.

The students are able to utilize the expertise in language to create operations that have been described appropriately. This will allow other people to use these computer programs. A good example is a computer program to describe an operation. The students learn reading, writing, and translation of different representations. This includes statements that are written in English, representations of plans, and the computer codes. Despite the fact that solutions are easily created in many ways, there is an expectation of all students to go through the experience of creation of many different solutions on the computer. This allows the students to see that the computer makes sure it causes implementation of what the students have been able to write, and also allows them to practice how to debug.

Subjects running through the Significant Aspects of Learning: Information and Process: Being able to run through the three aspects means understanding the notion of information and processes. Computers are mainly gadgets that help with carrying out and manipulating various operations. It is not shocking that everything we do in our day to day functions, such as video calls, online banking, playing games on the computer, are all operations designed by a computer program. Therefore, it is important to ensure the development of proper comprehension on operations and information, so as to fully comprehend computer science and be able to think in a computational manner (Barton, 2004).

A computer system does not make decisions on its own, including the decisions on what to do and what to manipulate. There is a need for certain instructions that will tell the computer what it needs to do. These instructions are found in a computer program. They are written in a language that is used to program. These languages are not in any way similar to what we hear or see daily. It is important to know that they are different, by taking the time to understand the language extensively, so as to be able to ensure reading and comprehension of what the written programs means.

This comprehension will allow the student to predict what the computer will be able to do before it is done, as well as have knowledge on the information that the program will manipulate due to the instructions that have been set. So as to be able to achieve this, it is important to have an understanding on the different instructions, and how they affect the computer. This is quite complicated because the operations that are found within the computer are out of our reach. It is not possible to view what is happening as it happens inside the computer, and this means that the reliance is on the models that are mental so as to know and grasp what is happening (Woollard, 2007).

Figure 1.4. *It is important to fully understand the three aspects so as to understand how the computer processes information.*

Source: https://thaiembdc.org/2019/08/19/thai-primary-schools-start-teaching-coding-to-kids/.

Despite these difficulties and a large number of various devices that are used for computing, they are quite the same, and therefore, learning the main concepts is very beneficial. The second significant aspect of learning deals with how the mixture of languages that need to be grasped, their representation, as well are how they affect the computers that they work in.

The main focus of the computing courses is seen in the third significant aspect of learning. This involves being able to take a certain task and write a program that allows the computer to ensure that the task is solved. This aspect covers how the programs are created to ensure the solving of problems, as well as how the determination is done of knowing if they are correct, and if not, how they are fixed.

Despite the fact that the discussion so far has mainly been about computers and languages that are used to program, the main aspect is much larger. This same information on the main aspects as well as the expertise that is needed also deals with systems of the web, networks that are found digitally, the systems if the mobile, etc. They all utilize different forms of operations and data and they also all have instructional languages. Most of the skills and aspects that are understood are able to be used in many other different contexts of computer science. Even when computers are not directly involved, there are many different complex aspects on life today that use these aspects (Singh, 2008).

1.3. HOW THE CONCEPTS PROGRESS

1.3.1. Significant Aspects of Learning (SAL)

The significant aspects of learning have proven to provide the teachers with a way to organize the best way for the students to learn the concepts of computing. There is a wide range of computing concepts that are individual, and they have undergone incorporation into the framework of progression.

How information concepts progress in SAL-1: Being able to understand the world through thinking in a computational manner.

- Early level: The students are able to classify and group patterns into simpler categories. For example, it is possible to group books based on their topic, size, color, etc. The students are also able to make identification of different sequences in structures and data. The students are also able to make identifications of the start and end of operations as well as those that occur in between. An example of this includes being able to give directions to a certain place that is familiar.
- First level: The students are able to make classifications on the basis of a number of categories. They have a wide variety of methods to perform a collection of data and also grouping this

information in a way that is logical and well organized, by using methods that they have created, or those created by others. This makes then able to make classifications and decide on things based on thinking in a logical manner. The students are also able to make demonstrations on their what they know about the different operations by following rules that are written in a recipe, or comprehending what they need to do when cleaning a room. The students make constructions of a set of instructions on how to find a clue in a treasure hunt, ways to get to certain locations, etc. They are able to make descriptions of how each step may affect the computer. The students have the opportunity to interpret certain instructions and make predictions on how they will work.

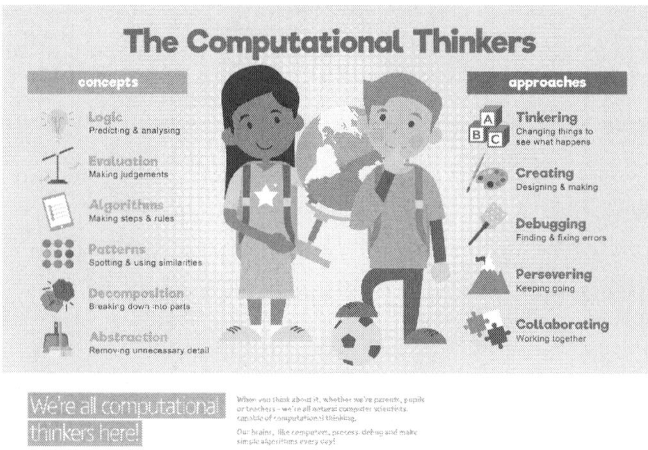

Figure 1.5. *Students are encouraged to use computational thinking to be able to recognize patterns and even predict how an algorithm will affect the computer.*

Source: https://callysto.ca/computational-thinking-101/.

The students are able to make identifications on how the instruction of certain operations may be similar or different. They are able to know the sequences that are the same, repetitive or fairly similar. The students are able to make descriptions on how the sequences may be the same.

- Second Level: The students know how to sort information and create efficient algorithms to analyze patterns. Additionally, the students are capable of arranging data into meaningful groups. They can also identify whether the operations consist of one pattern or a combination of many patterns that have been organized in a parallel manner. The students learn how to make predictions on how the operations work or make identifications of when the operation cannot be predicted. The students are able to find out if the sequences are repetitive and fixed, or based on a certain condition. They will be able to see sequences when it comes to solving problems as well as the identification of answers to the problems that have been used initially. Later on, the students are able to use SAL-3 for the creation of games, by using segments of codes that had been used before for functions that are different from the previous ones. They will be able to make evaluations on various answers to problems and check on them to see how fast and efficient they are.

How languages progress in SAL-2: Being able to understand and analyze computing technology.

- Early Level: The students are able to comprehend how the symbols that are used in the creation of instructions related to how the computer behaves after it has followed the set of instructions it has been given, when utilizing simple robots. The main cognitive progression is being able to see that being able to press a button to ensure that the robot moves immediately differs from the comprehension of an arrow button as an instruction that will lead to a behavior that has been defined later on in its time. The student is then also supposed to be able to comprehend a pattern of instructions when a symbolic language that is simple is used, such as arrows that have been shown on a paper. They are also supposed to know how to make predictions of what the robot is intending to do after it has gotten the set of rules it needs to follow.
- First Level: Student that do not have literacy skills for reading instructions that are provided textually are still able to make explorations of concepts of computing by using pictures instead of texts due to the ability to use a block environment that is based on icons, such as The Foos. They allow for the students to have more confidence when it comes to comprehension of the exact meaning of the specific individual blocks. An example of this includes how an instruction can affect the visual display when running a program. This comprehension of the definition is

also supposed to have the incorporation of being able to run the entire program, with the set of rules being followed to the latter according to how the blocks of the program are laid out. This involves comprehending how the specific block of rules have an effect on the operation of the world cumulatively. This includes the updating of the visual display.

- Second level: Utilizing development environments that are based on blocks, such as Scratch, allows the students to make explanations of the definitions of programs that are complex, which also involves blocks that are used to select and repeat. They get to comprehend that it is possible to use variables to make changes as a program is running through each block that is providing instructions. This allows them to make predictions on what happens when the program is running.

How languages progress in SAL-3: Being able to design, build and test computing solutions.

- Early level: The students get to learn how the behaviors are modeled in a robot or characters of a computer, by utilizing a pattern of instructions that are simple. For example, being able to make a floor robot model the behavior of being able to move in the direction of a box with a set of rules such as "turning right," "moving ahead," etc. In general, the students are supposed to know how to choose where the robot will move to, make designs of a pattern of rules that will allow the robot to head for the direction set, and also be able to input those rules and test if they are able to perform the desired function. If this end state is not a state that was planned, learners should identify and correct errors in their set of instructions. It is evident that the student will not be able to design and build the solutions for computing without knowledge on the important nature of the sequential process (SAL-1) and how the robot is affected by the running of the program step by step (SAL-2). Despite the fact that all the three aspects may seem easy in the examples that have been given, it is important to ensure that the students fully understand these aspects before they move on to concepts that are much more complicated.
- First level: In this section, systems and languages such as Scratch are utilized in the designing of programs that help in fulfilling tasks that are much more sophisticated and abstract in comparison to

making commands in movements. Although, it is still important to use the language skills of computing that are achieved in SAL-2, so as to be able to succeed in the designing of processes that are abstract.

- Second level: At this stage the students should be able to comprehend that there are various methods of being able to achieve similar outcomes, and also that these outcomes may be much better than the other ones. The students need to have seen this in the other Significant Aspects of Learning through the exploration of concepts to do with effectiveness and speed. The students get to comprehend how the definition of programming constructs such as repetitiveness and the conditions relate to how these can be utilized in achieving behaviors that are desirable when running a program.

1.4. EXPERIENCES AND OUTCOMES

1.4.1. SAL-1: Being Able to Use Computational Thinking to Understand the World

Early Level: It is important for the student to be able to explore processes of thinking that are computational, and they should be involved in the various daily tasks, as well as be able to identify sequences in certain structures as well as data.

The benchmark for this is the following:

- The student should have the ability to make identifications and sequence the major steps that occur in a task that is done daily, so as to develop an algorithm.
- The student should also be able to make classifications of structures and group them into simple categories.
- The student should be able to identify sequences, differences, and similarities in structures or even data such as their size, color, and other ways in which they are related.

First level: This ensures that one is able to make an exploration and comments when it comes to the processes around them, by using the core concepts of computational thinking, as well as being able to organize data in a manner that is logical.

The benchmark for this is the following:

- The student should have the ability to follow a sequence of an algorithm from situations that are seen every day.
- The student should be able to make identifications of steps in a sequence and make descriptions of how each step works.
- The student should also be able to decide by thinking logically.
- He/she should be able to collect, group and order data in a manner that is logical and organized, based on set criteria.

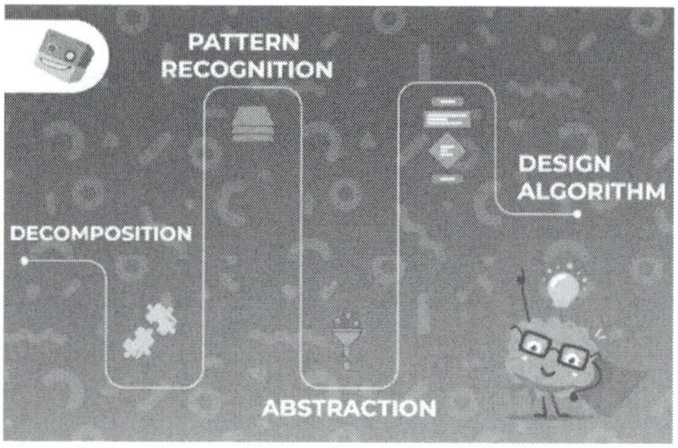

Figure 1.6. *There are three main aspects of computational thinking: decomposition, pattern recognition, abstraction and designing an algorithm.*

Source: https://robogarden.ca/blog/a-traditional-approach-to-computational-thinking-in-daily-life.

Second level: There should be an understanding of the processes in certain computational operations, as well as their outcomes. One should be able to structure the items of information that are related.

The benchmark for this is:

- The student should be able to make comparisons on certain activities that have one sequence of steps and those that have many parallel steps.
- The student should make identifications of algorithms that have a group of instructions that have been repeated in a fixed manner, or in a loop, until they meet the condition.
- The student should identify processes that cannot be predicted due to its random element.
- The student should utilize sets of instructions that have been recognized to deal with daily tasks.

1.4.2. SAL-2: Being Able to Understand and Analyze Computing Technology

Early level: The ability to comprehend that computing technology is controlled by sequences of instructions. In addition, also being able to experiment using and also identifying uses of the various technology for computing.

The benchmark for this is:

- The student is able to demonstrate a comprehension of the manner in which symbols are used for the representation of processes and data.
- The student should be able to predict what the computer will do when a certain sequence is presented to it.
- The student learns to identify the computing devices found around them.

First level: There is a need to understand the rules of a visual programming language and make predictions for the outcome of any program that has been written using the language. In addition, the students need to know how information is processed by a computer.

The benchmark for this is:

- The student should demonstrate that one comprehends the definition of the specific instructions when using programming languages that are visual.
- The student should make explanations and predictions on how the program will function while running.

Second level: One should be able to give explanations on the main concepts of the programming language using the technical language. There is also a need to understand the manner in which information is stored.

The benchmark for this is:

- The student should be able to explain what the individual instructions mean in a visual programming language.
- The student should make predictions on how certain programs in the visual programming language will work when running.
- The student should explain and predict how the activities that are parallel will work.
- The student should make demonstrations on the comprehension that all computer information is written in binary.

- The student should make descriptions on what the processor, memory, and storage are supposed to do, and how they are related.
- The student should understand how network connections are made and what there are used for.

1.4.3. SAL-3: Being Able to Design, Build and Test Computing Solutions

Early level: The student should be able to develop a set of rules that can be run on programmable devices.

The benchmark for this is:

- The student should design a sequence of an algorithm, that is simple, for devices that can be programmed, so that they can carry out tasks.
- The student should identify and correct any problems that may occur in the program.

First level: The student should be able to make a demonstration on the various ways of solving problems, through the building of programs that are simple, for carrying out certain tasks, with a language that is appropriate.

The benchmark for this is:

- The student should be able to simplify issues by dealing with them in smaller parts that can be managed easily.
- The student should construct a set of instructions that can be used in solving tasks, as well as in explaining the output that is expected from each set.
- The student should create programs that can carry out certain activities in a visual programming language.
- The student should also be able to identify when the set of instructions are not working appropriately, and also be able to correct the errors.
- The student should make evaluations on solutions and make suggestions on how to improve them.

Figure 1.7. *Students should be able to use programming languages to create programs that work as computing solutions.*

Source: https://www.slideshare.net/Infostreaminc/cloud-computing-solutions-implementation.

Second level: The student should be able to make creations, developments, and evaluations on the solutions of computing when there is a challenge in designing.

The benchmark for this is:

- The student should be able to create a program in a visual programming language, that involves a variable and repetition that is conditional.
- They should also be able to identify sequences in solving of problems, and also make use of the solutions that were previously provided, appropriately.
- He/she should also be able to identify any parts that have not been matched well, between the description of the task and the solution that is being programmed, and also state how it should be fixed.

1.5. THE GUIDE TO TEACH THE OUTCOMES AND EXPERIENCES

1.5.1. Early Level

SAL- 1

- Process: The students should be able to make identifications on of all the steps of the process, through being aware on the tasks and objects that they see every day. They get to comprehend the causes and effects as they see the sequences transforming a structure from start to end. As the students make different experiments, they are able to note the specific steps that help in providing the end state that is desired. The teacher should find a different example of how to illustrate the changing of different states, for example, water.

- Information: The students can make identifications on the main characteristics of certain objects, such as size, etc. They can also note how the structures are similar and different, as well as how they relate. There can also be the identification of sequences in objects. The students get to gain knowledge in the identification of the basic characteristics of certain objects, as well as classifying them. The teacher can ask the student to make comparisons on the characteristics of the objects. The teacher should note if the student chose to classify according to color or size. The teacher needs to make sure that the student is well aware that there are many different ways to classify objects, due to their many attributes. The students should be asked to think about these many classifications.

SAL- 2:

- Process: The students can do some reading and understanding of the different ways to represent simple processes, when they read from the various representations, such as a flow diagram.
- Information: They can also comprehend physical representations that are simple so as to be able to create deductions about the world as it is right now from these representations.
- Computing technology: The students need to appreciate their environment with many different computing devices that help with performing useful activities.

The students are able to utilize various representations. They can then make predictions on how the toy robot would function if it is given that set of instructions. This can be done as a simulation as well, with another student playing the part of the robot, in case there is no access to one. The students can also comprehend the easy ways to display information and utilize this for reasoning about their environment. The students should be introduced to an object that is used daily, with computer technology that has been embedded.

SAL- 3:

The students are able to comprehend the manner in which a short sequence of instructions that are precise can undergo interpretation by a computer. They also have the ability to comprehend the difference between an instruction sequence that is correct, and one that is incorrect. The students should be able to fix any issues in the instructions they create.

At this level, the main focus is being able to learn instructions that are simple. They should be able to make corrections on instructions that contain errors when the robot does not respond to what they wanted it to do. Despite the fact that Beebots have been used for a number of years in primary schools, they do not have instructions that are visible to the students. They are deep inside the bot. There is, however, an alternative called Ozobot, which functions by following a lime that has been illustrated on a surface, and perform various functions when the color of the line changes.

Figure 1.8. *Above is an image of a Beebot that is used in primary schools to teach commands.*

Source: https://www.robot-advance.com/EN/art-beebot-classroom-pack-1508.htm.

The instructions for the Ozobot normally have undergone encoding on a surface. The students should be encouraged by the teacher to understand the rules and make predictions on the actions the bot will perform. This bot can be used in the first three levels. Apart from the Ozobot, there are also other bots that can be used, such as Ollie, Dot, etc. Most of the other various ones in the shops have block interface controlling systems on a tablet or computer application. This allows the student to follow the steps as they are carried out by the bot. Some of these bots can be controlled in many different ways. These include using lines that have been drawn using the draw tool, commands that are direct, or applications that are based on blocks.

For the schools that are not able to but these bots, due to their high costs, there are applications that have been developed to allow the students to have the same experience. There are also some of these bots that have an emulator on the web. In addition to all this, it is possible to have a board game available as well, such as Robot Turtle.

1.5.2. First Level

SAL- 1:

- Process: The students are able to make identifications and utilize the concepts of controlling flow, of sequences, selections, and repetitions. They are supposed to familiarize with this sequence from the Early level, as sequential instructions. The students are able to understand sequences that are simplified, and they will also be carrying out the role that they have been given in a certain operation. The students will have the ability to make demonstrations of their knowledge on the operations by their ability to follow instructions, no matter how small the role is, even just sweeping the class. They can also be given work to identify and make descriptions of the steps that are being carried out in a certain game. The students can also be given a couple of processes that have steps, so as to make identifications of how they are similar and how they differ. They can also use the same processes to note for any repetitive sequences, identical patterns, and similar steps.
- Information: The students will start to gain an understanding for logical constructs that are much more complicated, so as to make groupings of objects that are found in the real world, or also following instructions that are verbal that need them to make certain decisions. To achieve this, they can use OR, AND NOT to follow instructions that are logical.

SAL- 2:

- Process: The students should be able to achieve reading, understanding, and explaining of representations of operations that have been expressed in the language used for programming, while incorporating repetition that is fixed, selection, and control flow elements of sequence. The students should comprehend how the conditions can be utilized for making decisions between sequences of steps that are alternative.
- Information: The students can comprehend images that show illustrations of important aspects of information. Diagrams and Tables can be added into the lesson as a manner of making representation of information about objects that have been collected.
- Computing technology: The students should know about the various input devices, such as the keyboard, mouse, and various output devices. This allows them to understand the process concepts together with whatever is happening inside the computer.

Figure 1.9. *Scratch is programming language that is used in teaching computer science to younger students. Above is its logo.*

Source: https://v4t.pixel-online.org/videogames_view.php?id_videogames=NDg=.

The students can achieve this by reading the blocks that are found in the visual programming language that is based on icons such as Scratch, so as to gain an understanding on what the simple programs do. They are then able to make identifications of any mistakes that are found in the program that has been written in a visual language that is simple. They are then able to comprehend the various types of diagrams that help in displaying information. They can be given diagrams to look at so as to give solutions to the data that has been presented.

The students can also learn on the various output and input devices, so that they are able to understand how information is inputted, processed, and outputted by the computer.

The students should also have an opportunity to make explorations on the different systems of the computer such as mobile phones, so as to also identify the input and output devices that are used. If an old computer is available, the students can be given the opportunity to explore the inside of it. This allows them to make a link on the concepts that are used for programming that they are being taught, and also what happens in the daily use devices.

SAL-3:

The students will begin to comprehend how to effectively utilize programming constructs that are simple, such as repetition, to ensure achievement of the behavior that is desired in a manner that is much more concise.

They get to have an introduction to the ideology that instructions that differ can be utilized for the achievement of similar behaviors and that there are some that may be better than the others.

The students are able to utilize a visual programming language for the creation of programs and animations that are simple. An environment that is based on icons would be very appropriate because they have no reliance on good literacy skills.

For the schools that are able to afford tablet, there are various applications that allow the students to perform programming in a manner that is simple. Scratch Jr is one of these applications that can really help students who prefer to learn using symbols and images instead of texts. The teachers can give the students problems that are more interesting and complicated to do by giving them programs that are partly completed so as to write a code that can add onto the incomplete one.

Bots are an interesting way for the students to learn the development algorithms that are simple. The students that are utilizing the Ozobot have expectations for starting to utilize color codes for programming the bot.

1.5.3. Second Level

SAL-1:

Process: The students can make an identification and description of the characteristics of systems that are simple such as processes that are parallel. The students can play a game that involves physicality where the activities are done in a manner that is parallel. It could be done in a manner that allows the students to compete in completing processes. The students will then be able to have a discussion on how effective the different strategies of the teams are.

Figure 1.10. *Above is an Ozobot which is programmed based on color. It follows the colors and have different actions for any different colors.*

Source: https://www.stem-supplies.com/technology/robotics-and-coding/ozobot-set.

It is possible to carry out more than one activity at a time. They can then be able to make an identification of two activities that may occur at the same time, and how they have an interaction. This is important for the students to gain an awareness on the fact that data can undergo sorting using algorithms in the world right now.

SAL-2:

Process: The students have the ability to read and reason on codes that are much more complex in the visual programming language. They are able to perform these skills by using exercises that involve a pencil and paper, to record the information in a manner that is sequential. They can also use their voice to speak in what they have understood on how programs operate in discussions with their fellow students and teachers.

Information: There are many activities that can be utilized in assisting students to comprehend how different forms of data undergo representation by the computer. These activities are mostly useful in all SAL levels.

Computing technology: The students will have additional knowledge on how the computer networks work. Having this knowledge can allow the students to be aware of the daily uses of communication networks.

SAL-3:

In this level, the students utilize their knowledge and comprehension from the levels before so as to be able to achieve designing and building of solutions for the computational processes, such as games. When using an environment that is based on blocks, it is advisable for the student to begin with animations, utilizing repetition and loops. Thereafter, they should be able to create algorithms with variables so as to make descriptions of control flow processes that are complicated, including handling events. They should also be able to build and make designs of robotics as solutions for computing.

Chapter

2 The Aims and Objectives of Teaching Computer Science and Technology

CONTENTS

2.1. INTRODUCTION

Computer science is the study of computer and the computational systems. It mainly involves the study of computer software. In the study of computer science, the key principal units of study include the following:

- Networks
- Database systems
- Artificial intelligence
- Computer interactions
- Software engineering
- Theory of computing

Computer scientist therefore have the ability to design and analyses logarithms to solve programs and study the performance of computer software. They can also design computer software to carry out certain instructions. A computer network is a set of computers connected together for the purpose of sharing resources. Database systems is the structure and relationship between stored data, a database, users and the hardware. Computer scientists are required to be familiar with these terms and many more (Singh, 2008).

Computer science is a very important concept in our lives because it shapes everything from objects around people to ways in which people communicate, travel, work, and play. Computer science knowledge enabled the emergence of innovation and discoveries that aid individuals in their everyday study. Computer Science knowledge has been used to invent the future by discovering and inventing techniques and technologies that are using complex computing and applications that operate in this work frame are developed.

Computer science can be divided into several fields which can further be divided into several theoretical and practical disciplines. The fields include:

- Computation complexity theory
- Computer graphics
- Programming language theory
- Computer programming
- Human5-computer interaction

These fields are discussed more to get a better understanding of computer science below.

Computation complexity theory is a theory that shows computational problems according to their inherent difficulty and relating these problems to each other (Singh, 2008). A computation problem is a problem that is meant to be solved using a computer by computer programs such as an algorithm. An inherent problem that is a problem that requires significant resources to solve it such as logarithm is a computation problem. A computation problem explores the fundamental properties of computation. Computations complexity theory's main goal is the practical difficulty of solving problems.

Computer graphics is anything involved in creation of images using the computer It may include animated images or drawings or paintings. Painting and drawings are three-dimensional graphics but, in most cases,, the end results are usually two dimensional. Two-dimensional graphics include pixels coordinates and colors. Computer graphics emphasize visual application in real-life (Singh, 2008).

Programming language theory deals with design, implementation, analysis, characterization, and classification of programming languages. Programming language includes the lambda calculus which was developed by Alonzo Church and Stephen Cole Kleene in the year 1930 being among the first computer languages. Programmable language theory makes great use of other mathematical prances which include computation theory or category theory.

Computer programming is the process of designing a computer programmer to perform certain functions. It involves tasks such as analysis, generating algorithms, resource consumptions and implementations of algorithms. Those who study computer programming can get jobs as coders, debugging, integration, maintenance, software architecture, software testing, specification, and documentation. It investigates several aspects of the use of computing language (Singh, 2008).

The aims of teaching computer science include; To produce computer scientists who understand fundamental computational concepts underlying most programming language. When one studies computer science they become computer scientists who have the ability to know several computational concepts which are underlying programming language. The computational concepts are the action of mathematical calculation or the use of computers especially as a subject of research or study. Therefore, computer scientists understand a computer and they can apply the knowledge to use the computer to perform calculations or to use it for study.

Computer scientists gain the knowledge problem-solving techniques using computers. There are problems that a computer has the ability to solve while some problems it cannot solve (Hazzan, Lapidot, & Ragonis, 2015). An undecidable problem that is a problem requiring a yes or a no answer may not be solved by a computer. Examples of these problems include; Kolmogorov complexity, wang tile problem and the halting problem. The halting problem determines if a programmer will finish running. Kolmogorov complexity deals with compressing and the impossibility of perfectly compressing any file. A computer can never solve problems that include, the halting problem where a computer can never be a determinant of when a programmer stops. No program can compress any file making it smaller and it cannot take any given tiles and tell if it will tile the plane.

Figure 2.1. *Computer scientists are able to know the role of programming in the process of developing a software.*

Source: https://www.businessinsider.com/climate-change-and-evolution-science-education-2017-6?IR=T.

Programming is the process of building a computer program to perform a given task. Programming can be used to develop a software. It requires programming languages for software development. The programming languages include; python which is a high-level programming language used for general-purpose programming. Testers use it as debugging and is quite easy in this language, its advantages include; it is portable across operating systems, idly supported, contain user-friendly data structures, object-oriented language and it is easy to use. Another language is the Java, which is a programming language that can be written on any device and can work even on a close platform basis. It is most commonly used to develop applications for mobile phones. Many testers use it due to the ability to use even on cross-platform. Its advantages include, it is platform-independent in both binary and source level. It is user and design-friendly; it is very secure as it can disrupt corruption or errors and it has an automatic garbage collection and memory allocation. Another programming language is Ruby which is a simple programming language that the programmer does not require to have, programming vocabulary or commands. Testing a program designed using Ruby is very easy. The advantages of these programming languages include, it is fast and user-friendly, it is efficient, it consists of simple syntax, has a lot of online tutorials and resources to learn it and it builds web apps very quickly. Another language is the C which is the most difficult programming language. Other programming languages include; LISP, PERL, MATLAB, and SQL. These programming languages are used widely in the developing of programs (Hazzan, Lapidot, & Ragonis, 2015).

Computer scientists are also equipped with attitudes and appropriate working practices. The working practices for a professional programmer include; they should be good communicators. This is where they should have the skill and compatibility to pass information and listen attentively so as to receive accurate and correct information. Computer scientists also have problem-solving skills where they have the knowledge of solving a problem at hand. In the development of a computer software, many problems arise hence the computer scientists develop solutions for them and these gives them the skills to solve problems. Computer scientists also develop a knack for learning where that continuously research and add information about the computer and software development so that they remain relevant on the field (Singh, 2008).

Computer scientists are also equipped with skills supporting solution of small problems using easy programming language which is Java, Python and C, they get clear expressions of solutions at different level of abstraction and they also get independent and the self-motivated study in competing science. This is where the computer scientist can study on their own without being invigilated.

The main objectives of computer science is that a student should posses the technical skills for solving various problems. These could be every-day problems, which enable the students to test their strategies in order to gain knowledge on software development.

The students learn to appreciate and program. Both of these require commitment and perseverance. They are able to communicate ideas, build technical skills for solving problems, and write efficient programs.

Figure 2.2. *There is a great need of teaching computer science in schools.*

Source: https://hechingerreport.org/should-computer-assisted-teaching-expand-its-reach-to-more-states/.

Teaching computer science in schools enables a student to get a basic knowledge of what computer science is to enable them to further their studies in computer science. In schools, they teach the basics of computer science enabling the students to get the basic knowledge of what computer is and what revolves around computer science. In case one wants to further studies in computer science in the higher level of education they will have the basic knowledge of what the studies involve hence they will be able to relate to what they are being taught (Singh, 2008).

Students get the basic understanding of a computer and the related technology and its applications. The study of computer science enables a student to know what a computer is and hence they become familiar with a computer hence they can use the computer.

They also get knowledge of technologies which are associated to the computer hence they can use technology that has the concept of a computer. The study helps students to apply the computer to solve problems and to perform various tasks that help the students in their learning.

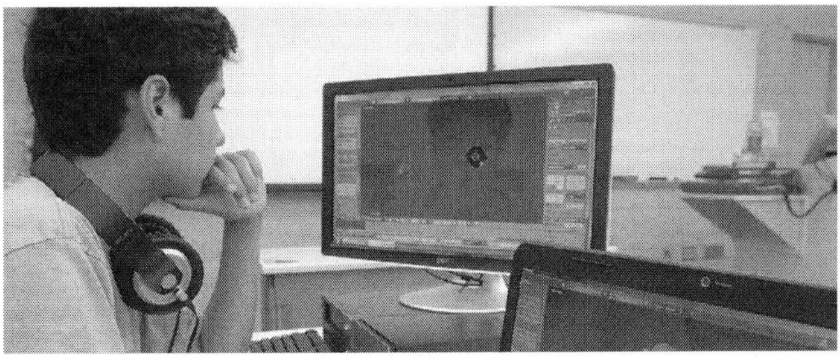

Figure 2.3. *Computer science enable students to have the ability to think deeply and further and apply this solving their daily life problems.*

Source: https://www.neiu.edu/academics/college-of-arts-and-sciences/departments/computer-science.

Students have to think widely when they study computer science especially in units like programming and hence this improves the thinking capacity of the students. Students also face various problems when dealing with specific units like the programming hence they should develop the solutions for this problem. This enables students to have the ability to solve problems that they face in their everyday lives and hence they can apply this concept (Singh, 2008).

Science technology is being introduced in everyday life. It is essential for students to be familiar with the various types of technology and computer science enables the students to do this.

Computer science in schools' subject is a body of knowledge because students gain knowledge that they did not have. They get awareness of what a computer is and the technologies that surround it. They are also equipped with knowledge of how to apply the knowledge they gain to solve problems and to perform duties. It is also an attitude developer towards life thinking and growing. By studying computer science students develop an attitude towards life on how to take it and what revolves around life. They also improve their thinking as the students thinking capacity is increased and they can grow significantly.

For the computer students to gain the qualities appropriately then the quality of the content of computer science being given to the student must be very high and accurate. It should have certain qualities. The knowledge being offered to the students should be beneficial to the students. It should help the students solve problems in the future hence it should be information that is relevant to the student and not information that will not be of any help to the student. It should also be timely such that it should be given to the student at the required time. It should be given with consideration that the students can relate to the materials being used so that it may create a positive impact. The knowledge must fit to a sequence that leads to broad objectives. The content being taught must enable the students to gain broad objectives and hence achieve a lot of things (Singh, 2008). The content must be appropriate to the learners such that it fits in their level of maturity and their background of the students. It should be introduced to the students according to their mind capacity to understand and how much information they can retain and improved as the level of understanding increases. This means that students who are in the lower grades are given the basics of what a computer is and as they mature more complex information is introduced to them such as the programming languages. Lastly, the experiences required for the development of aims and objectives learning should be possible. The content offered should be able to be used to develop aims and objectives for learning. This means that is should be practicable such that one can apply the knowledge in learning process. IT is therefore important that the content offered to preserve these aims so that the students gain computer science knowledge.

The objectives of teaching computer science in schools include; must ensure better match between the industries requirement and outputs of education sector emphasizing the quality needs. This means that the student gains the required knowledge and skills that are required to gain a position in the industrial sector. Computer science must aim to ensure that students are prepared enough to get a job once they have completed their studies. This student can get a job as a programmer, computer science teacher or lecturer, computer scientist or IT manager (Singh, 2008).

2.2. COGNITIVE DOMAIN

Cognitive domain is a branch in the bloom's taxonomy of learning domains. The blooms taxonomy was created in 1956 by Dr. Benjamin Bloom who was an educational psychologist. He invented it with the aim to promote higher forms of thinking in education such that the students can think with a higher capacity than they did before. This includes the capability to analyze and evaluate concepts, processes, procedures, and principles rather than just remembering facts. It enables students to think and gain information from in-depth search rather than just gaining a brief overview and cramming that is not beneficial. There are three domains which include; cognitive, affective and psychomotor (Singh, 2008).

Cognitive domain involves knowledge and development of intellectual skills from Bloom 1956 theory. The cognitive domain is in six major categories starting from the simplest to the most complex as stated below. They include;

- Knowledge
- Compression
- Application
- Analysis
- Synthesis
- Evaluation

Knowledge is the basic information that one has about a certain thing. In cognitive domain, knowledge is basically what one knows about a certain thing. For one to have in-depth understanding on what something is they must first have the basic understanding of what it is that is they must know what it involves or how the use it (Singh, 2008).

Comprehension is the understanding that one has about a certain thing. If one has comprehended something it means that they can interpreted what it involves. They can also use the information gained to utilize information to solve problems. Comprehension is important because the students do not get the literal meaning but the in depth meaning that promotes understanding. For one to gain appropriate capability to analyses and evaluate concepts they need to comprehend what they are dealing with first so that they can interpreted it correctly and appropriately.

Application is the ability to use the concept gained in everyday life. If one can apply the information gained then it means they have developed an understanding for it and they have knowledge about it. This means that for one to have application skills they require to have understanding and knowledge of it. That is why it is said as the categories go down their complexity increases. Application is important because it shows that the student can use the skills, he has gained to solve problems or come up with ideas to improve their lives and the lives of others (Singh, 2008).

The analysis is the detailed examination of the elements or structure of something. It is the process of breaking down a complex topic into smaller parts in order to gain a better understudying of it.

Synthesis and evaluation are the among last steps and they are the most important since the student has the ability to evaluate and synthesize the information they have acquired. It is therefore important that students be able to synthesize and evaluate a piece of information they have acquired for them to be termed as having a gained understanding of the topic appropriately, effectively and totally.

Phys Cho motor domain is to instill skills in students which include drawing skill, computation skill, construction skill, observation skill, problem-solving skill, dissection skill.The objectives of an effective domain include; receiving, responding, valuing, conceptualization, organization, and characterization.Receiving as an objective state that the domain can sensitiveness the desire or stimulus to accept anything is receiving. It has three levels which include awareness of the phenomena, willing to receive the phenomenon and controlled or selected scheme. The domain can receive or get awareness about a certain ting, occurrence or phenomena. The willingness to receive the phenomena is hen the domain is ready to accept any occurrence that may appear. Controlled or selected scheme is the ability of the domain to select what it receives and control the information it gets (Singh, 2008).Responding is an active reaction for the domain. It has three levels which include acquaintance in responding, willingness to respond and satisfaction in responding. Acquaintance in responding is the conviction of responding to the domain. Willingness to respond is when the domain wants to respond without having to be forced. Lastly, satisfaction in responding is when the domain gets satisfied after it has responded to the issue.

Valuing. The behavior of child by which he represents his feelings about superiority value, and characteristics of anything, fact event and behavior. Since it is related to faith for values therefore for specific value acceptance, priority and conviction adds three levels. They include; acceptance of a value, preference for a value and commitment or conviction. Acceptance of a value is when the child accepts a value and is ready to use them. The child has no problem in adjusting to the value and its requirements. Commitment is the wanting of the child to be dedicated to the task and conviction to the ability of the child to achieve a goal by faith (Singh, 2008).

Conceptualization is the base of construction of thinking or concepts is similarity and dissimilarity. Even when students build concepts by establishing similarity difference in relationship in existing values then their behavior comes in this objective. As a result of variation of values concept making for solving problems comes in this.

It is therefore important to learn all these objectives of the domains as they explain more about the domains and bring a clearer understanding of them. The domains help to bring understanding of how to improve the understanding of students to eliminate memorization (Singh, 2008).

2.3. TEACHING OF COMPUTER SCIENCE AT DIFFERENT LEVELS IN SCHOOLS

Figure 2.4. *Computer science is the teaching of computers and instilling knowledge about computers and the technology surrounding computers to students.*

Source: https://blogs.microsoft.com/on-the-issues/2016/11/17/teaching-kids-computer-science-no-computer-required/.

Computer science is a very important subject that should be introduced in schools today. Teaching computer science skills in schools is important because it gives students vital skills. These skills include the ability of students to innovate new technologies that are used to solve economic problems and other problems in the world. The acquiring of these skills, therefore, strengthens the local community, national innovation and creates many opportunities for youth hence eliminating idleness, drug, and substance abuse and spread of diseases among the youth (Singh, 2008).

Computer science also offers rewarding careers that the students can take up once they are done with their education. These careers include software engineering, information technologist, computer scientists, computing that involves arts, film finance health care, journalism and manufacturing, and IT technician. According to the United States study, they have discovered that computer-related jobs are among the fastest upcoming jobs in the world. For one to be employed they require to have the knowledge of the computer in the recent worlds therefore, it is among the skills that should be included when one is writing their curriculum vitae.

Before computer science is introduced in schools, decision-makers in school should be informed that computer science differs from computer literacy. Computer literacy is knowing to use technology to manipulate computer software and hardware whereas computer science is the study of computers and computational systems. Computer science needs to be part of math, science, technology reform. They should understand that teaching computer science is not about giving students the basic knowledge of a computer and teaching them how to manipulate the software and hardware of the computer but it is much more than that like the computational systems and computer languages (Singh, 2008).

They also need to be informed that computer skills can make the curriculum more relevant to students. This means that students can computer science courses that can tap into students' interests in technology helping them become technology inventors. Most technology being invented require computer skills and knowledge (Singh, 2008). By introducing computer science to schools' students are given skills which they can use to develop technologies to solve various problems. Other teachers can build these skills by allowing students to design technical solutions to problems in science, math, social studies, arts, and literacy. This, therefore, makes many courses available to the youth in future.

The decision-makers should also be made aware that the studying of computer science can help students meet better accountability goals and provide the students with skills necessary for innovation and translates to better-paying jobs. The probability of computer science students failing to acquire a job is very low and also the probability of computer science-related jobs disappearing is also very low. This is because new technology is being invented daily that require computer science skills to operate. Students can also develop accountable goals because a key component of computer science involves the use of critical thinking and problem-solving.

For a school to incorporate computer science in the school they should ensure certain factors are put to place to avoid failure of incorporation. These factors include;

- They should form computer science lessons and implement them. Although the computer may be incorporated in certain subjects like language and science a computer lesson must be introduced to ensure students have the time set to study computer science. The computer skills that are incorporated in the other subjects are shallow and do not give a lot of information hence in the computer science lesson students can dig deeper and acquire more information about it.

- Schools should make computer science a count towards graduation. Students have a lot to study about hence they may ignore computer science with the mindset that mathematics and science are more important and beneficial. By making computer science a count towards graduation means that students will not be able to graduate if they have not passed in computer science. This will make students realize the importance of computer science and hence they will spare time to study it. It will also give them the motivation to study it so that they ensure they have passed hence they will graduate.
- Schools should make the computer science course accessible to all. Introducing computer science is a way of making it accessible to students, however, some factors may hinder some students from taking up the course. These factors include; the course may be given at a very high cost. This may disadvantage the children from a humble background since they may fail to acquire the required amount. This can be solved by the school taking into consideration all students from all backgrounds and offering the cost at a fair price. They can include the course fee in the student's total fees to allow parents to pay in installments and also to discourage parents who may fail to pay due to their consideration of computer science not being an important course at all.
- Schools also need to improve teacher's preparation and professional development. For computer science to be taught there is a need for the availability of a teacher who is equipped with the required skills to take up this course. When they are employing teachers, they may take into consideration teachers who have graduated with computer science knowledge and skills so that they may be employed to teach this course to the students. Also, the school may provide professional development for teachers who teach or who may like to teach computer science to improve their teaching skills and ensure the proper delivery of these skills to the students.

- Lastly, schools need to have the necessary resources for teaching computer science in school. These resources include the necessary textbooks, writing material and also the computers for student's practical use. In case these resources are not available then the delivery of the course may not be efficient and the students may fail to grab everything that was being taught. It is, therefore, necessary that schools should invest in this.
- Introducing computer science in schools is not an easy task. It is not as easy as adding a simple computing workshop or class into the schedule since there is adding of computer science into the whole curriculum. Just like the core subjects, students can learn computer science by learning incrementally laying a foundation from pre-school. The information about computers taught in pre-school is not the same as that taught in higher grades because the students in pre-school have a different level of understanding from those in high grades. They are therefore taught according to their level of understanding (Singh, 2008).

Figure 2.5. *Computer science at primary level involves displaying the lessons in the form of rhymes, games and browsing and interactive mode using the computer.*

Source: https://www.businesscloud.co.uk/news/computer-science-teaching-set-for-boost.

The level of understanding for a primary student is very low therefore teachers should simply introduce computer science in a way that the students will comprehend easily. If they introduce comprehensive things to them, they may fail to understand and they may get discouraged. Jean Piaget invented a theory called cognitive development theory that states that children move through 4 different stages of mental development. These stages include; the sensorimotor stage where children who lie in this stage are those born to the age of 2 years. There is the preoperational stage where the children who lie in this stage are ages two to seven years. Next to the preoperational stage is the concrete operational stage in which children who land on this level of brain development are those from the age of seven years to eleven years. Lastly is the formal operational stage which includes people from the age of eleven and above. Jean Piaget invented this theory when he was eleven years in the late 1800s and published his first scientific paper (Singh, 2008).

Primary school students are majorly from the age of two years to seven years therefore they fall in the preoperational stage. According to Jean Pignut, he states that these children think symbolically and learn to use words and pictures to represent objects. They are very egocentric, which means that they think only of themselves without regarding the feelings of others. Hence they struggle to see things from other's perspective. Finally, the students tend to think about concepts using only concrete terms. These kids learn through looking at pictures and pretend play yet still struggle with logic and taking things from other people's point of view. They learn through senses, icons, and effective modes of representation. When learning computer science, they are taught using simple applications that they can comprehend well and also ones that enable them to be associated with looking at pictures, senses, icons and effective mode of representation. Some of the concepts taught to children at this stage include LOGO and Microsoft Paint. These two are basic applications and the students can interact with them well and freely and easily suit the student's levels of understanding for example in Microsoft paint students can draw images and fill them with a color which is a fun process (Singh, 2008).

Secondary students are mainly from the age of seven to eleven which is the concrete operational stage according to Jean Piaget's theory. This stage is characterized by logical thought. Thinking still tends to be very concrete, children become much more logical and sophisticated in their thinking during this stage of development. Jean argued that children at this stage become more logic in thinking and hence their thinking capacity is higher than the preoperational stage. In this stage, the children become less egocentric and they start looking at things at other people's point of view rather than their own alone.

At the secondary level, computer skills are developed. Here the students have a more developed thinking capacity such that they can use software like Microsoft Excel, Microsoft PowerPoint, and Microsoft word. This enables students to develop their fundamental computer skills. Also, various advanced computer languages are introduced, such as Basic and Fortran. Using Microsoft Word, students can write articles and assignments. This not only improves student's computer writing skills but also enables the student to correct their language mistakes.

Higher secondary level falls in the last category which is the formal operational stage. In this stage children are either eleven years old or older. In this stage development thinking become more sophisticated such that the person can reason and their thinking capacity is high. In this stage, the students can be taught complex things and they reason and come into understanding. Skills such as logical thought, deductive reasoning, and systematic planning also emerge during this stage. When they are faced with a problem or an idea, they can reason on it and find a logical solution (Hazzan, Lapidot, & Ragonis, 2015).

Computer science is more complex and more advanced exercises are being introduced. Programming at this level requires a lot of thinking and reasoning. Some students may be discouraged but most continue working on developing their programming skills using C, C++, Java, and Visual Basic. They are also introduced to web languages, such as HTML. This helps develop their arithmetic and logical thinking which is shown in their programming skills.

By observing the development levels of the mind before knowing what will be integrated into the curriculum has several benefits. One, it will help teachers to know what to teach to a particular age of students. It also enables the students to gain understanding rather than memorizing. It also enables the students to apply the knowledge they gain and come up with ways to solve world problems using technology invented using computer science skills that they acquire. It is therefore important that all the stages of development be considered first before coming up with the curriculum.

The place of computer science in the school curriculum is mainly to instill fundamental skills to children necessary for their future. Students when they study core subjects, they gain understanding and gain skills which they use in the future when they are seeking employment or when they want to employ themselves. For example, when they study languages, they gain skills of communication and when they study mathematics, they gain skills of business and critical thinking. Likewise, when students learn computer science, they acquire skills which enable them to acquire employment later in future (Hazzan, Lapidot, & Ragonis, 2015).

The skills acquired from learning computer science include; analytical skills, problem-solving skills, creativity, critical thinking skills, and resilience.

Analytical skills are the ability to identify a problem and finding a suitable solution for them. When students are learning computer science, they are faced with several problems example in the process of programming where they need to find solutions to them. Students hence acquire the skill of analytical skills and once they are employed, they can identify a problem that others had not identified and they can find the solutions. Employers today employ individuals with analytical skills since they are assured that they will be able to solve their problems (Lakshmi, 2009).

Problem-solving skills is the ability of an individual to identify systematically solve complex problems and effectively. Most projects that students work on require students to take a concept and transform it into reality. When students can solve problems, no challenge can come the way that they may fail to find a solution to it. Problem-solving skills are very vital and important because individuals and business organizations face problems daily and they are required to be solved for a smooth run of the organization therefore students should aim to acquire this skill.

Creativity goes hand in hand with problem-solving since a creative person can solve problems and an individual with problem-solving skills is creative. Creativity is the ability to think and come up with new inventions and ideas that were not present before. One gains creativity when studying computer science because when they are working on projects, they are required to be creative and think broadly to come up with new ideas. They also require creativity when they are writing their reports after they complete the projects. Creativity is important in employment because the organization needs to invent new things to keep their market or gain new market.

Critical thinking skills are gained from computer science when they are carrying out their projects because they need to think critically about the methodologies they need to apply. By thinking critically, they can identify procedures and methods that will not work hence it prevents them from wasting time applying this method. Critical thinking is the ability to think deeply and eliminate any impossibilities. It is still connected to problem-solving because for one to solve a problem they need to think about it very deeply and come up with solutions. Critical thinking is important in employment since employers need people who can think critically to eliminate time wastage in trying out procedures that will later on fail (Lakshmi, 2009).

Lastly, resilience is the ability to understand that failing is part of the process of success. Students who study computer science face a lot of failure during programming since it is a difficult task. Students, therefore, keep the failure aside and start again until they achieve a positive result. An individual with resilience can face any problem and still overcome it and move on. Employers need employees who can overcome situations they face to eliminate the wastage of time when individuals' take-offs to have time to adjust and also those that can adjust very easily to new working conditions or new environments when they are given transfers.

2.4. MAIN REASONS WHY COMPUTER SCIENCE IS TAUGHT IN SCHOOLS

The following are the main reason why computer science is taught in schools:

- It is necessary to know how to use computer gadgets and electronic gadgets in all fields.
- Computer science equips individuals with the skills necessary to use any electronic gadget example mobile devices and phones and since the world is revolving technologically in such a way that all works will be performed using mobile gadgets and electronic devices there is need for people to know how to use electronic devices.
- Computer science courses are also taught for students to be on part with ever-increasing societal needs and expectations. The society demands a lot of things and among them, it demands that a person should be computer literate failure to which the individual may fail to fit-in appropriately.
- Most tasks in the current society are performed using the computer hence if an individual does not know about the computer and how to use it then they are outdated and they may go to the extent of lacking jobs and even being conned by malicious individuals out there.
- Computer science skills are also taught for students to become equipped for new business and industries dimension. As stated

above most functions today are performed using the computer and other electronic devices. Therefore, if a person does not have computer skills they may fail to fit in and they are rarely employed.

- The need for students to become competent employees. The global competitions that require computer science include; image cup where students team up to use their creativity, passion and knowledge of technology to create applications and compete for cash, travel tickets and other prices. These competitions are important because they enable the country to gain prestige and also it enables the individual to benefit too. Other competitions include important stem competitions.
- Lastly, the teaching of computer science in schools enable students to work with finance. Students can do calculations using the computers as it is faster and give accurate answers. They can also work out other financial computations, for example, preparing a balance sheet or acquiring a financial statement easily and fast. It is therefore noted that computer science is a vital and very important subject for study in schools and should be incorporated into the curriculum.

2.5. IMPORTANCE OF COMPUTER SCIENCE IN HIGHER EDUCATIONAL LEVEL

The purpose of education in higher schools is to provide that kind of atmosphere through which pupils can acquire the knowledge of computer science, skills of application and the right attitude that makes pupils useful citizens in the society. Computer science instills skills in a student example analytical skill, critical thinking skills, and resilience skills. It can also help students to understand comprehend global functions of computer science and act locally to meet their needs. The main reasons for teaching computer science in schools include:

- It enables diverse thinking in students and enables them to solve any computer-related problem. As discussed, earlier computer science gives the student the skill of thinking critically and problem-solving skills. A student who studies computer science in high school will be in a position to be able to solve problems easily as they advance in their education. They will also be able to think critically and come up with new things.

- Students also develop the right kind of attitude to develop and acquire the knowledge and skills that are required in the current technological world. Students who learn computer science can acquire skills that are required to operate any technological or electrical appliance. Due to the technology revolution, these students will acquire jobs from any field.
- Students are also trained to develop scientifically to appreciate the technological advances and adapt in their lives. Students who learn computer science appreciate when new technology is introduced or when the existing technology is improved. Since they have the required skills they can easily adapt to this change as they can fit in and use the new technology of any kind or version. This is due to their understanding that they gained earlier and also the skills such as analytical skills that enable them to analyses the new technology, evaluate it and figure out how it works.
- The students are also trained to make meaningful contributions to make the world and society proud of. Many computer students have developed new technologies, software, and hardware that not only speed up work but also enable communication and transfer of information. For instance, mobile phones that are being invented daily and new versions being made daily have been manufactured by students who know computer science. These technologies are of great importance to society and the nation at large. This makes the society and nation to become very proud of the students who invented the new technologies.

Using the computer and related technologies requires teamwork. Teamwork is the ability of people to work together regardless of their background to achieve a certain goal. Students need to be trained to work as a team. Computer science promotes teamwork since the students are grouped into small groups that will work together when doing their projects. When they work as a group, they can share the knowledge to come up with a comprehensive and perfect project. Since two heads are better than one when people work as a group, they can accomplish so much than when one works alone. Teamwork also helps build harmony therefore people interrelate together appropriately and they can stay together in peace (Reçi & Bollin, 2017).

When students learn computer science at higher educational levels, teachers can identify their mistakes from the mistakes they do when writing their report when delivering their report or even from their project itself, therefore, teachers can help students to correct their mistakes early enough and avoid them from making the same mistakes in future. Also, the teachers can identify students' talents. For example, if the student is talented in coding, they can build and help the student to grow their talent by guiding them through the process. This talent can come to develop into the student's future career or employment.Just like any other core subject computer science enables the students to listen attentively and come up with solutions or gain the required information. This is enabled in class when other students are presenting their projects the other children sit silently and listen attentively to what is being communicated. IT also benefits the student by enabling them to be open-minded since they are open to other people's ideas and from that they can gain new information, new ideas or even discover where they make have made a mess in their project so that they can correct on it early enough.Higher secondary schools are a bridge between school and society. Ones one is done with their higher secondary school they are fully integrated as members of the society. For those who decide to stop their education when they complete their higher secondary school, computer science can help them gain employment but for those who decide to continue with their education, it helps them seek higher education and continue with their studies. Computer science teachers, therefore, give their students the necessary information and skills that enable them to fit into the world. The current world terms these skills as very important and requires all students to acquire them (Lakshmi, 2009).

Students gain decision-making skills and grow into complete personalities who are mature in words, actions, and deeds. When students study computer science they can make logical decisions on their own. Students gain decision making skills by solving problems and writing algorithms, which are basic computer science skills that they gain during their daily lessons. It is therefore important that students who are in high school to learn computer science to prepare them for their future careers.

Students need to be proficient and professional in learning computer science. They must be trained to acquire the principles of electronic devices and get the diversity of operations. Most students who do not have the opportunity to study computer science in schools should find their way into it. Some vocational training facilities, for example, offer computer science and these students should ensure they enroll in them because it is for their benefit. This will help them to be overcomers of any competition they may get from those with computer science skills hence they can be equal (Singh, 2008).

2.6. TEACHING OF COMPUTER SCIENCE IN RELATION TO OTHER SUBJECTS

Computer science has been proven to have a relation with other subjects such that they borrow ideas from one another, they share ideas or one contributes ideas to explain the other one.

Computer Science is the main factor that helps students when deciding what career path, they want to take, learn to make informed decisions, and learn to make decisions on their own without having to depend on others, lifelong learners.

There is a difference between working smart and working smarter because technically in working smarter, the mind is the key factor and it must be fit and ready but working hard involves wit that is strength and effort that one puts in a certain task. In our current world, technology is changing very fast that it gives people very little time to adapt to a new one. A certain version of a phone may be the most recent fashion and in weeks a new one is introduced. Teaching mathematics has no special method of teaching it but by using computers to practice basic skills one may acquire special benefits that they might not acquire anywhere else like learning new methods of calculating that are easier and faster as opposed to the methods they are used to (Singh, 2008).

Computer-based exercises enable students to be more motivated and have a greater psych to perform a certain task. A computer can easily make things visible that is it can be seen by the eye rather than being imagined. It is among the major strengths of the computer. It can make visual abstract processes that are otherwise indescribable and impossible. For us to ensure that students excel very well in mathematics, we must consider adapting to change and using the best tools available to us especially using technology that always plays a role by offering tools that enable and assist in the study of mathematics, for example, using Computer-Guided Learning (CGL) that enables teachers to be guided in a certain direction that they are to move in, while being confident they have a resource correlated to the curriculum outcomes they are mandated to teach. Computer Guided Learning refers to high-quality world-class CD-ROM materials supported resources for teaching and learning that can be printed and offered to the students (Singh, 2008).

2.6.1. Computer Science and Chemistry

Chemistry is the branch of science that deals with the identification of the substances of which matter is composed; the investigation of their properties and how they interact, combine, and change; and the use of these processes to form new substances. In synthetic chemistry, new compounds are formed or synthesized from the older ones or other compounds. Chemists rely on techniques that require an optical device for producing and observing a spectrum of light or radiation from any source to analyses and determine the compounds that have been formed (Rocha et al., 2018).

Some equipment used in chemistry which include nuclear magnetic resonance, mass, infrared and ultraviolet spectrometry most commonly depend on computers to control the sensitive equipment and obtain results and record detailed measurements. These techniques for analysis have allowed chemists to know how a compound looks like and its structure, which was previously guesswork based on observations from chemical properties. This means that scientists do not have to imagine how the compound looks like but they can find out how it looks like by the use of this equipment.

Molecular masses are known to the microgram, which would be impossible without the aid of the computer. Measuring the mass of a molecule is close to impossible and is only made possible by measuring it using the microgram. The microgram only operates with the aid of the computer.

Computers are very important in taking measurements but they can also be used to predict measurements. There is some very powerful software available for predicting physical properties of compounds. Bond lengths, melting points, vibrational frequencies and properties such as solubility can be predicted using dedicated software based on theories known. Software like this can, therefore, help you to design a molecule to the specific needs of the chemist. Without the software, it would take hours of calculations to predict the properties (Rocha et al., 2018).

Another important area of chemistry is analyzing data obtained from experiments, to look for patterns to prove theories. This can be done by hand but involves a lot of calculations, which is time-consuming and liable to mistakes.

Analyzing of data is often done using a spreadsheet. These spreadsheets are found in the computer and they can quickly work out calculations required and they go to the extent of plotting graphs showing a pictorial representation of the data that if it was offered to a human being they may fail to complete the task as it is tedious, involving and tiring. Spreadsheets are usually very good at calculating the equation of a best-fit line of a graph accurately, which is often important in chemistry for deriving the accuracy of the experiment and deriving results that are needed for calculations like finding out the errors. If a student could be given the task to do without the aid of the computer, they may have a lot of errors causing the experiment to be inaccurate.

Having used computers to obtain accurate data, it seems sensible to store it where it can easily be retrieved for reference. Traditionally before the invention of the computer people used to store data in the form of writings on papers or by filling them and storing them away. IT still worked but had several disadvantages like the information could easily get lost or tampered with and since in chemistry a lot of information is stored from even very early years and storing them in this form could be very hectic to find a specific document that one wants from those years it is also very cumbersome and the information can easily get mixed up. An example is if one wants to find data on a group of compounds such as the alcohols, or those with a melting point above 100 centigrade. Computers offer the opportunity of people or scientists to store information electronically with a database. This makes the searching of data very easy for different criteria such as temperatures, solubility or mass. This leads on to communications and the sharing of data (Rocha et al., 2018).

Networks are very useful in large companies. They allow communication between different computers, and more importantly, the exchange of data. This means a company could have a central database with all the records. Therefore, companies can share data about chemistry easily with one another and help solve problems together.

2.6.2. Computer Science and Physics

Computers have great influence in the field of physics. Computers influence physics in the fields such as; Atom energy, Astronomy, finding weather reports, Moments of particles and their functions and Research in the field of Physics is enhanced and sophisticated by computer and its applications. Atom energy is the energy that is given out by changes in the nucleus of the atom. Using a computer, students' study about the atom and they can find results from past study making their study easier and faster. Astronomy is the study of objects and matter outside the earth's atmosphere and of their physical and chemical properties. Computer science knowledge is used to invent satellites that are sent out into outside the earth's atmosphere to observe and send signals that are interpreted to determine and learn about the atmosphere. Finding weather reports is aided by computer skills because the study of the weather is done by pieces of equipment that are manufactured by the use of computer science knowledge (Wang et al., 2009).

Figure 2.6. *Computers are used in Mechanical Engineering through CAD, CAM, ANSYS, and CATIA as designing and analyzing software programs.*

Source: https://stock.adobe.com/ee/images/at-the-factory-female-mechanical-engineer-designs-3d-engine-on-her-personal-computer-male-automation-engineer-uses-laptop-for-programming-robotic-arm/254487300.

2.6.3. Computer Science and Biology

Computer science is used in Biological Science as follows:

The use of computer technology has greatly enhanced the medical fields, such as in hospital environments where reliability and quality are very essential factors. In hospitals the details and information of the patients are stored in the computer for accessing their data easily and faster. Traditionally, the hospitals used files to store information about the patient and this was hectic and cumbersome especially in retrieving the files this made the processes of the hospital to be slow hence most patients went home untreated but with the integrating of computers a lot of this problems have been solved by many computer applications, such as patient information systems, monitoring, and control systems and diagnostic systems, have been used to enhance healthcare.

In the hospital patient information systems allow doctors at different locations to access permanent patient records from a centralized database. This type of computer application enables doctors and or nurses to easily find and send notices to patients who need follow up treatment/medication at the comfort of their homes rather than having them visit to know their next appointment. This system also allows for doctors to compare methods of treating illnesses. According to computer and information technology, the use of computers can store a lot of data as compared to writing (Wang et al., 2009).

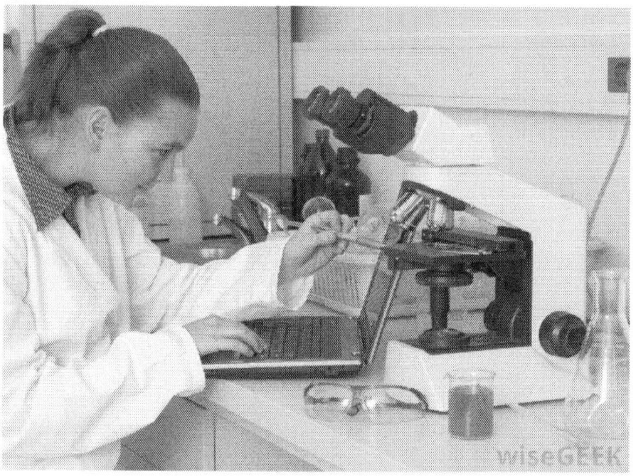

Figure 2.7. *Computers are a great influence in the field of Microbiology, Genetic Engineering and Tissue culture monitoring.*

Source:http://www.aljanh.net/the-biologist-in-the-lab-wallpapers/2349463329.html.

2.6.4. Computer Science and Social Science

The computer is used to review the past with documentary shreds of evidence. The computer is used to research to find out what was happening in the past and dig into the past since most history books and other documents that contain documented information of what took place in the past are being digitalized using the computer. The books and all other old documents are easily found in the computer and it saves people time that they would have taken to go into the libraries and search for the historical book as and taken time to read them. They are also cheaper than buying a new book as long one has internet access, they can access the books and information freely or at very little cost (Wang et al., 2009).

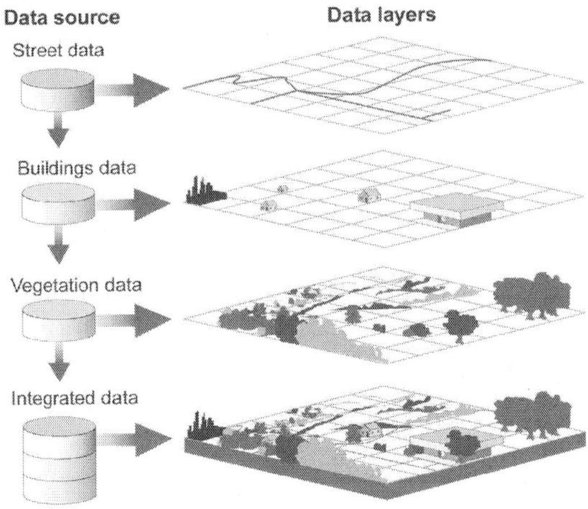

Figure 2.8. *Computer has great influence in developing Global Positioning System (GPS) that determines where a country or place is positioned.*

Source: https://www.nationalgeographic.org/encyclopedia/geographic-information-system-gis/.

2.6.5. Computer Science and Languages

Figure 2.9. *Computer science is used to develop software in languages.*

Source: https://blog.edx.org/the-4-most-lucrative-programming-skills-you-can-learn-online/.

Computers can therefore spread the languages throughout the world. There are many different languages in the world and the computer has assisted in the spread of this languages through various ways like; People can learn new languages through the computer, and the computer offers translations of texts into other languages and the computers can offer training and lessons on other languages thus enhancing the spread of the languages. People can learn new languages using the computer because the computer is designed in a way that it incorporates all languages and only offers the selected language to the researchers. In case one does not understand a certain word that is in a different language in his study they can look up the word in the computer and the computer will give the meaning of the word in the language that the researcher will comprehend easily. This enables people to come across so many words that are not in their language and they can know the definition hence they can learn new languages (Wang et al., 2009).

The computer also offers translations of words for instance if one is in a foreign country and they are not able to understand what the citizens of that country are communicating they can use the software developed by computer scientists to translate the words to them in a way and language they will understand therefore it eases communication.

Lastly, the computer can offer foreign languages such that students learn other languages through the computer. Some foreign languages, for example, French and Germany are taught via the computer or students may also use YouTube videos to enable them to learn the languages (Wang et al., 2009).

Chapter 3 Applying Micro-Teaching in Computer Science and Technology

CONTENTS

3.1. INTRODUCTION

Microteaching is a perfect way to develop a wide horizon of teaching designs, improve on one's feedback skills, and build up self-confidence. It gives teachers a safe space to place themselves in someone's shoes and observe others' performance.

Microteaching is beneficial for improving tutoring skills. It is normally done around small group of people especially teacher colleagues. Video recordings are used in aiding microteaching.

The group of people judge the teacher as they perform their teaching skills then the necessary feedback is given.

Microteaching helps in sharpening the instructors' skills of handling students since they assume the role of a student and this enables them to get an idea of what other students need and expect during learning.

This eventually improves teaching methods and also helps them learn new teaching strategies. Instructors observe each other tutor in an organized manner. Then feedback is given to every teacher then they discuss their performances that is their strengths and weaknesses.

3.2. EARNING OF MICROTEACHING

Microteaching is a tutoring tool that is used to modify and advance teacher's behavior as it is a simulated social skill tutoring that helps in providing the teacher trainees with accurate feedback on their teaching mannerisms. It provides teacher trainees with an environment with instructions which cannot be found in normal classrooms.

The trainee tutors form a small group of colleagues (fellow teachers) for a short period of time (5-10 minutes).

The group pays attention to a specific skill in order to identify teacher's strengths and weaknesses. Feedback is given systematically on the teaching skill the trainee has and then the trainee moves on to another skill.

Microteaching is systematic as it trains teachers to improve their skills starting from less complex skills as it advances to more complex ones. This exposes the teacher to an organized curriculum of miniature teacher experience (Lakshmi, 2009).

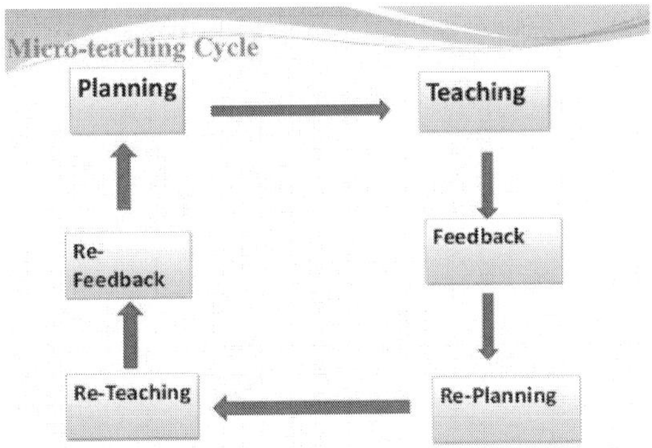

Figure 3.1. *Microteaching cycle.*

Source: https://www.quora.com/What-is-micro-teaching-cycle.

Microteaching has a very basic rule. A public tutor will teach a class which comprises of a public group for about five minutes at the end of the lesson the group takes a break and the student-teacher discusses with the supervisor about their performance during the lesson. After the discussion, the trainee teacher gets a short feedback and from the feedback the trainee tried to improve his or her next lesson from the previous one.

There has been a number of definitions over the years by different educators. Some of these definitions are;

In 1976 Allen defined microteaching as "scaled down teaching encounter in class size and class time". Recently, microteaching has been defined as "a teacher training procedure that reduces the teaching situation to a simpler and more controlled encounter by limiting the practice teaching to a specific skill and reducing teaching time and class size." Encyclopedia defines it as "a real constructed scaled-down teaching encounter which is used for teacher training, curriculum development and research."

In 1970 McAleese and Urwin suggested that microteaching is the most utilized technique in the use of closed circuit television (CCTV) to provide instant feedback of the student-teacher performance in an environment that is simple but also points out that microteaching is best seen as a form of a simulated tutoring technique which incorporates minimized complication and feedback "along a simulated spectrum ranging from the purely abstract textbooks of teaching practice through actual classroom teaching."

Also, microteaching is defined as "a teacher education technique that allows teachers to utilize and apply well-defined tutoring skills to a carefully prepared lesson in a planned series of five to 10 minutes and encounters with a small group of real classroom students often with an opportunity to observe the performance on videotape" Bush define this in the year 1968.

The following are some of the main differences between microteaching and traditional teaching:

- In microteaching the approach of objective mainly focuses on behavioral terms whereas objectives in traditional teaching is not specified but general.
- In the former, class comprises of about 6 to 10 students but in traditional the class consists of about 40 to 60 students.
- In microteaching the teacher focuses on one skill at a time whereas in traditional teaching the teacher uses all the skill at a time.
- In microteaching the duration for teaching is approximately 5 to 10 minutes but 8n traditional teaching it takes about 40 to 45 minutes.
- In microteaching there is immediate feedback but in traditional teaching there is no provision of feedback.
- In microteaching tutoring is done under a controlled environment but in traditional teaching there is no control over the scenario.
- Tutoring is rather simple in microteaching but in traditional teaching it is complicated.
- The job of the supervisor is clearly outlined in microteaching but in traditional teaching it is not specified.
- In microteaching, the pattern of interaction can be studied objectively but patterns in traditional teaching cannot be studied objectively.

3.3. THE OBJECTIVES OF STUDYING MICROTEACHING

- To comprehend the idea of microteaching cycle and its components
- To elaborate on the procedures used in microteaching
- To elaborate stimulus variations
- Skill reinforcement probing questioning

- Demonstrations and use of blackboard
- To elaborate the need for link lesson

In the field of teacher practice, the most crucial development is microteaching. It was initially being practiced in the university of Stanford in 1963. Students in the research department created a strategy to aid in a practical way of training teachers and they considered it as a way of providing feedback in teacher training.

3.4. ORIGIN AND DEVELOPMENT OF MICROTEACHING

As stated earlier, microteaching originated from Stanford University during an experimental research on identifying teaching skills. Their research was supervised by Professors Bush, McDonald, and other faculty. Kettering and Ford foundation steered the research.

Testing and evaluating tools were designed by experts who were assigned to develop them. The tools were meant to measure the achievement of teaching skills. At the same time, a research expert Acheson was experimenting about the use of video recording in the growth of technical teaching skills.

The video recorder was used to pick every teacher reactions and interaction with the students in an accurate procedure. This enabled for an elaborate feedback to be given to the trainee. Throughout this process, a microteaching technique was formulated and in 1963 microteaching started to become known as the essential training skills. Ever since this teaching technique has been applied in many universities all over the world (Lakshmi, 2009).

3.5. ASSUMPTIONS OF MICROTEACHING

Microteaching brought five propositions:

- Microteaching is an actual teaching focused on developing specific tutoring skills as opposed to focused on the growth of a student's ability.
- It reduced the complications of a normal class setting by a toned-down classroom size content and duration.
- It leads to the growth of particular training skills which leads to the mastering of that skill

- It allows for a heightened control of practice as it provides feedback to the trainee.
- It immensely increases the general skills of results of feedback to tutoring. It individualizes training to a single person.

3.6. PRINCIPLES UNDERLYING MICROTEACHING

- *Principle of one skill at a time*: A trainee takes up one skill and they get skilled to a level where they have mastered then another skill is picked up and the same procedure is followed.
- *Principle of limited content*: Very little information is provided to the student-teacher and is required to only train using that limited content provided this helps teachers who have who are beginners.
- *Principal of practice*: Since one skill is being picked up at a time, by the time the trainee has mastered the skill, he or she would have done a lot of practice which will lead to perfection.
- *Principle of experimentation*: Experiments are done many times. They are normally done under controlled situation which with factors like them, content and number people being considered.
- *Principle of immediate feedback*: This will lead to improvement of teaching skills since the trainee learns from the mistakes we have made in the previous lessons.
- *Principle of education*: After every short lesson the student is evaluated and evaluates themselves also so as to identify errors and rectify them thus enhancing proper learning.
- *Principle of continuity*: Learning is a continuous process as skills are slowly picked up by the trainee overtime. This enhances effectiveness during skill utilization.
- *Principle of individualized training*: The student-teacher is seriously and clinically trained and maximum attention is given to the students.

3.7. STEPS OF MICROTEACHING

- The specific skills that are to be practiced are elaborated to the teacher in terms of the functions and elements of the skills giving appropriate examples.
- The supervisor demonstrates to the other trainees how the skills will be practiced

- The trainee prepares a brief lesson of the given skill.
- The student-teacher then teaches a class as he or she gets supervised by their colleagues.
- After supervising and observations made a feedback is given to the trainee teacher. The supervisor points out errors and how to improve on it and also emphasizes on a strength
- The teacher training plans using the feedback given and tries to improve skills in the next lesson.
- After re-planning the rectified lesson is taught again using other people.
- After observing the supervisor gives a re-feedback with convincing facts.
- The process goes on until the trainee teacher masters the skills(teach re-teach).

3.8. CYCLE OF MICROTEACHING

Tutoring is considered to be a gained skill and each and every tutoring skill is a combination of related tutoring behavior which enhances students learning, defining, practicing, controlling and evaluating of skills can be done (Kadijevich, Angeli, & Schulte, 2013). A teacher is required to develop the necessary skills so as to improve their ability to teach. There are six steps involved in microteaching and it involves:

- Planning: This pertains picking up a topic then the skill being tested is put under practice the topic is scrutinized into various activities and they are planned in a logical criterion that optimizes the skill.
- Teaching: Here the trainee utilizes the skill in teaching the students. In the event, a different situation occurs in class the trainee is expected to modify his temperamental as per the demand of the situation and should be courageous enough to contain the situation.
- Given feedback: This is giving back information to the teacher trainee regarding his performance strengths and weaknesses are identified.
- Re-planning: The training strategies are his lesson using the feedback given and tries to improve from the previous lesson.

- Re-teaching: Hear the trainee teaches a different group of students with the same topic or vice versa in order to break monotony using the feedback the teacher trainee teaches with a different energy source to improve on the lesson.
- Re-feedback: This is the most vital step for behavior modification as it steers the trainee to the desired route of teaching.

However, there can be slight variations depending on the skill sets being trained.

3.9. PHASES OF MICROTEACHING

There are three phases of microteaching namely knowledge acquisition, skill acquisition, and transfer phase

Pre-active phase/knowledge acquisition phase: This phase involves activities like provision of knowledge about teaching skills, observing the demonstration of teaching skills and analyzing the demonstration of the teaching skills.

Skill acquisition phase/interactive phase: This phase involves planning and preparation of micro lessons of the skill, practice of the skill, evaluating the skills, re-planning, re-teaching and re- feedback until the mastery of the skill is achieved.

Transfer phase/post-active phase: This involves giving the trainee a chance to practice the skills acquired in a normal class setting and incorporating the different skills practiced.

3.10. ADVANTAGES OF MICROTEACHING

- Aids in developing and mastering skills.
- Aids in accomplishing particular teacher competence
- It caters for the need of individual difference in teacher training
- It is an individualized training technique
- It gives a deeper knowledge behind the art of tutoring
- It minimizes the complication of the process of teaching
- It uses real-life teaching scenarios for growing skills.

3.11. DISADVANTAGES OF MICROTEACHING

- Micro-teaching does not emphasize on content in that it is skill oriented
- Most of the trainees are not given a chance for re-teaching and re-planning
- The technique is time involving
- It caters for only a few sets of skills
- It lingers away from a normalized class teaching
- There might be the occurrence of management issues while arranging micro lessons.

3.12. SKILLS AND ACTIVITIES IN MICROTEACHING

Tutoring is considered as a work of art. A well-qualified teacher will use all the effective skills to cultivate quality learning in the class. Microteaching is a tool that gives instant feedback and it is used in growing tutoring skills. Tutoring skill is the collection of teacher activity and behavior which when practiced brings about an effective and desired behavioral shift among teachers and students. There are specific tutoring skills that have been noticed by tutors/educators and can be instilled among teacher trainees. Among the list of skills identified by Alan and Ryan in 1969 are stimulus variation, set induction, closure, silence and nonverbal cues, reinforcement of student participation, asking questions, probing questions divergent questions, attending behavior, illustrating, lecturing higher-order questions, planned repetition, and completeness. BK Parsi describes that with these skills one becomes a whole teacher in his book "becoming a better teacher" these skills are fluency in questioning, probing questions, noting down goals, introducing a lesson, elaborating with examples, stimulus variation, silence and nonverbal cues, reinforcing students to participate, increasing people's involvement, use of blackboard, getting closure and recognizing attending behavior (Kadijevich, Angeli, & Schulte, 2013).

3.13. EVALUATING MICROTEACHING

Teaching skills being nurtured and developed through microteaching is thoroughly evaluated and analyzed by a supervisor or fellow colleagues. It is measured using the rating schedule. The common tool used to evaluate the effectiveness of micro-teaching is the Stanford teacher competency appraisal guide (STAG) evaluating microteaching effectiveness is a challenge rather we need to ask ourselves if the experience gotten from microteaching is developing and improving teaching skills in a normal class setting. An evaluated sheet was provided by Allen and Ryan to assist in the assessment of skills reinforcement it is four-dimensional.

- The accurate answer by the student is gifted by saying using words like "good" or "fine," etc.
- Use of nonverbal cues by Teachers, for example, smiling to encourage and motivate the students.
- If the student partially gets an answer correct the teacher should give him credit for trying.
- The tutor should emphasize on the positive aspects of the pupil.

These dimensions are noted down in form of frequency of which the tutor has used them in a lesson. A hanging scale of 3 to 7 points is used to scale the categories. STAG comprises of scale ratings rates different aspects of the performance by the teacher.

The chances of a purpose happening again is usually increased by reinforcement. The teacher in a class can use positive reinforcement techniques to alter student's behavior. Negative reinforcement usually skills a student's imitation.

The elements used in reinforcement are:

- *Positive verbal reinforcement (PVR)*: the teacher uses verbal expression to give a student positive reinforcement by and by doing this the tutor accepts the feelings of the student, for example, "good job."
- *Positive non- verbal reinforcement*: use of gestures, facial expressions and body movements by Teachers so as to encourage students has been very effective in recent teaching.
- Nonverbal reinforcement: the teacher points out the mistake done by the student so as to make them reduce the chance of making the same mistakes again. Comments should not be degrading, for example, "I hate your behavior."
- *Nonverbal reinforcement (NNVR)*: this is when a teacher neglects a student as he or she is trying to answer a question due to a previous misbehavior they did this is discouraged.
- *Writing pupil answer on the blackboard (W.P.A.B)*: this enhances and boosts pupil involvement and participation. This also

enhances alertness in the class and leads to more understanding of concepts.

- Description of the skill of explaining:
- *Cognitive link (CL)*: This is a procedure trying to connect an original concept with the current concept. Using examples can help in the connection process.
- *Illustrations (ILL)*: Use of illustrations such as diagrams, real-life situations, and models will help in concept understanding as it creates a mental picture of the situation which will make it hard for a student to forget the concept.
- *Comparing and contrasting (CC)*: It is the procedure used to discriminate similar concepts of a specific attitude.
- *Meaningful repetition (MR)*: the tutor repeats a concept numerous times this can be done by repeating questions. This will enable for both slow and fast learners to be involved in the learning process and it enables students to instill the idea in their mind.

3.14. SKILL OF STIMULUS VARIATION IN TEACHING COMPUTER SCIENCE AND TECHNOLOGY

The technique used in variation of stimulus involves behavioral factors, namely movement of teacher, teacher gesture, eye contact and eye movement, changes in pattern of speech, pausing, changes in sensory focus, student talk, and student movement. It is defined at the intentional shift in the teacher's behavior so as to capture and sustain the attention span of the student throughout out the teaching process. Stimulation variation significantly affects the mood of the class as it determines tutor's zeal and liveliness in the classroom situation. According to research and numerous psychological experiments, there is evidence and proof that a student's attention and focus tends to change from one stimulus to another stimulus at a fast rate and therefore the mental psychology of an individual needs to be kept in check and monitored quite often so as to sustain attention (Lakshmi, 2009). It is challenging for a student's stimulus to focus on one thing for more than a few seconds as it is extremely volatile thus it changes a lot and due to this reason, for a student's attention to be secured and sustained throughout the lesson constant variation of stimulus should be practiced as it creates effectiveness in the general teaching process (Lakshmi, 2009).

3.14.1. Components of Stimulus Variation

Teacher movement (TM): The tutor makes very meticulous and purposeful movements in the class so as to secure and retain attention in the mind of students. The physical movement of the teacher in the class aids in capturing the attention of students in the class as their attention wanders off due to boredom. Abrupt shift in the movement of the teacher's body and also sudden stopping of teacher movement all aid in capturing the attention of students at high levels. Though, in as much as body movement is desirable, excessive body movement is not advised as it will lead to confusion of students.

Teacher gesture (TG): Use of gesture consists of movements of the head, hand and facial gesture such as laughing, raising of eyebrows, emotions and many others. Use of gestures assists the tutor to be more expressive and dynamic in presenting the concept in the class. Gestures and body movements are used by teachers in the class so as to draw attention and to elaborate a certain concept. Use of gesture and body movement in class enables the tutor to be more expressive and dynamic in presentation and this creates a mental picture to students which enhances retention of information.

Changes in patterns of speech (CSP)/Change in voice: The teacher should make use of voice fluctuations in his or her voice during teaching. Normally, the students develop boredom when the teacher's speech remains the same in pitch and this brings about deviation of student's attention. The teacher usually changes his or her tone of voice so as to portray a certain feeling or emotion and this helps to capture attention of students.

Changes in sensory focus (CSF): Normally, the teacher utilizes different frameworks to create various scenarios and introduce the new terms in the event students are not being attentive in class. The tutor utilizes and applies some sensory focuses which makes them to listen and pay attention. Focusing involves capturing attention of the learners regarding a specific concept point which the tutor considers important and needs to emphasize. Such technique involves verbal focusing, gestural focusing or verbal-gestural focusing.

People talk (PT): the teacher engages the students to talk in class by asking questions and holding discussions to maintain their attention and keep them alert.

Pupil movement (PM): during the teaching process the teacher can request the students to come to the front and write on the blackboard or tell them to open the windows observe the environment and describe the things he or she has observed.

Eye contact and eye movement: Use of eye movement and eye contact aids in portraying emotion and moderating interaction between the parties that is the teacher and the student. To enhance sustainability of attention of the students, the teacher should make use of eye contact and eye movement.

Pausing: pausing involves short, intentional intervals of silence used when elaborating and delivering a concept during teaching. This helps to capture the attention of students and also sustain their attention span. On the other hand, long pauses can be annoying and irritating.

3.14.2. Describing the Skill of Questioning

Use of questions is an essential skill in good teaching. Tutors normally use questions to check if the students have been attentive in class and it also engages the students. It is also used to assess the degree to which students are understanding the topic being discussed. It is important to understand that it is not only the questions being asked that are important, but the relevance of the question and if it matters. For example, the teacher can ask questions such as 'are we together?' or 'are you following' so as to see whether they have been attentive in class and also to gauge their level of understanding (Lakshmi, 2009).

However, students can lie and insist that they are following so as to be left alone and avoid embarrassment. Because of this, it is important to have a follow-up question like asking the students to make a summary on the topic of discussion or ask for their opinion regarding the subject matter. With this, you will ascertain they were attentive and they were understanding. The nature of the questions being asked should be open-ended so as to enable for divergent thinking and make the students think outside the box and at the same time, the intent of the questions still sticks. Asking questions using this technique, the tutor will be able to meticulously analyze and evaluate the level of attentiveness and comprehension of the students regarding the topic of discussion. Not only does asking open questions enable outside the box thinking but also it motivates sharing of ideas by students which leads to learning that is active and collaborative. This illustrates the need to be able to ask the right sort of questions to engage students (Lakshmi, 2009).

3.14.3. Questions That Tap Higher Level Thinking

During microteaching, one of the questioning techniques that have been employed in almost every institution is the use of the 5 W and the 1H, that is Who, What, Where, When, Why and How questions. Although this form of questioning technique is used and it is essential, to some extent they tend to be close-ended and most of the times it elicits a factual response. Even though getting true responses is desirable, a skilled teacher needs to encourage and develop high level of thinking skills. A perfect way of promoting high thinking level skills is by using Bloom's taxonomy of thinking skills as a guideline to be used in asking of questions. For instance, to check whether a learner has been attentive and has understood the topic, the teacher can go ahead and ask a student to judge and critique a theoretical difficult scenario or situation (Singh, 2008).

The bloom technology suggests that a student should have content and knowledge on the topic of discussion before they can be able to comprehend it and they need to be able to comprehend it prior to applying it to different contexts and situation. Students should be able to manage the lower order skills stated above that is knowledge, understanding, and application before they can be able to analyze and critic the concept. This is critical to the students before they are able to go ahead and consolidate various types of knowledge and intelligence to come up with new concepts and evaluation of "highest order" follows afterwards. Advancing between these phases requires a heightened level of thinking by the student.

There are slight variations and exceptions to this though bloom's techniques come in handy when unfolding such questions. If students are unable to answer certain questions of a particular type, the tutor can go ahead and lower the order of asking the question so at to take them back to what they are able to do and build up the asking of questions from there. Overtime, the teacher should ensure that he or she is increasing the cognitive demands so as to make it difficult (Singh, 2008).

3.14.4. Strategies to Improve the Distribution of Your Questioning

Introduction of hands-down questioning is where the students are not allowed to raise up their hands but instead the teacher picks a student who will answer the question. The teacher clearly states to the pupils that this is going to be s hands down answering session and that the teacher expects everyone to be able to answer the questions posed to them even though the response will be of a nature like "I am not sure." This might take some training but it is worthwhile.

During asking of questions, the teacher should be walking around the class so as to be able to distribute questions to every student thus asking a wider range of student's questions. Teachers seem to ask those pupils seated in a sort of "shifting spotlight."

At the beginning of the class, distribute slips of paper/card at the beginning of the lesson. Once the student answers a question the card is handed over to the next pupil. This will enable teachers to clearly identify students who still have their cards and can target an appropriate question to ask. This technique also allows teachers to engage reluctant pupils, who may be given fewer cards.

The teacher should address the question directly to the named pupil. At the same time, keep other students engaged by asking them if they have a point to add or whether they agree with the response given to that question, e.g., "Caleb, do you believe that John is the true son of the king? do you believe that proper planning leads to better results? think that Macbeth really wants to kill the King at this point? Sam, do you agree? What evidence can you find? Does anyone think something different?"

Give the students the 'thinking time' pause after posing a question so as to point out who has already answered questions. The teacher can strategize and ask the student who often answers questions to pick out other students to assist him in answering the question. This will keep the other students involved.

Allocate an observer who will keep tabs by tallying the class performance of the distribution of questions. This will aid in revealing how the questions have been distributed either in terms of gender or location. This can be done by a fellow student so as to engage others in the discussion about the answers.

3.14.5. Options to Recalling Questions and Answering Sessions

Recall questions are particularly important as they help lay out the scope of the teaching and fix key vocabularies. The teacher should use questioning techniques that will require all students to participate in recalling information that can ensure engagement of students and pace, avoiding the teacher-pupil process which limits engagement. Some of the strategies used are:

Utilization of mini whiteboard – students have to write and show their response on the board and from this teacher will be able to know the students who have grasped the concept and those students who need more learning and guidance.

Games such as "Key-word Bingo" can be used to make learning entertaining. This is where students note down words from the board. The teacher then reads out aloud the definitions of the words and the students tick out or match the correct definition they had written down.

"Here is the answer, I want you to give me the question" kind of technique can quickly stir up the kind of thinking required to make students connect. For example, if the question is: "The correct response is 24 – what could possibly be the correct question to the answer?", then the teacher can compare and contrast students' answers.

During planning, the teacher should rework the lower order questions so as to heighten the degree of thinking that is required. For instance, consider the difference between "construct and equilateral triangle" and "construct different types of triangles" from these, "what is different and what is similar?".

Using quiz-type programs on the whiteboard is great for interacting with students. Using colored pencils or fingers is also considered an alternative.

In case there is a right answer, strategize a way in which all pupils will be able to participate and give it. This is a quick way of enabling the teachers identify students who know and students who do not know and modify the tutoring accordingly.

3.14.6. Making It Okay to Get Incorrect Answers

The techniques used in questioning is meant to build a student's self-confidence. For students to be effective in the learning process they need to be able to take risks and try new things and make mistakes. A skilled teacher should be able to effectively handle wrong answers in order to raise the degree of difficulty instead of the degree of stress and at the same time, help students grow a broader understanding by connecting bits of concepts.

- 3.14.7. Tutors Ways:
- Give students time to think in order to motivate them to reflect on their answer and edit them accordingly.
- Preview the question in advance so as to give time for them to prepare.
- Echoing – for example, "So what you mean by saying "Does anyone beg to differ?""
- After a student gave a wrong answer, let the class take other responses after which let the student reconsider the response he or she had given and let them decide if it is correct or not.

Moving further, it would be extremely helpful and motivating for the teacher and the student to make the entire class to engage and participate in the discussion which enhances cross-breeding of concepts and ideas. This differs to the style of questioning which involves have a one on one questioning technique that is the teacher and the student. For a teacher to initiate a discussion in class, a proper initiation point would be to raise a question on the topic being discussed or make a statement that will lead to students making divergent responses and this will lead to a buildup of further discussion. The teacher can achieve this by making prior preparation before class like planning the type of questions to ask so as to manage the questions and ensure that all questions have been handled within the time given.

During the planning process, it is not only the type of questions that only matters but also the clarity of questions, the sequence of asking questions and the timing of asking the questions during the discussion. During asking of questions, it is important to give students time to analyze and think about the question so as to come with a sensible, well thought and modified answer though the student should not be given too much time so as to prevent time-wasting.

If the student has taken a long time to answer the questions can be given another student to answer as the other student keeps on thinking and in the event the student does not answer, it is the teacher's responsibility to check whether the question lacked clarity. If that is the case, then the teacher can go ahead and rephrase the question and pose it again to the student or try to figure which part of the question is bringing challenges to the student and why so. If the teacher realizes the question is too difficult for the student due to insufficient prior knowledge on the topic of discussion, he or she should take the initiative to bridge that gap as it will help the student connect the dots and lead to an accurate response.

Overall, teachers should not only aim towards providing clear intent questions, but also to learn to ask the right type of questions. A good teacher should always question and think about the learning outcome that is content understanding student thinking and the process of learning.

It is crucial for a teacher to develop good questioning skills as it is important in the learning process. A computer science teacher will greatly be advantaged when he or she uses questions during teaching because it stimulates a student's thinking process and assists in clarification of concepts which were not understood.

Asking questions can serve many functions as listed below.

- Asking questions stimulates the students thinking process.
- Asking questions creates a channel of thinking
- Asking question challenges the students
- Asking questions helps in recalling and relating of relevant and related concepts and facts
- Asking question helps in keeping students actively engaged in class
- Asking questions ensure the students attention is focused on the topic of discussion
- Asking question heightens the level of curiosity of the student and the topic being discussed. It develops interest and motivates the students.

3.14.8. Components of the Skills of Basic Question

The components used in asking questions include structure, variety, pause, voice, reinforcement, fluency, and distribution.

- Structure: structure should be grammatically correct, relevant that is it should be related to the topic being discussed, specific in that It should call for an individual and particular response and concise that is it should not contain redundant words.
- Variety: that is, one should apply recalling and recognizing type of questions that for example define RAM. In higher order, it should simulate high levels of intellectual skills for example how or why type of skills.
- Pause: this involves the speed of thinking and sufficiency in time for students to think and answer
- Voice: the teacher's voice should be clear, elaborate and audible.
- Reinforcement: teachers should encourage correct responses and try to reduce incorrect responses by students.
- Distribution: the teacher should redistribute questions to students so as to ensure everyone is participating actively.
- Fluency the teacher should provide a sufficient number of relevant questions.

3.14.9. Probing of Questioning

The technique of probing is used when a student has given a correct answer but it lacks proper elaboration and depth. The teacher then goes ahead and asks more question about the vague response given by the students. This technique of asking questions in response to a question is inclusive in the skill of probing questioning and it is an important skill not only to the teacher but also the student.

The five elements of the skill of probing questions are;

- *Prompting technique*: this technique involves having an in-depth scrutiny of a response which was given by the student. This helps and guides the student to come closer to the required response. The tutor provides hints and clues and asking leading questions to the students.
- *Seeking further information*: this involves asking follow-up questions to the student in accordance with the response he or she had given so as to provide additional information which actually steers the response to the expected level.
- *Re-focusing*: this technique involves providing the student with time to focus and view their response in relation to other similar scenarios. A completely acceptable response is related to the students' response. The acceptable answer comes from a topic that the student has already studied.
- *Redirection technique*: this style involves asking the same questions to other students and listening to their response. This acts as a probing technique and also enhances the participation of students in class.
- Increasing critical awareness techniques: when a student gives a correct answer or expected response the teacher goes ahead and asks 'how' and 'why' and this is used elaborate the rationale and worthiness of the answer.

3.14.10. Skill of Using a Blackboard

The use of blackboard is a really vital tutoring tool. It acts as a visual aid and its use is widely spread all over the world in the education in training sector. There also exists whiteboard which acts like a blackboard. Though, due to mechanization of our recent world the use of blackboards and whiteboards is greatly reducing due to mechanization. The ICT department is growing at the rapid rate. The use of blackboards enhances clarity in concept perception and it is effective in the use of displaying notes and diagrams during a lesson. The elements of the skill of the utilization of blackboards are;

- *Legibility (L)*: the tutor should ensure there is a proper distribution of every letter and there is enough spacing between words. This makes the handwriting to be more legible and more appealing to the eyes of students which enhances the grasping of concepts.
- *Size and alignment (SA)*: the sizing and aligning of letters is very important in blackboard writing. Uniformity of letters and the size of the capital letters should be nearly vertical as possible without getting out of line.
- *Highlighting main points (HMP)*: the content written on the Blackboard should be well highlighted so as to emphasize on the main points. Underlining and use of different colors of chalk sticks can be applied so as to draw attention to the main points.
- *Utilization of space (US)*: essential contents should be written on the blackboard. Overwriting should be avoided as it makes the work untidy and this makes the work confusing to the students which limits understanding.
- *Correctness (C)*: high-quality should be observed. Correct spelling, punctuation, and grammar should be maintained during construction of sentences in the Blackboard. Inadequate knowledge in English and errors done by teachers limits and reduces the attentiveness of learners in a classroom situation
- *Positioning of the teacher (PT)*: when the teacher is writing on the blackboard he or she should be positioned strategically at an angle of 45° so as to ensure that every student in class has a clear view of the written work on the Blackboard.
- *Eye contact with pupils (ECP)*: when the teacher is writing on the board he or she should maintain periodical eye contact with the pupils so as to maintain discipline and sustain attention of the learners throughout the lesson.
- *Clearing the board (CB)*: the teacher should systematically clean the board from top to the bottom so as to reduce the amount of chalk dust that may spreads to the class which might affect the students during learning. Once the class is over, the teacher should clean the blackboard to pave way for the next teacher to teach.

3.14.11. Demonstration of Skills

Demonstration is an act of showing that something exists by giving out evidence or proof that will support its existence. In microteaching, it is the procedure of teaching which involves showing of specimens, experiments, and devices to elaborate and illustrate the concept at hand, idea or teaching point, in the tutoring and learning process. Demonstration aids in consolidating the subject matter with real-life situation. Demonstration also makes teaching easier and meaningful to the learner

The elements used in demonstrating skills are;

- Appropriate topic concept, ideas and teaching points (A)
- Sequential order of presentation (SOP)
- Adequacy of manipulative skills (AMS)
- Creation of appropriate situation (CAS)
- Generalization

Appropriate topic, concept and teaching points (A): When demonstrating ensure it is appropriate and within the scope of the topic concept, idea and teaching point. The tools being used to demonstrate the concept that is specimens, experiments or devices should be ensured that they are related to the teaching point, concept and topic of the discussion. This leads to effective teaching as the attention of students don't go off topic as it makes grasping of the concept more difficult and the aim is to enhance teaching skills.

Sequence Order of Presentation (SOP): During presentation, the tools that will be used that is devices, experiments and specimens should be arranged in a manner that is sequential and should be presented in a systematic order this is to ensure that every demonstration tool has emphasized the evidence being presented. This sequential order of presentation indicates that there was better preparation before the actual demonstration and this shows that the skills are getting well mastered by the teacher student.

Adequacy of manipulative skills (AMP): During the demonstration process the presentation materials such as experiment; specimens or devices should be displayed to the students repeatedly during demonstration or learning process. When the teacher continues displaying these materials the students will be able to see more of the concept trying to be driven home and this has an effect of building interest in the Minds of the learners and. Enhancing mental picture of the students through repetition cements understanding of the concept.

Creation of appropriate situation (CAS): Use of nonverbal cues during presentation process is important some of the cues involve body movements, gesture etcetera. During demonstration proper physical situation with the appropriate tools, instruments and diagrams should be applied during the learning process so as to convey the concept idea in an appropriate manner. This will arouse the curiosity of the students.

Generalization: Once the demonstration has been performed and come to an end, the teacher should go ahead and generalize what has been demonstrated with the students participating so as to cement and consolidate the concept that was being demonstrated.

Once the trainee teacher has mastered all the necessary skills, he or she combines all the skills learnt in one class and utilizes them together. The separate training of subskills program to integrate other isolated skills is called link practice. This technique assists the teacher trainee to transfer skills learnt in an effective manner during the microteaching session It aids in bridging the gap created during training of isolated teaching skills and the real-life training situation experience by the trainee teacher. During the practice, the following criteria is put into play; the desirable number of students is 15 to 20, the desirable time horizon is 20 minutes and the desirable number of skills to be consolidated is 3 to 4.

Having equipped the teacher trainees with a handful of teaching sub-skills, what follows is the integration phase of the skills mastered by the teacher trainee into a major skill that they can practice in their teaching careers. Another definition of link lesson is the intentional creation of a program that is used in consolidating the sub-skills mastered by the teacher trainee. There are a number of procedures for practicing link practice. One of the procedures is that after the sub-skills have been mastered separately by the teacher trainee, three skills are combined and are practiced in a lesson for about 10 minutes. The teacher trainee then practices another three sub-skills separately and puts them together. He then puts together all the six sub-skills in a single lesson of 15 to 20 minutes. This process of linking skills goes on until all the skills that had been mastered separately have been linked together. This leads to a macro lesson that will take a normal class duration of 40 minutes which sums up to a full class session.

Link practice or integration of skills can be practiced in two ways that is integration by parts and integration as a whole.

- *Integration in parts*: Here, 3 to 4 skills of teaching are consolidated and transferred to a session that involves 15 to 20 minutes' time duration and also the 3 to 4 skills are linked and are all transferred to one lesson. Though this varies in most institutions but with an error of 3 minutes in time and 1 skill.
- *Integration as a whole:* Student-teacher links all the individual teaching skills that were mastered by the teacher and consolidates them then transfers them to a macro lesson and incorporates it to a real-life teaching scenario.

The link process starts with a sequential series of hands-on experiments which is also termed as 'make your own magic.' This help in maximizing the student's attention and interest towards the subject matter. Working materials that is 'students' material' are given out to students with each student being distributed with a worksheet number one which resembles a quiz though it is mostly empty and blank a part for spaces designated to write your name, admission number, and class. The element of "fake quiz" alters the students' perception as it makes them have an added interest thus capturing their attention. The students are then given instructions on the experiment. For example, they are told to inflate the long balloons and try two experiments which is to rub one of the balloons over another students' hair and observe whether it will make their hair stand. Also, place the rubbed side of the balloon next to a wall and check if it will defy the law of gravity (instead of the balloon falling down due to gravitational force, it will stick to the wall.

The teacher will then tell the students to tear up the worksheet one they were given into will then be told to smaller pieces. The required size of the torn pieces of paper will be shown in the OHP guideline. This will give the kinesthetic student learners a chance to participate in the hands-on activity which will contribute to a heightened and expanded participation involvement in their own process of learning. The students will then rub rulers they have been given against their piece of clothing to generate static electricity then use the ruler that has static to pick the pieces of paper on the table that were torn earlier. As you bring the ruler over the piece of paper, students will notice through observation that the pieces of paper will 'magically' be attracted by the ruler and this in its own accord, seems to defy the law of gravity.

At this point of the lesson, juggle the students' mind and ask them what are the other kinds of forces they know about apart from the force of gravity. After the students' answer, you then introduce the topic of study which is static electricity and now begin the discussion. Further hooks and bridges into the topic of discussion can slowly be introduced by providing real-life examples with regards to static electricity. For example, the creation of thunderstorms through rubbing of clouds and anecdotes of static shocks.

Chapter 4

Methods and Tactics of Teaching Computing and Computer Science Aided Instruction

CONTENTS

4.1. INTRODUCTION

The concept of teaching computer coding and data structure in schools involves analyzing the problem, using specific methods to represent the issue, problem-solving and validating the solution. Furthermore, it is essential to change the problem-solution into a simple program using a unique coding language.

Figure 4.1. *Effective computer science teaching should engage and inspire the students.*

Source: http://etec.ctlt.ubc.ca/510wiki/Computers_and_Instructional_Design_in_Foreign_Languages.

Of importance is also testing the computer instruction program to check for logical or syntactical errors, in order to ensure the output is accurate. Finally, maintenance is the last practice in application of the program based on the users' wants. The maintenance may also need to be varied depending on disparities in user applications.

4.2. FUNDAMENTALS OF INTERNET COMPUTING

4.2.1. Developing a Lesson Plan

The lesson plan refers to a methodical preparation performed in a scientific way. Effectual and successful training largely depends on flawless lesson planning. The lesson plan embodies a single teaching component meant for a learning duration. Mostly, a lesson plan refers to the teacher's cognitive and emotional conception of classroom activities.

By definition, the lesson plan is a report of the goal to be realized plus the particular method by which they are to be achieved, due to outcomes of the activities participated in during the duration. Daily lesson planning includes describing the goals, selecting and organizing the subject matter plus determining the technique and procedure. Furthermore, the lesson plan doesn't permit the educator to deviate plus it facilitates students on the way (Wang et al., 2009).

During the process of training, lesson plan is required due to these reasons. Through lesson planning, teachers regularly realize the teaching goals and process in form of elaborate objectives and processes. Furthermore, a lesson plan promotes the possibilities of modifications in the classroom setting which makes the education effective. It helps in mentioning every step of syllabus unit, as well as planning the procedure of training on the context of class control, inspiration and personal uniqueness of students (Wang et al., 2009).

4.2.2. Significance of Lesson Planning

Planning is vital and required in nearly every part of human activities, including in preparing computer science creating lessons. In a coherent lesson plan, goals are fixed while the teaching strategies, methodologies and content aid are planned beforehand. In the event that a good teaching system is created, the training work goes in a more organized way. Additionally, based on preceding knowledge, when preparing course plans the instructor provides fresh knowledge as the context of preceding knowledge that the pupils will gain. This allows the students to gain the fresh knowledge very easily on one side, while the teacher succeeds in meeting his objectives on the other hand.

In terms of psychological training, the teacher uses appropriate teaching strategies, methods and instruments to remember the interests, abilities, needs, aptitudes, and abilities that pupils have when preparing for teaching lessons. This ensures that the teaching is comprehensive by covering both psychological, emotional and cognitive aspects (Wang et al., 2009).

When making lesson plans, typically the subject material becomes limited. This allows the educator to let go of irrelevant things. They only remember material and limited content and its demonstration before the learners become easy. Students also obtain the necessary knowledge in a methodical and organized way.

For the determination of activities, generally both educator and student activities are pre-arranged depending on the class level. Ultimately, this ensures the teaching methods are significant and purposeful. During the time of formulating a lesson plan, teachers determine what facts should be clarified in respect to the strategies, procedures and instruments being used, plus what aid should be used and at what period. This allows for preparation of the necessary and effectual aids before beginning the teaching role.

The teach shall also improve their teaching skills, generally, the lesson plan functions as a crucial means for building teaching skills in pupil-teacher environments. This eventually promotes teaching with confidence. Preparation of a course plan ensures the computer science subject, plus other associated subjects are clearer to teachers (Wang et al., 2009).Eventually, this stimulates self-confidence among them. Once a teacher develops the feeling of self-assurance, he or she can easily present the fresh knowledge to the students with more interest and pleasure. Through preparing lesson plans, the educator becomes cognizant of what, how and when matters are done within the class. Ultimately, this absorbs all learners in their individual tasks, resulting in significant classroom discipline. For the perfect lesson plan, both development and thought striking questions must be asked. Furthermore, there must be some effort to expand the training from basic memory level to a more engaging contemplative level (Wang et al., 2009).

4.2.3. Qualities of an Effective Lesson Plan

Figure 4.2. *A well-prepared teacher is organized and usually effective in class.*

Source: https://education.illinois.edu/about/news-events/news/article/2019/07/25/inaugural-summit-to-convene-on-statewide-k-12-computer-science-education.

First, the lesson plan must be objective-based. An effective lesson plan should be based on certain objectives that the teacher has. While preparing this, objectives need to be clearly written and defined since its main aim is to realize some goals. The decision on proper material aids also matters. This is an important instrument of the teacher, therefore appropriate decision concerning the charts, pictures, graphs, maps, and diagrams must be taken when preparing the perfect lesson plan, plus these should further be marked at appropriate places whereby the teacher must apply them when teaching (Singh, 2008).

Likewise, a good lesson plan needs to be based upon the preceding knowledge of the students. This shall prevent difficulties in acquiring fresh knowledge by the students. The teacher further needs to subdivide their lesson plan into units.

The lessons can be subdivided into three classes which are skill, knowledge and appreciation lesson. For a perfect lesson plan, all these relevant steps must be determined and included in the classroom setting. Every lesson needs to be subdivided into appropriate units so that students can comprehend the lesson progressively. The teacher-pupil activities should be decided before-hand and there must further be a homework provision in the suitable lesson plan. It will allow students to understand the significance of the gained knowledge through practice. Furthermore, a good lesson plan should have a convenient strategy for self-criticism. The instructor must present some questions to students so that they can determine the answer, therefore judging the efficacy of the lesson planning (Singh, 2008).

4.3. HERBARTIAN TEACHING METHOD

Herbartianism is a pedagogical learning system developed by German instructor Johann Friedrich Herbart. His educational concepts, which applied mostly to the teaching of adolescents, had an immense impact on late nineteenth-century learning practices, particularly in the U.S, where teachers formed the Herbart Society back in 1895. The Herbartian Teaching style promotes 5 formal stages in teaching which include the following:

- Preparation: The process of connecting new content to be blended to relevant past concepts or memories, so as to give the student a greater interest in the subject under consideration, which in this case is computer science.
- Presentation: Offering new material through means of solid objects or real-time experience.

- Association: By integration of the new concept through association with previous ideas and contemplation of their comparisons and discrepancies in order to cultivate the new concept in the mind.
- Generalization: This procedure is especially essential to the teaching of adolescents and developed to condition the mind past the level of perception and the solid.
- Application: It involves using learned knowledge not merely in a fully utilitarian way, but such that every learned concept becomes an aspect of the practical mind and a facilitator to a clear, essential analysis of life. The step is considered possible only when the pupil directly applies the acquired idea, eventually making it his personal activity.

While enthusiasm for Herbartianism teaching declining following the emergence of new pedagogical principles, particularly those associated with John Dewey, still some schools continue practicing it up to date.

4.4. CLASSROOM USAGE

Presentation is the main step by which the actual teaching process takes place. In this phase, the goal of the lesson must be stated visibly and the title should be inscribed on the blackboard. There should be provided a situation for the tutor and the pupils to partake in the procedure of training and learning. The ultimate goal of the demonstration is to ensure the concepts are comprehensible to the pupils. This basic language is used.

Proper and accurate examples and depictions of the concepts shall make the comprehension better. The attention of the pupils on the subject context should be maintained always through asking relevant questions continually in this phase. The educator should sensibly and competently organize his material such that the pupils can clearly and easily grasp it. The instructor should make good use of graphs, pictures, charts, models, questions and various other illustrative tools for showcasing and explanation. By the end of every section, some questions regarding that segment only should be inquired to whether the students are now capable of acquiring new knowledge (Lakshmi, 2009).

Additionally, the Comparison of Association phase should be given considerable weight for comparing the facts witnessed by the pupils with another model by way of providing examples. Through using this comparison, scholars can come up with descriptions or theories that can aid in their learning. The learners are encouraged to provide new appropriate models for the concept, rather than the examples mentioned in the book in order to make them reason in an inventive way.

As for the generalization phase, it is concerned with getting at some general concepts or deriving the essential conclusions by the pupils on the context of the various comparisons, contracts, and connections in the learning content presented by the instructor. Possibly, the work of formulation must be left to pupils. The instructor at this stage must try to stay in the background and providing only essential guidance and correction (Lakshmi, 2009).

In application, teachers make the learner to use the learnt knowledge in a new environment. Except the knowledge of computer science is practiced in new environments or our daily life, any study of this subject shall be completely pointless. This practical application of computer scientific principles shall reinforce learning and further make the learning long-lasting. Finally, the recapitulation phase is meant for instructors to know if pupils have understood by revising a lesson, or providing special assignments to the pupils. It is mostly through this phase that achieving some form of closure is possible (Lakshmi, 2009).

4.5. PROGRESSIVE EDUCATION

Progressive education is a teaching movement which began in Europe and the U.S. During the late nineteenth century, being a response to the supposed narrowness and linear style of traditional education. Among its key objectives was educating the "holistic child"—which is, attending to their physical, emotional, cognitive and growth needs. The methodology was originally imagined of as an experiment where the learner was to participate actively—by learning through practice. The concept was that a child learns best through actually performing duties related to learning. Innovative and manual arts became considerably significant in the syllabus, and kids were inspired toward exploration and independent thinking (Lakshmi, 2009).

The class setting, in regard to Progressivism, is considered a democracy microcosm. The roots of progressive education movement can be found partially in European pedagogical reformations, which took place between 17th to 19th century, eventually stemming relatively from the Jean-Jacques Rousseau theories of teaching that emerged later on.

Right from its onset, progressive education sparked sharp and continual opposition from various critics. Idealists and Humanists condemned its naturalistic orientation, including its Rousseauean stress on motivating and freeing the child.

4.6. INSTRUCTIONAL OBJECTIVES

Instructional goals represent the expected change in the student who goes through teaching in a class lesson. Generally, there are two forms of instructional objectives which are General Instructional and Specific Instructional Objectives. During planning, the instructor should ask themselves "What is the purpose of teach the lesson?" Final answer to this query makes up the Instructional objectives. Every instruction will prompt learning which consequently bring about modifications in the learners' behavior (Singh, 2008).

General Instructional Objectives (GIOs) stand for the objectives mentioned in a general or vague manner. Typically, they comprise non-behavioral or non-action verbs. For instance, the learner would gain understanding of the different branches of computer science being taught with ease. They should also be able to build relevant skills in operating or manipulating digital apparatus.

In this context, the words 'acquire' and 'develop' are taken as non-action verbs that can't measure nor observe material directly since they're in form of an inward development or even passive attribute of mental activity. Specifically, the student understands the physical concept of friction and applies the acquired knowledge of friction practically in appropriate unfamiliar situations. Furthermore, the students will develop relevant skill in performing experiments, plus build interest in experimenting (Singh, 2008).

As for Specific Instructional Objectives or SIO's, the goals are mentioned in specific, and then they're referred to as specific objectives. Essentially, they feature behavioral verb such as 'action' verbs. The visible and quantifiable behavioral changes that emerge from realizing a goal is considered to be specific instructional goals or even specification.

Before any form of training is developed, teaching designers first recognize the instructional goals of the program. Instructional goals are measurable terms which describe what learners may be able to perform after the instruction. It's crucial to have clearly outlined instructional goals to ensure that what's taught in the programs matches the intended results. The abbreviation S.M.A.R.T. is applied to recollect the aims for writing clear goals.

Describing S.M.A.R.T:

- *Specific:* Instructional goals should exactly describe what's required of a learner. Specifically, the pupil shall be able to address all manner of situations or problems that come their way. This may be enhanced by mentioning how the student will address the issue step by step.
- *Measurable:* A measurable teaching objective is one which can be witnessed or one which generates data points. The student may apply compassion skills when handling their peers. They may also log and further report the consequence of each call at the final week of the semester. The log provides data concerning how the learner's reacted to the approach.
- *Attainable*: Students can't feel defeated from the intended results of the knowledge goals. Instructional objectives shouldn't ask students to prove themselves in whichever circumstances. Give students sufficient time to verify their new abilities. For instance, in the goal above, the student has around a month to verify they are effectively practically the new abilities. This is sufficient time for the pupil to do so.
- *Relevant*: Majority of learners don't care about learning content that they can't use straight away. The data availed in the training course, plus the outcomes must be significant to their private lives or daily work.
- *Time-framed*: Students need a deadline defining when they must achieve and exhibit the use of a skill set. Roughly one month is the duration for the above-mentioned goal. A learning goal that isn't time-framed provides learners the false hope that they got an indefinite quantity time for learning the skill and applying it.

4.7. THE DEDUCTIVE APPROACH

Figure 4.3. *Deductive teaching prepares students for careers of the future like software engineering.*

Source: https://www.kentuckyteacher.org/features/2018/05/spreading-computer-science-across-kentucky/.

Deduction is the procedure by which a given fact is attained from some overall known truth. Therefore, in the deductive technique of teaching the student advances from common to particular, theoretical to concrete plus from procedurals to examples. In this teaching arrangement, a pre-established policy or formula is provided to the learners plus they're requested to solve the associated problems by applying that formula. Hence, in this technique, the learner must perform just calculation or simplifying the substituted recognized values in the particular formula to arrive at a solution for the problem. Scholars like Joseph London say that "Deductive teaching safeguards first the understanding of description or law."

A deductive method to teaching usually starts by providing learners with rules, followed by examples, and practice. It is a teacher-centric approach for presenting fresh content. It is compared to an inductive method, which begins with examples and requires learners to identify rules, and thus is more learner-centric (Hazzan, Lapidot, & Ragonis, 2015).

The procedure and application of third conditional may be explained to scholars, then they got a gap-fill training to complete, before preparing their own examples.

4.7.1. Classroom Setting in a Deductive Approach

The deductive method might be appropriate with lower-level students who require a strong base from where to start with a fresh language set, or with students who are used to a more conventional approach, besides those that lack the necessary training will still be able to detect the rules themselves.

4.7.2. Planning the Activity

As a computer science teacher, first determine the theory or generalization to be taught. For demonstration purposes, this could be the point where the teacher selects generalization. Having chosen the lesson, you should choose examples which promote this generalization.

You can prepare a specific list of sentences which showcase precisely punctuated words in direct quotations. Next, open Microsoft Word document on your laptop and switch on the virtual projector which is linked to it. When you're ready to start the lesson, start by typing the first example sentence which could be a sentence like: "Stop!" Grace's father shouted as the girl raced toward the street.

Throughout the years most teachers have used inductive training methods to instruct students on concepts and generalizations, they have presented pupils with data, asking them to make open observations of that information, plus on the context of those observations, you can ask learners to mention the theory or generalization that's being taught.

Teachers have discovered this to be quite an effective training strategy since it promotes participation, which assists any action to be more exciting. As you may realize, the more captivating an action is, the simpler it is to have pupils focused and engaged in the course.

The inductive teaching system is also effectual for building perceptual and observational abilities. Pupils not only understand content but they further learn techniques for processing data and applying it for arriving at proper conclusions. This training method comprises of three overall initiatives which are: activity planning, executing and assessment of the outcome (Hazzan, Lapidot, & Ragonis, 2015).

There are many techniques that can be used to teach computer science in schools, however, teachers should ensure that the method they ultimately choose is easy to understand and practical so that it can be of great value to the students.

4.8. INDIVIDUALIZED COMPUTER SCIENCE INSTRUCTION

Figure 4.4. *Students helping each other out to solve a computer problem.*

Source: https://www.understood.org/en/school-learning/partnering-with-childs-school/instructional-strategies/individualized-instruction-vs-differentiated-instruction.

Individualized instruction emphasizes the specific needs of each student. Instruction is specific and focuses on one need per time. This instruction method may be applied on its own. Alternatively, it can be an attribute of differentiated teaching. A few pupils who get individualized instruction require teachers to assist them in understanding and learning. Other pupils using a similar teaching method may skip topics which they already know, plus progress on to more technical information.

Personalized learning is closely associated to differentiated instruction. Whereas differentiated instruction concentrates on flexible organization of learners, individualized instruction emphasizes more on the requirements of specific children. Effective classrooms should balance both individualized and differentiated approaches to develop an engaging and exciting learning environment.

4.8.1. History

Individualized instruction has its origins in B.F. Skinner psychology theory. More emphasis is placed on the particular qualities of individual learners. Teaching no longer becomes a single-size-fits-all approach, but is rather adapted to fit each individuals' needs. This form of instruction concentrated on an individualized system, and incorporated "small group training, teaching machines, coded instruction, teaching, project work, and autonomous study."

Different methods were applied to individualize instruction, such as presenting the content at varying rates for different students, changing the presentation style depending on learner social preferences, plus using materials and goals tailored to specific students. Case in point, the course work at a local school may include single lecturing sessions per week, or individual self-paced library practice with a unique worksheet. In this format, the learner can be availed with a brief overview of the study procedure, the specific library resource getting taught, and particular critical-thinking abilities to promote the study procedure and usage of a specific library resource (Reçi & Bollin, 2017).

4.8.2. Practical Application

Intelligent teaching is an aspect of computer-based instructional learning that's founded on the basis that learning based on personalized instruction by a skilled tutor is way more superior than classroom-format group instruction. Great human instructors should be 'intelligent' by continuously adjusting the material and format of their instruction, so as to ideally meet the requirements of the learner.

The historical progress of intelligent teaching systems has been drastic. The beginning point was programmed teaching which started during the late 60s, then knowledge-based trainers sought to inspire effective human trainers through the integration of teaching knowledge, domain knowledge, and understandıng about the particular student.

Ultimately, some popular current trends such as collaborative, distance and internet-based learning are defined. The presentation is availed within a cognitive science perspective. From this viewpoint, the study on intelligent teaching has shown various fruitful collaborations between scholarly research and application-based research in regards to topics such as knowledge representation, digitized assessment of knowledge, competency research, learning and acquisition of knowledge acquisition (Reçi & Bollin, 2017).

4.8.3. Perspectives on Applying ICT in Education

It is widely recognized that information and communications technology (ICT) is also affecting teaching and learning. Others expect that ICT may reduce various problems in modern-day education, such as the requirement for individualized teaching and the minimal exchange between school knowledge and actual life.

Furthermore, emerging demands from society need the education to concentrate on information administration and communication abilities. ICT is a valuable and indispensable tool in grasping these skills. Likewise, in constructivist techniques to training and learning, pupils are held answerable for their individual learning. IT is considered to provide suitable environments and implements for supporting this process (Gal-Ezer & Stephenson, 2014).

The high application capacity of ICT in education systems is well-captured in a research by Dede, carried out in 2000. This study focused on ICT abilities for improving learning: centering the syllabus around authentic issues parallel to the real-world settings; covering students in digital communities of practice, applying advanced tools such as those in modern day high-tech workplaces.

It was found that technology-facilitated guided, contemplative inquiry through lengthened projects that back complex concepts and skills plus generate more complex products; applying modeling and conception as powerful techniques for bridging the gap between abstraction and experience. When used appropriately, computer science can promote students' collaborative development of meaning through various viewpoints on shared experiences, plus includes learners as partners in building learning experiences and growing knowledge; while nurturing success for all pupils through unique measures to assist the disabled as well as the disenfranchised (Lakshmi, 2009).

In 1994, researchers made concerted efforts to interpret advancements in ICT with regards to educational innovations. They postulated that the possibilities of technology determine the way in which education develops. From their perspective, there are certain key stages which be identified. The 'substitution' phase marks the technology applications which are able to mechanize aspects of the instructional procedure. In this phase, ICT gets used solely as a substitute for various tasks of the instructor, with a specific goal to make learning more effective, while providing increased possibilities for customizing education.

For 'transition' stage, ICT isn't just used for substituting existing tasks, but further requires that instructional activities and material are changed. During this stage, technology applications don't just shape the learning process, instead students themselves must progressively structure their individual learning process. During the 'transformation' phase, not only should instructional activities and content be changed, but even the underlying basis of education must change. A good example of the final case is the advancement in network technology which may trigger digital learning communities whereby pupils, instructors, and scientists are directly involved. The situation provides greater opportunities for education to occur in collaboration with practicing experts than may otherwise be conceivable with just a few field excursions per year (Lakshmi, 2009).

4.8.4. The Importance of Individualized Instruction

Meeting the diverse needs of learners can be an overwhelming task for teachers. It most probably requires planning and evaluation of student progress, even though the benefits greatly outweigh the demerits. Individualized teaching prepares kids to become active plus effective learners, building the skills necessary for becoming life-long students in an ever-progressing world. With the varied ability levels of kids, individualized instruction assists instructors to notice the differences of kids to improve moral standing, retain useful information, and enhance kids' engagements in their daily learning (Lakshmi, 2009).

There are certain essential steps to developing a successful personalized learning classroom. First, they should be setting specific, achievable, realistic, measurable and timely. Not to mention instructors must also be able to review the goals regularly, and allow pupils to own their learning progress. Teachers must plan prudently and cooperatively to ensure they're applying meaningful information to gain insights into how individual students are progressing towards achieving a particular goal. There's a movement away from extended full-group lessons to more engaging instructional and question-based projects.The schools and learning projects that compliment strategic usage of modern technological resources permit teachers to develop engaging lessons, which address the natural curiosity of every child. Trainers provide opportunities for kids to address their learning process in various ways, providing increased opportunities for retaining information that enhances moral understanding and interest for learning. Individualized learning fundamentally allows pupils to learn content at their individual pace with instructor direction. While the students are still striving towards meeting rigorous and complex learning outcomes, nevertheless they're provided with multiple ways to showcase their learning (Lakshmi, 2009).

4.9. PROGRAMMED LEARNING

Figure 4.5. *Programmed Learning promotes cooperation and is an effective way of teaching computer science in schools.*

Source: https://www.learncomputerscienceonline.com/computer-programming/.

Programmed Learning refers to a method of providing individualized instructions through applying different educational instruments, which may be done with or without assistance from a teacher. The educational material is organized in a particular order and subdivided into small sections or parts known as frames. Once an instructional content is prepared by the teacher, the pupil's entry behavior is deliberated (Wang et al., 2009).

The instructor then designs the educational material which will help the learner to attain the terminal conditioning necessary for the lesson. The pupil is provided with a frame and assisted to learn that frame. Furthermore, the learners can evaluate themselves or allow the instructor to evaluate them. Upon mastering the frame, they can advance to the subsequent frame. This provides for increased understanding of the topic. A pupil will realize if they understand the subject well, or if they require any improvement and should study the computer science topic more. During programmed learning, students are highly motivated because they often get a quick response from their activities.

They quickly get to know whether they have the necessary knowledge for advancing on to the subsequent topic. The learner moves in his individual speed, which is known as Self-Pacing. In case determining a frame or topic proves to be difficult, the person can spend as much duration as they want to learn the subject. It is only after mastering the particular topic or frame that they proceed over to the next, an aspect that works similar to Formative Evaluation.

There is less contact between learners and students, and increased interaction between learners and their education material consisting of book, computers and other such resources. Programmed Learning may take place in school or at home, plus students don't need to be within the school setting. Essentially, there are three forms of Program Learning which are Linear, Branch and Mathematics (Wang et al., 2009).

4.9.1. Origins of Programmed Learning

Socrates is believed to be the original programmer, who created a special program in geometry that was later detailed by his follower Plato. Others believe that the beginnings of programmed learning content can be traced back to Bhagvat-Geeta, who successfully developed the first coding text. Moreover, programmed instructions derive its origin from learning psychology advocated by one E.L. Thorndike, who gave certain laws on learning. Based on one of these laws, known as the effects law, the learner has a habit of repeating their program, though they may also take interest in increasingly understanding the learning curve that provides great contentment (Seendani, 2014).

Pressey also developed the teaching device in 1926. The instrument is also related with the origins of coding instruction. The device comprised of the structure of having expressive texts with the collection of objects having provision for quick feedback or multiple-choice questions. Multiple-choice questions present only one correct answer, which the learner has to identify. The machine he developed had some aspects of programming which have been brought forward to today's education system (Seendani, 2014).

Additionally, Skinner's operant conditioning plays a lot to the expansion of programmed instruction or teaching. In this theory, an organism's response is voluntary and unstructured and the occurrence predictability of these reactions is increased considerably. Skinner attempted to formulate the key philosophies of learning plus through these models he eventually developed an instruction model, commonly referred to as Skinnerian, programmed instruction or the linear model. In the 60s, organizations like NCERT began making coded teaching materials in different languages, so that they can be available to as many students as possible (Seendani, 2014).

4.9.2. Programmed Learning Principles

The most common one is principle of objective. This means detecting the terminal manners that the student is required to have by the conclusion of the course or program. Generally, the terminal behavior must be based upon the entry behavior. In case the entry, behavior has been ranked as weak or poor, educators should have minimal anticipation of terminal behavior. The next one is Small Steps Principle. Here, the teaching program should be separated into smaller steps or frames since it makes learning a whole lot simpler. The teacher should design the program so that the frames can move from basic topics to more complex and multifaceted topics (Seendani, 2014).

Additionally, students learn much quicker when they are active. For program learning, the student is constantly kept active since each frame needs them to actively participate in activities such as learning, self-evaluation and knowledge application. These frames also need to be meaningful. In case the frames are excessively easy or too complex then students might become sedentary and bored.

Also, of great importance is the Minimal Error Principle, this simply means that error and failure must be avoided at any cost since they're considered as impediments to learning. A student can't go from a given frame to another if they keep making errors. As for the Model of Immediate Feedback. The learner is motivated upon getting immediate response. For program learning, the student can swiftly know if they are right or wrong. For guaranteeing success and satisfaction, pupils should realize that this activity is correct.

In addition, it involves Self Pacing which is a method of individualized teaching. Learners don't need to wait in order keep up with other students. So long as they've mastered a particular frame or topic, they can rapidly advance over to the subsequent topic or frame. For slow learners, they can gradually learn at their own unique speed (Singh, 2008).

Additionally, Programmed Learning can be a great way for students to test their learning abilities, since it constantly tests the learners' knowledge. Pupils are expected to give some form of response for every frame. In case the pupil is correct, then this means that they have understood the frame, plus they can advance over to the succeeding frame. This is a form of formative evaluation, which further helps in improving instructional programs.

Programmed learning, also called programmed instruction, basically is a research-based structure that assists learners to work successfully. This method is determined by research conducted by various educators and applied psychologists. The teaching content is in a form of textbook, computer or instructions machine. Furthermore, the medium typically offers the content in a rational and tested sequence. Typically, the text is presented in small phases or larger chunks. Following each step, students are provided with a query to examine their comprehension. Then instantly the accurate answer is shown. It means that the student at all phases makes responses, plus is given instant knowledge of their results (Singh, 2008).

4.10. BRANCHED PROGRAMMING

Figure 4.6. *Chinese students in a practical computer science class.*

Source: https://theirworld.org/news/chinese-school-children-learn-computer-coding-digital-skills.

The originator of Branching programming method is Norman A. Crowder. This is a problem-solving technique where frames have been arranged to appear like a tree branch. He believed that learners must be able to rectify their own mistakes. While in Linear Systems students must check the answer key and determine if they are correct or otherwise. For the Branch Method, if their answer is wrong then they advance to Remedial Frames that further expound on the topic.

Ultimately, the pupil moves forward once they answer correctly, though is still diverted or branched onto one or several remedial frames in case they don't. The frames clarify the matter anew, ask the student questions to prompt the correct answer and divulge any previous mistakes they may have made, next return them back to the original frame. Essentially, this cycle persists until the pupil passes through the entire instructional content at their own pace (Lakshmi, 2009).

Considering that this method depends on self-learning, it is ideal for higher education levels like universities and colleges. It is why Branching Programmed Teaching is also referred to as Intrinsic Programming. This means the learner by themselves can make the necessary decision, to conform the Learning process to their needs. Additionally, solutions may be realized by the pupils themselves. They won't depend on any external sources such as teachers or answer keys for finding answers.

4.10.1. Key Features of the Branching Program

The frames are normally huge and lots of data is provided in each frame. The frame might comprise two or several paragraphs and occasionally a full page. Equally, multiple-choice queries may be asked while every response for the question should be keyed to varying Remedial Frames. In case where the learner chooses the correct response, their response is given and for cases where they pick the wrong response, it means that they must move onto Remedial Frames from where learners can determine why they were wrong in the first place (Lakshmi, 2009).

Furthermore, learners have the freedom to determine their unique path of action depending on the subject matter's background. The pupil controls the unique sequence which they will follow, a learner may either consider typical frames or advanced remedial frames. Also, the programming allows students to express their opinions better since it's not objective-based questions such as Linear Style. Students are further impelled to focus on the subject content more carefully in order to understand and better focus on the subject material.

In his theory, Crowder assumes that making errors now and then is a normal process of learning, which allows students to apply some of these techniques in their community. If any adjustments are to be made, then based on their eventual spectator or goals that are set up students' needs should be focused to understand them (Seendani, 2014).

The Branching model allows for at least 20% of errors which do not affect the student's overall performance in class. Nevertheless, the branching program is a bit difficult and complicated and learners may make several errors that could still impact on their ability to grasp the concepts. Also, the frames which a student covers will depend on their knowledge. In case they are very smart, the learner may not need to consider Remedial Frames. However, when the learning content is in the form of a book, then the book is known as a scrambled book since the pages don't run in a normal structure.

For instance, if a pupil makes a mistake, then the instruction shall direct them to visit the subsequent page for further detail. This approach is quite useful or applicable to concept learning, even in cases where the content is availed in much larger steps. Overall there are fewer interactions between students. Students aren't provided with the answer straight away, but are rather brought to discover the final answer by themselves (Reçi & Bollin, 2017).

Programmed learning helps to provide "stimulus control" in the entire learning process, through which it broadly affects or impacts on the teaching content itself. Furthermore, in programmed learning, there may be a complete system proposed that includes several stages. A pre-test may be given, or alternatively the original behavior stated with a post-test provided as well. The content can also be tried out and reviewed depending on the final results.

4.11. LINEAR PROGRAMMING

Figure 4.7. *A classroom with a modern computer projector that makes learning more exciting to students.*

Source: https://Twitter.com/mluebbecke/status/827495030424207360.

This teaching model immediately strengthens student responses in relation to the learning goal. Reactions that don't lead toward the objective go unreinforced. Every bit of knowledge is availed in a "frame," plus a student who's made an accurate response goes on to the subsequent frame. All learners work through a similar sequence, besides a low ratio of error is necessary to ensure continual positive reinforcement of accurate responses.

Linear education is an educational method which comprises of pedagogical strategies regarding program-centeredness and linear arrangements. This stands in contrast to flexible education.

A linear teaching format infers that to, for instance, understand the material of a learning module, one is needed to have grasped (through valuation processes) the material of learning program. For a linear learning system, this format focuses on a pre-determined line whereby the learning material is provided with none or minimal flexibility for participants. However, there is still an on-going debate regarding the practicability of linear learning (Singh, 2008).

The results of experiments done by education researchers like Benjamin Granger indicate that in some instances, linear could become more effective compared to flexible learning systems.

This finding would signify that this approach is reliant on the framework including learning styles and objective orientation/self-motivation techniques.

4.11.1. Research Finding

Linear programming is reinforced by Cognitive Load Theory (CLT), which draws attention to the amount of cognitive load present in the learning procedure, such as flexible teaching and face-to-face learning. The scenarios can either involve a basic content or more complex material.

Flexible learning is particularly effective in teaching simple content with superior results than the 'program control' method. When applied in a complex situation, the flexible technique loses roughly 50% of its effectiveness.

The experiment shows that flexible learning situations are in context a weak method when handling complex contents (Singh, 2008).

The dynamic learning method for complex material hasn't been presented to be unfavorable for every situation. Experts suggest that the ultimate performance of students placed in flexible learning settings was highly influenced by individual goal orientation, referring to the motivational ratio and learning traits of the learner. Eventually, the greater the goal orientation, the greater the output in learner-controlled (flexible) settings, no matter the content's complexity. This affirmation enforces the notion that flexible learning seems to highlight motivational personal differences, which are regarded as a disadvantage for the learning procedure (Singh, 2008).

4.11.2. Overcoming Personal Differences and Understanding Cognitive Load

According to researchers, individual mindsets can be influenced or even shaped so as to optimize scholar's use of student-control (in flexible teaching environments). The Learner Objective Orientation can be considerably high in some people, though can also be prompted or stimulated through external actors like trainers, supervisors and instructional designers via error encouragement, for instance; therefore, making it a personal difference which can be impacted prior to and in the course of training (Seendani, 2014).

Blended-learning techniques covering the use of linear as well as flexible learning sets, whereby the learner is given momentary control of learning actions, may further be considered as an option to overcome personal differences and mental overload.

4.11.3. Benefits of Linear Programming

Some of the practical applications of this teaching program involve scheduling, planning production, program management and fixation. The linear programming approach maintains a special structure which can be exploited by users, in order to derive computational advantages. Among the key benefits of Linear Programming include:

- Is well-suited for solving complicated problems.
- It helps in simplifying the lesson for students therefore giving much better outcomes.
- Enhances quality of decision. An improved learning quality can be achieved with the process by utilizing the linear programming model.
- Provides a methodology for unifying results coming from disparate zones of mechanism design.
- It is more flexible compared to other computer science learning systems, allowing for a broad range of problems to be solved easily.

4.12. COMPUTER-ASSISTED INSTRUCTION (CAI)

Figure 4.8. *Computer-aided learning can assist students from poor or rural communities increase their knowledge.*

Source:https://reap.fsi.stanford.edu/research/computer_assisted_learning_in_poor_rural_schools_phase_ii.

Many scholars believe that computer-assisted technology is the likely future of learning, plus that future is right now. Education, being a procedure and discipline, is particularly concerned with providing knowledge, techniques of teaching, and offering/maintaining a convenient learning setting rather than informal education and various other techniques of socialization. CAI, as the name suggests, is the application of electronic instruments/computers to deliver educational instruction plus to learn. Computer-aided learning may be used in nearly all sectors of education, varying from TV/DVD play/learn programs for kindergarten children to training complex theories in university. CAL is created by merging knowledge from various sectors of education/learning, cognition and human-computer interface (HCI).

Nowadays, classical education techniques are quickly being substituted with virtual learning, online schools, and distance learning structures. Enhanced by greater visualization and information transmission technologies, it is now rather easy to develop computer software courses that display and evaluate graphic multi-dimensional information for human interpretation. It has now become an integral aspect of education. Additionally, it is frequently applied to build and make smart presentations in topics that are hard for learners to comprehend without proper exhibition (Reçi & Bollin, 2017).

Computer-assisted training may be described as the training, learning, and cooperation process that is facilitated by the usage of computers. Essentially, the key advantage that CAL possesses over training approaches is interaction. Computers may motivate and rekindle the new interest of learners during the entire learning procedure at different levels. For instance, on one side, it promotes the interest of pupils in the education material or material being taught like a DVD tutorial showing how to perform certain procedures.

At a higher level, workstations can expedite live/active classroom interaction between the learners and the instructor, or among the pupils themselves and supervised by the trainer. The notion of human interface with workstations has been recurrent since the inception of home electronic appliances during the late 80s. Nevertheless, it only started to gain momentum during the last decade because of increased mobile innovation revolution, plus Internet which promotes affordable and reliable interaction across the globe.

Computer-based learning is sometimes referred to as PC assisted instruction. Through playing and using content stored on smartphones, DVDs, and other virtual-based resources, learning is made more appealing and dynamic, plus gives the students entertaining opportunities for showcasing their listening and knowledge acquisition skills. It improves the learners' confidence in handling the tasks they are given and therefore enhances the quality of content that they have learnt (Reçi & Bollin, 2017).

Since the Computer-assisted Instruction programs were set up as a modern training method, rather than a traditional teacher-centric classroom system, there have been growing concerns regarding the competences of this teaching method. Occasionally, teachers do express some concerns about this technology since they fear that computers may take over their careers.

Furthermore, a number of the technologies applied in CAI are fresh and thus teachers require teaching to get accustomed with the new innovation. Educators are needed to test-run the program before the class starts, and to expect and fix practical glitches which may happen during the lesson. If the generation distance is well considered, the instructor who seeks to apply the CAI program in class must adjust their focus and competence to something that seems like an entirely new teaching method (Reçi & Bollin, 2017).

4.12.1. Objectives of Computer-Assisted Instruction

The everyday use of IT and networks is getting indispensable in nearly every profession. Fresh changes in education models, including new business and technological innovations are mostly computer-centered. Therefore, educational institutions need to modify their course and training techniques to be computer-relevant.

The fundamental objective of CAI is to promote and develop the integration of this digital teaching methodology among students, whereas further increasing the efficiency and productivity of instructors with the assistance of computer-based technology, plus update students' familiarity to modern trends since most of the models outside the previous decade are increasingly becoming out of date. Hence computer technology must be an integral aspect of the schooling system. Another goal of CAL is developing easily understandable and striking tutorials and presentations of the topics or disciplines they are employed in (Reçi & Bollin, 2017).

4.12.2. Computer-Based Learning Evaluation Tools

The most popular tool is Multiple Choice Questions. It's mostly applied for computer-based tests, specifically this form of training is used to evaluate a student's comprehension of material that they have been taught. It is also closely related to Fill-in the Gap which is used for computer based tests as well. The learner is needed to write text in the spaces where a few have been left out. Here, the student must provide convenient words to complete the exercise. The exam can be easily completed in a few minutes, plus can be developed using affordable software like Hot Potato (Rocha et al., 2018).

Additionally, Digital Interactive Chat Group conversations can be a great learning path for learners and educators to share ideas virtually through speech or text. It is pretty simple to put up a group talk server through a social media instrument. Nevertheless, it may sometimes be hard to moderate plus it can become tedious if there are just a few users virtually in the chat box. When managed with tasks and appropriate groups of learners, in terms of their age and interests, chats can turn into inspiring communication, particularly when post chat duties are provided by the end of the instruction.

Equally, Listening Exercises can also be practiced. For these exercises, the workstation substitutes the tape recorder. Meanwhile, the computer is joined to a good sound system. Learners must listen keenly to the audio recorder that's being played using the computer, with audio CD/DVD, Podcasts and audio streams being among the most popular form of

Language art teachers will further be able to use simulated computer software to present complex concepts, which would have otherwise been impossible without technology (D'Atri et al., 2011).

Technology promotes essential structural improvements in learning, which may be integral to attaining significant enhancements in classroom productivity. It is used to advance both teaching and education, generally infusing classrooms with virtual learning tools, like computers and portable devices. Moreover, due to its versatility, course offerings, and learning materials can be improved and made available to more students in need of quality learning resources. Students will be equipped with the necessary skills for developing 21st-century skills which are relevant to the marketplace. Studies further show that learning technology and innovation can accelerate student engagement, motivation and enthusiasm to learn new concepts in school.

Equally, technology has the potential to transform learning by promoting a new concept of connected training. This model links educator to their learners and to expert content, resources, and structures to help them enhance their individual instruction and customize learning. Virtual learning opportunities, plus the use of public educational resources and different technologies can improve educational productivity through accelerating the level of learning, minimizing costs associated with educational content or program delivery, as well as better utilizing the instructor's time (D'Atri et al., 2011).

In the U.S., a total of 48 states including District of Columbia are presently supporting online learning opportunities which vary from complementing classroom training occasionally, to enrolling pupils in full-time courses. The opportunities provided to students through innovation include easy enrollment opportunities, and summer-school courses among others.

Chapter 5

Instructional Aids in Teaching Computer Science and Technology

CONTENTS

5.1. INTRODUCTION

There are many factors that can lead to having some difficulties in learning. It is, however, possible to promote intellectuality through sensory means. Sensory aids have helped to promote effective learning and they have also helped in improving the learning experience. There are many teachers, instructors, and educators who have seen the benefits of using audio-visual material in the classroom. These tools are versatile and help in improving student engagement. These tools have been very helpful in the teaching of computer science. One can never lack a way to explain a computer science-related aspect to the students when they are well equipped with these materials. There will always be a way to explain it using the audio-visual aids.

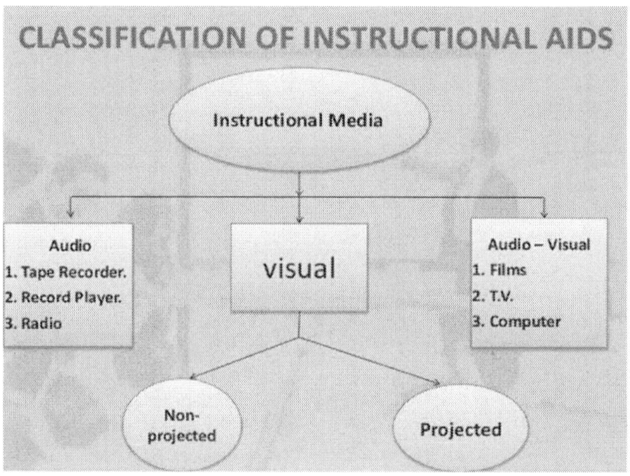

Figure 5.1. *Above are the main instructional media that are used in the classroom today.*

Source: https://www.slideshare.net/kanikaglr/instructional-aids.

There are many ways in which audio-visual material can be used to teach computer science, as seen in the following sections.

5.2. TEACHING COMPUTER SCIENCE USING INSTRUCTIONAL AIDS

Instructional aids are considered materials that help with teaching and learning. These materials help with reinforcing, supplementing, or supporting the aspects being taught. Instructional aids are different from training media because aids are materials by which instructional messages can be communicated to students.

Some of the examples include video cassettes, computer programs, the voice of the instructor, printed texts, or flight simulators. All these are considered training media (Reçi & Bollin, 2017).

Teachers choose and prepare instructional aids that they find appropriate in their schools and classrooms; however, most times they are already set up. There is a setting that allows the teacher to give independent instructions, and for these, the teacher may have to prepare this himself/herself.

This means that the teachers need to be well-prepared to use these materials.

There are some people who think that having audio-visual materials will make the teacher irrelevant but this is a misconception. The truth is that it helps to make the learning experience of the students and it also makes the teaching experience easier.

They help to make the learning experience much more attractive to the students.

There is a theory that helps in explaining how instructional aids work to promote student learning.

There are many different educators who have come up with many theories on how the brains of the students together with the part of the memory function works during the time in which they are hearing or viewing the materials. All the theories, however, have some specific aspects that are similar, and they have helped in the further understanding of these aids.

During the process in which the materials are being communicated, the memory section if the brain works to filter the information.

As the information is received, the sensory register of the student helps in sorting out the parts of the information that are important, leaving out the parts that are either considered ordinary, or unimportant.

Within a short period of time, around a few seconds, the information that is considered important, is sent to the short-term memory, where it undergoes processing for it to be later be stored in the long term memory (Reçi & Bollin, 2017).

Figure 5.2. *Visual aids are very impressive in classrooms. They help the students see what exactly they are being taught.*

Source: https://venngage.com/blog/visual-aids-for-learning-templates/.

This process is normally much more efficient by using appropriate instructional aids, which help in highlighting and emphasizing the major sections that are taught. The functions of the short-term memory are restricted by both the capacity and time. It is therefore important for the data that is being conveyed to be arranged in a manner that is effective. This includes piecing up the information in specific bits that are important so are to ensure the information is coded, rehearsed, and recorded in an effective manner. The level at which the instructional aid is effective is a major process.

Some of the aspects that help the students in understanding, and also retaining information that is important include charts, pictures, and graphs that have undergone selection in a proper manner, as well as any other visual aids that have been organized in a proper manner. All in all, instructional aids need to undergo designing in a manner that deals with major concepts and aspects. It is also important for the work being covered to be straight to the point and it should also have facts only, so that it makes it easier for the students to retain the information (Kadijevich, Angeli, & Schulte, 2013). There are many aids that are simple to use, and these should also be considered first.

5.3. FUNCTIONS OF INSTRUCTIONAL AIDS

Instructional aids are important in any and every classroom. They are considered one of the most important elements in ensuring effective learning as well as teaching experiences. There are many advantages of using instructional aids, including:

- They help the students in the development and enrichment of their reading skills, together with their skills of understanding.
- They help in the illustration, demonstration or reinforcement of specific aspects and skills.
- They aid in the differentiation of approaches that are instructional and also help in easing the anxiety that comes with learning new things. In addition, they help in eliminating the monotonous nature through using newer and innovative methods of conveying information.
- They also help in engaging all the sensory aspects of the students, considering the fact that these materials can be used to supplement or expound on aspects in the lesson.

5.3.1. Development and Enrichment of Skills on Reading and Understanding

Students normally find it hard to understand certain aspects of the information they are receiving. Using instructional aids, teachers are able to bridge this gap and also improve the understanding skills of the students. Some of the examples of instructional aids that can be used improve the comprehension skills of the students include the use of articles, newspapers, advertisements, comic books, etc.

5.3.2. Illustration, Demonstration or Reinforcement of Certain Aspects and Skills

Instructional aids are important for teachers when they want to illustrate, demonstrate, or reinforce certain concepts and skills. The students get more time to practice on their skills, and also the information is conveyed in a manner that allows then to have effective engagement with the information they are receiving in many different ways. They also achieve this by using the many different forms of learning in the classroom.

5.3.3. An Approach to Instruction That Is Diverse

These materials help the teachers to differentiate teaching allowing them to use the many different types of learning. Using aids, such as videos, charts, cards, helps with stimulation of the visual senses of the students, allowing them to get the opportunity to receive this content in different points of view. This allows the students to have interaction and engagement with the information that they are learning in a way that allows them to understand the content without having any hardships.

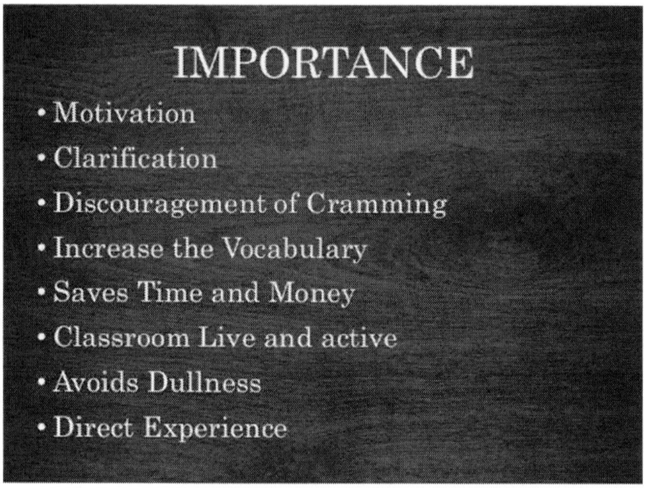

Figure 5.3. *Above is a summary of some of the main importances of using instructional aids in the classroom.*

Source: https://www.slideshare.net/jellyways/aids-and-applications-for-easier-learning-and-teaching-finals.

5.3.4. The Environment for Learning Becomes Interesting and Engaging

Today's world is digitalized and the students get exposure to technology at a very young age. Using computer devices, such as tablets and computer games, give them much more excitement than what they get at school, especially if the teachers use the lecture-type instruction. The students are always looking for ways to always get excited, making them detest boredom. Using technology in the classroom will help in eliminating boredom and therefore improving the quality of education that the students receive, due to the excitement that these devices bring.

5.3.5. They Discourage the Students from Cramming

Due to students' interest in audio-visual materials, students pay much more attention to audio-visual materials. These materials also promote faster understanding and retention because most of the student's senses are being utilized. The knowledge is interpreted through seeing, hearing, and doing, thus stabilizing the information that is being conveyed, thus preventing cramming, and promoting retention.

5.3.6. They Make Teaching Efficient

These materials make it easier for the students to understand, therefore making the teaching process much more effective and efficient. There are many aspects that students find hard to understand, especially when they are spoken or written on a blackboard; however, the use of instructional aids has helped to promote better student understanding. These aids help in making subjects that the students consider hard and boring, interesting and fun. The aids use factual materials that have been interpreted in a manner that is much easier to understand, allowing the students to grasp the concepts faster.

5.3.7. The Content in These Materials Can Be Updated Easily

Teachers create their content with certain things in mind: how long they are going to use the content, the number of times it may need to be updated, and the outcome of the content. They are well aware that technology is always changing, and they need to keep updating it. It may be harder to update material that is written on paper, in comparison to updating that on a portable keyboard. Being able to update the work in this efficient manner makes the teaching experience much more efficient and effective.

5.4. CHARACTERISTICS OF PROPER INSTRUCTIONAL AIDS

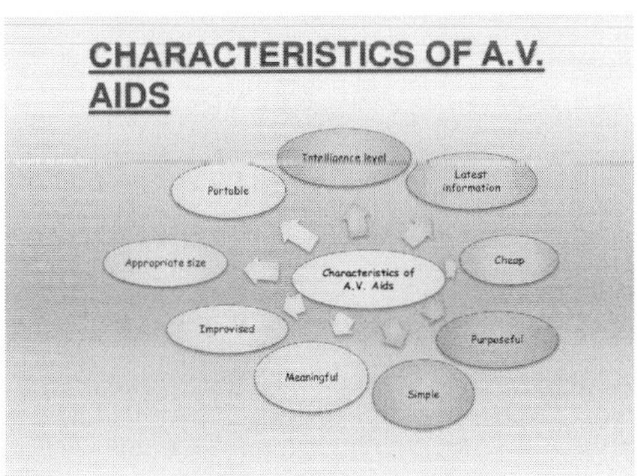

Figure 5.4. *This is a diagrammatic representation of some of the characteristics of visual aids.*

Source: https://www.slideshare.net/1302011987/audio-visual-aids-or-instructional-aids.

These materials are used to ensure effective conveying of information. It is important that the specific aids chosen are essential in doing so. The teacher needs to know how the instructional aids should be prepared and used so as to be efficient in the work they are supposed to do. It is important for the teacher to also appreciate the value of these materials, so that they can be able to use them to their highest potential.

Some of the main characteristics that these aids should have so as to be working in an efficient and effective manner include:

- They should be appealing to the senses and perceptions of the students.
- They should be able to cause attraction and also keep the attention and interest of the students.
- They should be able to develop comprehension of the information that is being relayed to the students.
- They should help the students attain faster learning and also reduce the time for instruction.
- They should allow the students to comprehend the relations between the different ideas and facts.

Instructional aids that are appropriate are required to help in the promotion of results that are desirable. They need to promote the stimulation of interest, engage the students, be easy to comprehend, and also ensure that the students have a positive reaction to them. They also need to be easy to use, and the instructions that are provided for their use need to be well written and explained, so that they are also easy to understand.

5.5. TYPES OF INSTRUCTIONAL AIDS

There are many different forms of instructional aids. Each of them has specific pros and cons. For the teacher to determine the appropriate instructional aid, they need to consider:

- *The instructor* – it is important to consider whether the teacher has the ability to form and use these tools. In addition, they should also be able to choose, from those that have already been created, in a manner that is suitable for his/her audience. All this depends on the experience the teacher has.

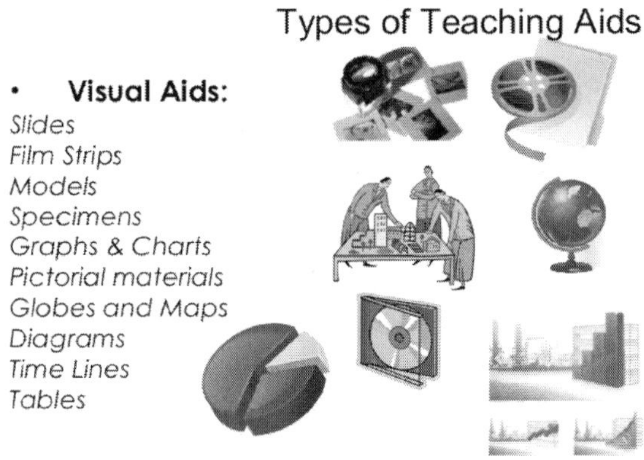

Figure 5.5. *There are many types of teaching aids, above are some of the examples.*

Source: https://pt.slideshare.net/7mukut/use-of-teaching-aids-in-the-teaching-learning-process.

- *The lesson being taught* – it is important to consider the specific aspect that is being taught in the lesson. Each specific instructional aid can be used in a different way to achieve different things. Others can be much more efficient than others with the different objectives that are being taught. For example, the teacher can use graphs to demonstrate a visual representation of a computer aspect.
- *The nature of the aspect that is being discussed* – the specific topic that is being taught helps in choosing the specific aid that will be used. An example includes having to choose an aid while considering the difficulty level of the topic being taught.
- There are two main classifications of instructional aids. The first classification include:
- *Visual aids* – These help in providing visual explanations and visual interpretations. They appeal to sight sensors. Some of these include pictures, posters, and graphs.
- *Audio-Visual Aids* – These help in providing both audio and visual information which allows the students to listen to and see the information being relayed. These include movies, slides, and motion pictures.

- *Auditory Aids* – These help in relaying information that the students can listen to. It uses the sense of hearing. These include podcasts, radio, and audio recordings.
- *Stimulation Devices* – These help to give representations of real objects or processes but are relayed in a smaller size. These help in the stimulation of the work of the actual devices. They help in the development of the feeling of the real function of the actual object.

5.6. HOW TO PREPARE INSTRUCTIONAL AIDS

There are many different places that one can acquire instructional aids. There are some that can be bought after being made and others can be created by the teachers. Most of the ones that undergo production for commercial use are hard to find and they are also quite expensive. The teacher then needs to ensure proper designing, construction, and utilization of the instructional aids that are desired. The method of creating their own instructional aids is called Improvisation.

The teachers are able to note any specific problems with the instructions that are set and these can be fixed by using a specific type of aid. Most of the instructional aids that are created from scratch are easy to make. To make an instructional plan that works effectively, it is important to consider the plan, the layout and the proportions.

The instructor should also remember to use colors at every single possibility that comes up so as to gain the interest of the students (Kadijevich, Angeli, & Schulte, 2013).

If the instructional aid is an object, it is important for the person designing it to choose the specific material.

It is important for the instructor to use materials that are easy to source out and they should also be affordable. If the tool is a model, it is important for the instructor to estimate and cost the materials. The teacher should also make sure to utilize the tools and paraphernalia that is found in the school where they teach.

They can also involve the students in creating these aids. It allows the students to improve their learning experience. It can also help them to better remember the aspects being detailed on the aids. It is very effective when the teacher is able to use visual aids in combination with verbal explanations (Kadijevich, Angeli, & Schulte, 2013).

The most common visual aid is the blackboard. If it is used in the correct manner, it can be very effective. It is important for the teacher to plan to use the blackboard in a manner that captures the attention of the students. This means having to use imagination and creativity. All the teacher will need is the ability to draw. Some of the ways the teachers can make the use of the blackboard more effective is:

- Planning the aspects that the instructor is trying to illustrate before attending the lesson.
- Drawing of pictures and diagrams that are complex before the beginning of the class.
- Using different colored chalks for the emphasis of certain points.
- Ensure that what you write on the blackboard is easy to read and understand.
- If the teacher is creating aids that are permanent, using the blackboard, they need to make sure that the images, posters, and charts are large.

While preparing these aids, it is advisable to ensure omission of any details that are not necessary, utilize a handwriting that is easy and simple to read, and make sure that the symbols used are appropriate.

Some of the factors that may influence the decision the teacher makes include:

- Audience factors: this includes the size of the class, the age of the students, the experience the students have, the level of understanding, and aptitude.
- Aspects that the teacher wants to change in the audience: this involves being able to learn a new skill, being able to gain information, and changing the attitude of the students.
- What exactly is being taught.
- The relative cost: this involves the time taken to teach the specific lesson, the money it will need, and the energy that is spent.
- The ability that the teacher has when it comes to handling the aid.

It is, however, important for the instructors to know that they will not be able to fix all the problems in student learning using instructional aids. These aids can be used to ensure that the teaching and learning experience is effectively carried out. These aids all in all require the instructor to have a lot of skill, as well a positive attitude while designing these aids and also while utilizing them in the classroom.

Depending on the situation that prevails at the time, the teacher is able to make the decision on whether or not to use certain instructional aids in the classroom. These situations may not have been caused by the teachers or the students, but by external aspects. An example can be seen by the use if a projector in class, which the teacher will not be able to utilize if there is no electricity in the school. In this situation, the teacher will have to look for a different aid to use, and try to explain the aspect to the students in a manner that is almost similar. Instructional aids might be the answer to improving the learning and teaching experience in many different ways and aspects; however, in the end the center of the whole scheme is the teacher and the students (Kadijevich, Angeli, & Schulte, 2013).

5.7. VISUAL MEDIA

This method of communication is used for the channeling of messages from an origin to the person meant to receive the message. After delivery, the message is conveyed in symbols that are visual. This form of media can be used to ensure that the attention of the person receiving the media is attracted, the ideas being relayed are clarified, and also make sure that the facts that may be forgotten easily, if not relayed visually, are illustrated and embellished. Some of the visual aids include charts, models, maps, figures, cartoons, etc.

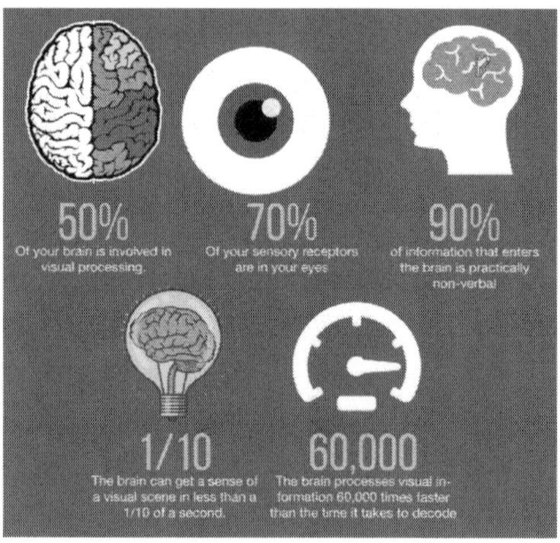

Figure 5.6. *The brain is the main center that processes visual information. Above shows how visual data is processed.*

Source: https://www.searchenginepeople.com/blog/how-to-create-the-perfect-visual-content-for-social-media.html.

Visual aids ensure that people viewing the aids understand the information that is being relayed. They represent a significant role in audience understanding. There are many different forms of aids that are visual. The form of aid that is used depends on the teacher that is presenting the information, depending in what the teacher prefers to use, as well as what exactly it is they are presenting. Being able to communicate in a visual manner is very important, even in our day to day lives. There are many things in the world that involve visual communication to a certain point. Some of these include presentations, advertisements, etc. (Lakshmi, 2009).

The different types of aids each have their own advantages and disadvantages that need to be considered before choosing one. It is important for the instructor to understand that he/she has to choose the correct visual aid for specific presentations. Teachers need to learn to prepare well before time before utilizing these tools. Visual aids need to be chosen appropriately for the specific information being relayed, and also for the specific audience (Lakshmi, 2009).

These tools can be very advantageous in enhancing the effectiveness of lessons and presentations. They are used to attract the attention of the audience, and thus being able to maintain student engagement. They should be used as additions to the effect and importance of the message being relayed, instead of being notes and written material. This will help in ensuring that the students understand, remember and retain what they see for a long period of time. Visual aids are especially important for students who understand concepts better by visualizing them.

5.7.1. Chalkboard

This is also known as a blackboard, and it is a surface that is used for writing and it can also be reused. These boards can be written on using pieces of chalk, that normally are made of Calcium Sulfate or Calcium Carbonate. Initially, these boards were created using thin panes of slate stone that were either black in color or a dark gray. These days the boards are mostly green, painted on using a dark matte paint. It is also possible to write on these boards using markers that can be erased.

Figure 5.7. *Blackboards are found in almost every single classroom. They are very good at displaying media that can be seen.*

Source: https://www.backdropexpress.com/Classroom-Chalkboard-Printed-Backdrop-p/kid-jk-005.htm.

Blackboards are normally almost always used to teach in most schools, colleges, and universities. Technology has been able to provide forms of the blackboard that are much more modern including the high visual interactive boards; however, the blackboard will always be impossible to replace. There are many pros that the blackboard can provide to both the instructor and the students. It provides a visual aid, promoting better understanding for the student, and easy teaching for the instructor (Lakshmi, 2009).

Many people take for granted the pros that the blackboard or whiteboard can provide. They work very effectively as visual aids and they help in making teaching and learning easier. They are advantageous to both the teachers and the students.

The ways in which they are advantageous to teachers include:

- *They make it easier for teachers to present their content* – they promote fast delivery of the information being relayed to the students by writing on the board as they teach. This allows the students to look back at what has been written in case they forget. Many students also do not like listening to lessons without seeing the content written on the blackboard.

- *Solving mathematical problems or explaining formulas* – the blackboard is an effective way of explaining the step by step methods of any mathematical problems. In computer science, they can be used to show step by step the formulas or computations to show proof that they work.
- *To spell out difficult words* – the teacher is able to show the students the spelling of words he/she might say that they do not know how to spell. It can also be used to write new terminologies for the students.
- *Drawing of diagrams* – It can be used to draw any graphs, timelines or diagrams so as to guide the students as they replicate them on their own notebooks, and also for them to visually understand the concept that is being explained.
- *Derivations* – it can be used to derive certain formulas that need to be explained upfront for the students to understand.
- *Outline the main objectives* – the teacher can use the blackboard to write the main topics that the students need to know by the end of the lesson.
- *Retaining student attention* – There are many students that are not fans of long lectures. Typically, students retain their attention for 10 to 15 minutes. After this, they get distracted or bored. This can be prevented by utilizing the blackboard where the teacher can combine writing and speaking, which will help in ensuring student engagement for a longer time. Using these boards to write some notes will also promote note writing for the students, which they can use to read and study for their exams.

Students also find blackboards advantageous for their learning experiences. Some of the ways in which they are advantaged include:

- *It makes it easier for them to understand* – it is much easier for the student to comprehend the aspects and even the methods of certain formulas, especially because they see it being done step by step as it is being taught.
- *It improves student memory* – when the students see a certain aspect being explained on the board, they find it easier to remember, in comparison to just hearing it. It has been proven that it is easier for students to remember something they have seen in comparison to something they have heard. Same way we have very good face memory when compared to name memory.

- *They find it easier to write notes* – when teachers use the blackboard to write notes, the students also find it easier to take down notes. This makes it easier for the student to learn because when they write notes in the same way the teacher wrote, they can read them later. The students get much more time to write notes when the teacher does it while teaching.
- *The students can see better* – students are able to see much better, especially if they are not able to hear the teacher speak, when the notes are written on a board. Even for students who are at the back of the class.
- Some of the disadvantages of using blackboards include:
- They consume a lot of time when using them, in comparison to interactive boards.
- They do not look as good and eye-catching as interactive boards.
- It is not possible to present videos that are visual using the blackboard.

5.7.2. Charts

These are use of symbols to represent data in a graphical manner. For example, using slices in a pie chart and lines in a line graph. They are used for the representation of tabular or qualitative data.

Most of the times, they are used to promote easier comprehension of large volumes of data as well as how the different parts of the data relate. They are normally much easier to read in comparison to data that has not been interpreted. They are utilized in very many different ways and aspects. It is possible to create a chart by hand, mostly on graph paper, and also using a computer device with specific software applications (Seendani, 2014).

When presenting work in the classroom, the teacher needs to consider that the different types of charts have different functions, and each has an appropriate use. There are some charts that much more helpful in the presentation of information in comparison to others. For example, it is easier to present percentages using a pie chart. There are many different types of charts, and each one of them has a different use. Some of the examples are seen below.

Column charts: These are normally very helpful when it comes to comparing one or more than one set of point of data. The charts have a Y-axis which is vertical and an X-axis which is horizontal. The former represents the values that are numerical, and the latter represents the time period. These are normally designed using Microsoft Excel which is a spreadsheet program, among other programs.

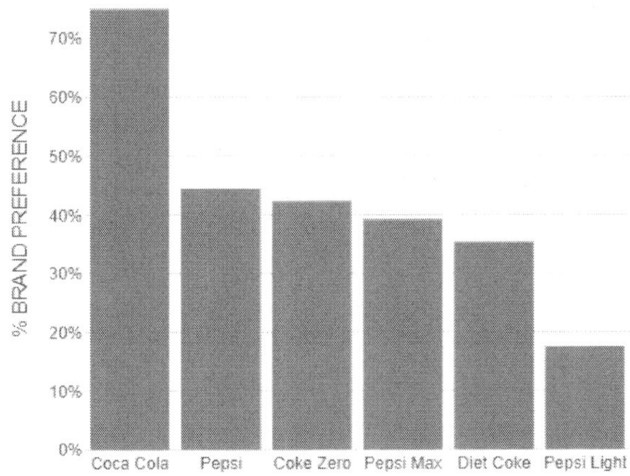

Figure 5.8. *This is also called a bar chart. It is used to present data that is categorical.*

Source: https://www.displayr.com/what-is-a-column-chart/.

Bar Charts: These are used for showing a comparison between percentages and concepts among a set of data. They are quite similar to column charts. They allow the person using them to apply different specific choices for their respondents. These are mostly used to compare large amount of data.

Pie Charts: These can be used to illustrate and show the breakdown of a sample in the dimension of the specific individual creating it. This chart is normally shaped like a pie so as to help in the illustration of how the main category and the sub-categories, of the data being relayed, relate. They are very effective especially in presenting data that has undergone categorization in groups, or in illustrating how data that is based on one variable differs.

Narrative Chart: These help in arranging thoughts and ideas so as to be able to express any events that are being developed of an issue that is important, to the point in which it is resolved.

Flow Chart: These help in showing relationships that are administrative or functional, as well as elements that are organizational. It involves a line that connects circles, lines, and rectangles so as to show the directional flow.

Tabulation chart: These help in showing individual schedules, or those of an activity. An example of this includes a class timetable. This helps improve the teaching experience by providing a visual aid when it comes to the breaking down of certain facts or statements that are supposed to be presented in a list. It also helps in creating a chart that can allow the students to see comparisons between two or more than two aspects. There are, however, some specific rules to making these charts. It is important to make sure that the chart is either 50 by 75 centimeters or more in size. It is also important to ensure that the chart labeled using bold letters. Lastly, the columns that are vertical need to only have short sentences instead of full ones.

5.7.3. Graphs

It is necessary to know the difference between a chart and a graph. Graphs represent values that are connected in a space that is multidimensional. They are much more efficient when it comes to the analysis of certain connections that are present in individual data units.

Graphs are considered very important computational tools, especially in mathematical subjects. The values that are found in graphs are called nodes and parts that connect them are called edges. These tools may be created in two ways: directed or undirected.

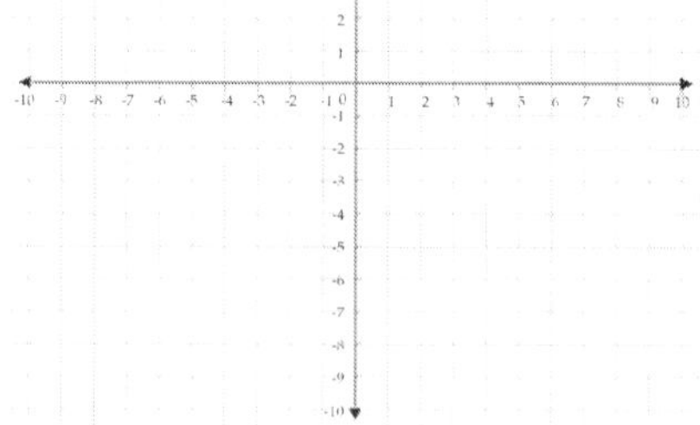

Figure 5.9. *Above shows the x and y axis of a graph.*

Source: https://authorguide.learnosity.com/hc/en-us/articles/360000448637-Graphing.

In computer science, graphs have proven to be very important. They have been applied in the analysis if social networks, search engines, and even systems that have been recommended, e.g., YouTube. Google uses Page Rank, which is a well-known graph analysis algorithm, for the generation of search results.

It is important for the instructor to know how the graph is created if he/ she will use it in the classroom. So as to prepare one, there is a list to follow:

- Draw a rough sketch of the graph that you want to make before you create the actual design.
- Make sure the paper you are using is 50 by 72cm in size.
- It is advisable to use contrasting colors for the different groups.
- The divided sections in the graph need to be spaced equally.
- The graph always has a key which needs to be written on right lower corner of the sheet of paper.

There are many different types of graphs. Some include:

Pie graph: This is also referred to as a circle diagram. The circle is divided into separate portions which are used to present the data. The teacher is to use pie to calculate the circumference of the circle and it should have a surface area that covers 360°.

Bar graph: This is a graph that is used in the presentation of data that has been categorized. This data is presented using bars that are rectangular in shape. These bars have lengths and widths that are proportional to the data that they are representing. These bars can be drawn either in a vertical or horizontal manner. This tool is used to compare within categories that are discrete. One part of the graph is supposed to show the main category that under comparison, and the other axis is supposed to show a value that is measured.

Line graph: This is a graph that is used in the visualization of values over a certain period of time. An example can be seen in seeing trends in the stock market over a period of time. This graph has an axis that is horizontal and one that is vertical. Most of these graphs only deal with number values that are positive. This graph is helpful in the visualization of finance and marketing related issues. It can also be used to monitor weather, research in the laboratory, etc.

5.7.4. Importance of Visual Aids

There are a couple of benefits of using visual aids in the classroom. Some of them include:

- *Improving success in the classroom* – Using visual aids can help students comprehend the work that is being taught faster. For example, when a teacher speaks of a certain part of the country, it will only be fully understood when the teacher includes a map to visually guide the students on what he is explaining. They also help in boosting creativity levels and also allows the students to think deeper. Students also tend to remember faster when they see images, which helps improve their retention.
- *Improving the level of engagement and interest among the students* – They help in improving student excitement in the topics that they are being taught. They have also been seen to help special needs students, especially those on the autistic spectrum. These students prefer to learn using visual aids, and they find it hard to sit in the traditional lesson that involves just speech. The students tend to be much more engaged when they see images of exactly what is being explained by the teacher.
- *Expansion of the learning scope* – Not much information can be provided by the teacher orally without the use of visual aids. These aids help in the expansion of the level of information that is being passed on to the students.
- *Promotes the integration of technology* – Technology is developing more and more in this world and it is important for teachers to ensure that their students are ready for this. The use of interactive whiteboards is a way of achieving this goal. This tool can help in displaying images, graphs, charts, etc. In addition, students are able to touch and move things around using this tool. The use of PowerPoint to create slide is also a good way of presenting lessons.

Figure 5.10. *Visual aids make lessons much easier than when speech is the only aspect used.*

Source: https://virtualspeech.com/blog/visual-aids-presentation.

Visual aids also help students who may have issues in the classroom such as:

- Attendance and concentration.
- Being able to process information that is sequenced.
- Being shy and socially isolated.
- Not being able to follow rules and instructions.
- Those who are anxious and have a problem accepting change.
- Those who lack motivation.

5.7.5. Principles That Need to Be Followed When Using Audio-Visual Aids

There are three main things that the teacher has to do as he/she introduces visual aids in the classroom.

- Firstly, there is a need to ensure that the students are well-prepared for this change in the learning experience
- Secondly, ensure reinforcement of values as the students share the experience
- Lastly, relate the new aids to the old lessons so as to stimulate further learning.

When using the aids, there are also other principles that need to be followed. The aids need to be able to cater for the needs on the students depending on their age, the environment, and even their previous experience with visual aids. There is a need to know all the pros and cons of the different aids before introducing them to the students. Not all may be advantageous. In addition, it is important for the teachers to know that they cannot fully replace oral and written methods with audio visuals. It is important to use them all in a manner that is appropriate. The teacher also needs to make sure that they plan the aids in a manner that the students do not confuse them for entertainment (Seendani, 2014).

5.7.6. Characteristics of Good Audio-Visual Aids

For audio-visual aids to be fully efficient and effective, they all need certain qualities. These include:

- They need to achieve the lesson's objectives.
- They need to be exciting and attractive in a manner that does not deviate the students from the main lesson.

- They need to neither be too big or too small, but they need to be made in a way that all the students in the class can see.
- Makes sure that they do not have any material that is not relevant. Irrelevant material can lead to indiscipline.
- They should be made in a way that makes the students curious, allowing them to be much more engaged.

5.7.7. Places in Which Audio-Visual Aids Can Be Used

Three of the main ways they can be used during the lesson includes at the beginning of the lesson, during the presentations, and while recapitulating. They can be used at the beginning of the lesson to draw the attention of the students. They can be used during the presentation to explain aspects that the students might find hard to understand without the aids, and lastly during the recapitulation for evaluation of the lesson.These aids should only be used to explain small sections of aspects that need to be understood. They should also be able to leave the students with an impression that is desirable, and this can be achieved by using aids that are interesting and easy to understand. Despite the fact that these aids are very helpful, it is important to only use them when need be. When they are used excessively, the students can lose track and end up perceiving it as a form of entertainment. Therefore, it is important how teachers use these aids. It is also important to use a variety of aids, because when the teacher reuses one for a long period of time, it becomes boring for the student (Seendani, 2014).

5.8. INTERACTIVE WHITEBOARD

This is a screen that can reacts to touching and works together with a computer and a projector. It is used for making presentations by creating an interface with the computer. It works by displaying images that are on the computer onto a board using a projector that is digital. It is possible to see and manipulate these images that are displayed on the board. It allows for the person using it to have access to controlling the software on both the computer and also the board. The teacher or student can use a pen or a tool for highlighting to add notations. It is also possible to use applications from the board, in a direct manner, using the fingers of the user at the time. In addition to all this, it allows for the user to save and print any information that was written down or drawn using the board. This tool is normally the same as the traditional whiteboard in size (Seendani, 2014).

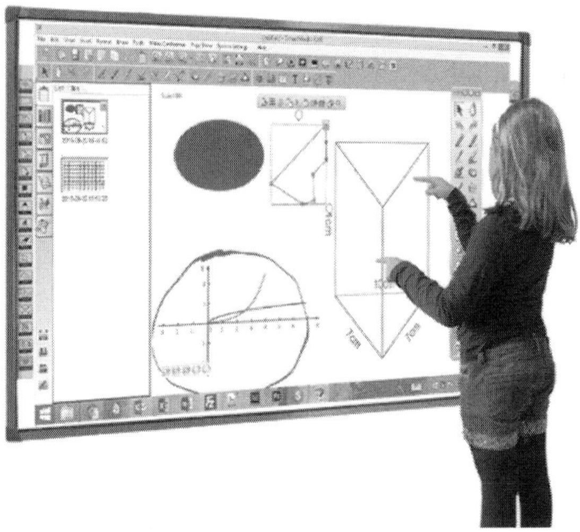

Figure 5.11. *Interactive whiteboard are a very interesting way of incorporating technology in the classroom.*

Source: https://www.indiamart.com/proddetail/finger-touch-digital-interactive-smart-whiteboard-8926402273.html.

5.8.1. Uses of the Interactive Whiteboard

This tool helps to promote interactions with content that is digital, as well as multimedia, in a learning environment that has multiple persons in an effective manner. Some of the ways this tool is used include:

- Being able to display and view certain websites together as a class.
- Manipulation of images and notes.
- Being able to save notes so as to allow reviewing of the notes at a later time.
- Writing notes in digital ink.
- Using images and other different forms of multimedia to create lesson activities that are digital.
- Being able to show the class ways in which they can use a certain application software without having to use the small screen in the computer.
- Adding notes over video clips that are educational.

- For the enhancement of materials that are used for learning.
- For the students to be able to display the work that they are presenting to the whole class.
- The board is equipped with presentation tools that the teacher or student can use to make presenting easier and efficient.

5.8.2. Promoting Student Learning Using Interactive Whiteboards

This tool has allowed teachers to transform the traditional methods of teaching to activities that allow interaction with the students. Students learn better using the interactive whiteboard and there are a couple of reasons why:

- *They help in enhancing the lessons* – they are able to ensure the integration of many different styles that are used for learning into one learning experience. Students are able to use most of their senses to learn, including sight, hearing, and even interaction through touch. This allows teachers to find many new different ways in which they can incorporate the specific topics they are trying to teach in this method. This variety helps to improve the learning experience of the students. They enjoy learning and also remember much more.
- *Interactive learning* – These boards allow students to have direct interaction with the materials that are being learnt. This allows them to become a part of the lesson and pass on the information to each other. They are able to touch, draw, or write on the interactive board. They are also able to play games that are based on their lesson materials. These games can be played by all the students in the classroom at the same time. They are also able to give feedback that is immediate, allowing both the teachers and the students to have access to the progress of the students.
- *They are quite easy to utilize* – they do not need high maintenance and remain clean. They do not require other writing materials such as a marker or a piece of chalk. They use a pen that has undergone specialization to modify data to allow for the teacher and students to highlight, draw, and write. This means that there is no mess that is caused when using the interactive whiteboard, and thus no clean up required.

- *They are very flexible to use in the classroom* – it is possible to use the interactive whiteboard to display many different forms of media. They can display maps, pictures, graphs, charts, photos, videos, etc., allowing the teacher to have many different options to choose from. The teachers can use this advantage to make sure that the lessons are creative so as to maintain the interest of their students.
- *You can connect them to the internet* – these tools are technologic and they can be connected to the internet, allowing the teachers and students to have a wide variety of tools and information that can be found online. They can access specific sources to attain specific data on what they would like to use to teach the class. They have different options such as videos, images, articles, etc. The students can also find a wide variety of research material.
- *Can be integrated to other different types of technology* – the ability of the boards to integrate with various other technologies helps in the enhancement of the student learning experience. They are able to integrate with microscopes, cameras, computers, and help by enhancing the instructions.
- *They have been proven to be effective* – Students tend to pay more attention in the classroom therefore helping in the improvement of understanding, exam scores, literacy, and even retention of the information. The students enjoy the lesson, allowing them to learn and remember better.

5.8.3. Activities in the Computer Science Classroom Using the Interactive Whiteboard

The computer language can be taught effectively using an Interactive Whiteboard due to two main reasons: it helps in promoting the development of oral skills, and it helps in ensuring the students interact and converse in the classroom. Using a traditional board and projector is very different from making projections on the interactive whiteboard.

Figure 5.12. *The interactive Whiteboard allows students to participate in the lessons. It promotes communication and brainstorming amongst the students.*

Source: https://www.viewsonic.com/library/education/jumpstart-engagement-interactive-whiteboard/.

The interactive whiteboard allows the person using it to navigate through the information using the board itself. This allows the teacher to remain at the front of the class while teaching, in comparison to having to walk back to his/her computer every time he/she wants to change something. This is very beneficial, as it allows the teacher to pay more attention to the process of teaching instead of the complications of the forms of technology. This can be very helpful in the computer science classroom.

The teacher is also able to manipulate functions in his computer using his fingers, as a writing or drawing material, on the board. The students are also able to do this, thus allowing many more opportunities for classroom activities (Seendani, 2014).

5.8.4. Activities That Help to Improve Oral Skills Using the Interactive Whiteboard

When a problem in the classroom is displayed using the interactive whiteboard, it allows the students to solve it in a whole new and different perspective. This display to the class can help in improving student interaction. It allows students to share and argue out their ideas and opinions.

The teacher can make an extension of the interactive whiteboard that allows for the student to be the one navigating the issues on the board. This helps in promoting oral skills because the other students will be able to give their opinions to the student that is actively navigating the board. They will be able to give directions in the computer language. It is evident that the interactive whiteboard has helped to encourage communication, thus bringing the students together (Seendani, 2014).

The students are also able to present their work to the whole class with the help of the interactive whiteboard. This helps in improving oral skills because they do not have to use the mouse when they are speaking, thus maintaining their concentration. With the simple touch of a finger, they are able to display videos, pictures, and other forms of multimedia.

5.9. POWERPOINT PRESENTATION

This is a presentation software application that was created by Microsoft. It helps in the creation of slideshows so as to display information, images, graphs, that are important to the user. These are normally used during presentations. Most of the times, it is used during student course work presentation, teachers presenting their lessons, businesses, etc.

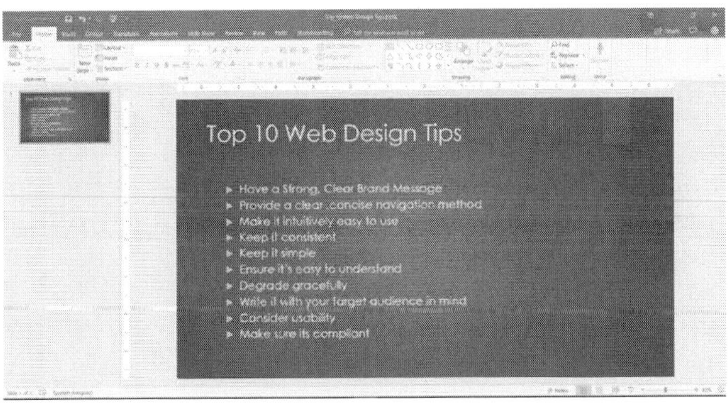

Figure 5.13. *Above is an example of a slide discussing tips on web design. This was created using Microsoft PowerPoint.*

Source: https://slidemodel.com/23-powerpoint-presentation-tips-creating-engaging-interactive-presentations/.

This software application mostly comes in the whole Microsoft Office Package as it is being installed into Microsoft Windows. This application can be found on the menu. This application has to be purchased and installed for it to work on the user's computer.

5.9.1. How Teachers Can Use PowerPoint to Improve the Teaching Experience

This is a tool that can be used to effectively present materials in the classroom during the lesson. It helps in encouraging the students to learn. It can be used for the projection of aspects that would be hard to understand without the visual aid. For example, the teacher can use maps to show the students the relevant areas that are mentioned during the lesson (Seendani, 2014).

It is considered the whole package when it comes to the presentation of graphical information. It has tools that allow the teacher to provide all the important information, in different ways, to the students. Some of the ways in which teachers are able to use PowerPoint to present lessons to their students include:

- Presentation of notes as well as lessons.
- Displaying images.
- As a routine that is used daily.
- For the students to present their work.
- To make sure that their agendas are met.
- To present different forms of multimedia such as videos and pictures.
- Displaying charts and graphs.
- Presenting audio files to the students.

5.9.2. How Students Can Use PowerPoint

Considering that the world today is very reliant on technology, it is evident that all employees need to be well accustomed with technology. Students need to know how to use the basic software applications in computer science. PowerPoint has proven to be very important, considering the fact that in the future, the students will have to use PowerPoint to present their work at the workplace. Ways in which the students should know how to use PowerPoint include:

- Writing articles in classes that involve creative writing.
- Providing an interpretation that is visual.
- Creation of charts and graphs.
- Being able to self-quiz themselves.
- Being able to do learning that is based on problems.
- Displaying work that they want to present to the class.
- Creation of instructions.

5.9.3. Steps in Creating an Effective Presentation Using PowerPoint

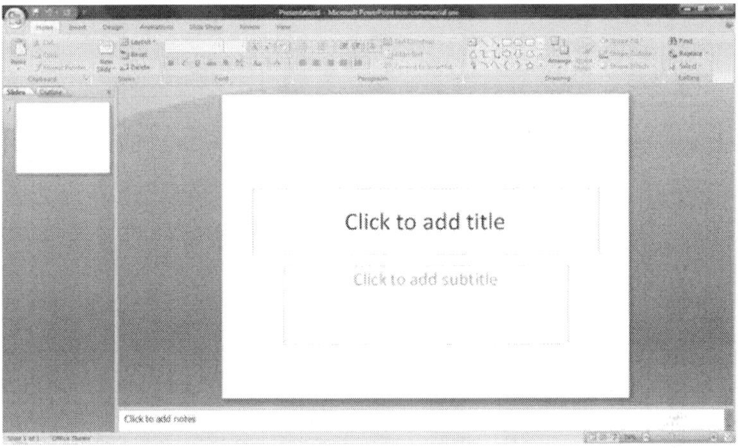

Figure 5.14. *Above shows the area in the PowerPoint presentation that one needs to input the title.*

Source: https://www.instructables.com/id/How-to-Create-a-PowerPoint-Presentation/.

So as to ensure that a PowerPoint presentation is effective, there are certain steps that need to be followed:

- First, one needs to ensure that they have opened the application, Microsoft PowerPoint.
- There is a section at the top labeled as 'the file.' On clicking this, one should open the box that says 'New Presentation.'
- One is then able to choose a design by choosing the design template that is found in the dialog box.
- One is then able to choose the design that they find appropriate. They are also able to choose the color that they want by selecting the box that is labeled as 'color schemes.'
- After this, the user can then select a layout for the slides. This is done by clicking on 'format' which is found at the top of the screen then 'slide layout.'
- After this, a text can be added by clicking and typing in the 'click to add text' box.

5.9.4. How to Design a PowerPoint Presentation

It is important to consider certain aspects when designing a PowerPoint presentation. Some of these include:

- Making sure that the time and effort put into making the presentation is enough.
- Is the presentation going to be in the classroom or online?
- Make sure that the material is compatible with student technology. This means that the videos and images need to be compressed.
- Make sure that the presentation is accessible to all students. It may be hard for the blind students to access the work and the teacher should consider adding audios.
- The materials provided should be cited appropriately. It is important to avoid copyrighted material.
- Make sure the information provided can be interpreted by the students.

So as to make sure that the PowerPoint presentation is effective, there are some things to consider when designing it. These include:

- *Make a choice on the color scheme* – it is important to choose colors that will attracts the attention of the student. This can be done using Adobe Color CC. This application even allows for the teacher to create his/her own color schemes.
- *Makes sure the number of slides is optimal* – it is important to balance the number of slides. The thumb rule involves showing one slide per minute. This time allows for the students to discuss, and also for absorption of the material. Make sure not to repeat content. This will help to reduce the number of slides, at the same time, have more content.
- *Make sure to emphasize content* – This can be done by using different fonts, colors, and even using different designs such as bold, italics, etc. It can also be achieved by using a light background and using a color that provides a dark font.
- *Including clip arts and graphics in a sparing manner* – There is research that has proven that it is only efficient to use clip arts and graphics when they are needed. They should be used a way to ensure that the content is supported. The teacher can use pictures and photos as a way to promote realism. These photos and images

need to well placed in the slides. In a way that they will not cover texts and notes. It is advisable to use pie-graphs and bar-graphs that are in 2D instead of 3D.

- *Including audios and animations* – audio and motion pictures should only be added when necessary. If you are not sure whether or not you should add them, it is advised to just avoid them. When they are used in excess, it is possible to lose the attention of the class.
- *The size of the point* – the font that is used should be able to read from any part of the classroom. The headings that are used should not be too long, and they need to be straight to the point, so as to ensure the students get the main point that is being explained.
- *Final checkup* – when creating the slides, it is important to check for grammatical errors, spelling errors, whether the material is flowing, and also how the presentation looks and flows. It is also helpful when you seek advice from your fellow colleagues. This can help in providing different points of view, especially in the checking of accuracy, and whether it will be interesting to the students. In addition to all this, it can be helpful to practice the sides just to know how long it will take, and whether the flow of content is appropriate. Just in case the presentation does not work, it is always important to have a plan B. This will to convey the message in case something happens, such as lack of electricity.

5.9.5. Ways to Enhance the Learning and Teaching Experience Using PowerPoint

It can be used for proper preparation of class presentations, as well as lessons. It is able to achieve this by providing tools that the teachers and students can use to refine their information into points that have been efficiently written out.

This tool also allows for the teacher to write the lessons in an outline format which can later be transformed into slides. These slides can even be printed and given to the students as notes.

Figure 5.15. *Using powerpoint presentations to teach can help in improving student retention.*

Source: http://togo.wpart.co/teacher-powerpoint/.

This tool also allows the teacher to learn the different teaching and learning styles that the students prefer. There are visual learners who prefer to use pictures, videos, photos, etc., and there are audio-visual learners who prefer to have a mixture of the visual forms as well as audio ones. This is like a YouTube video. There are also students who learn better using interactions. This tool helps in allowing for there to have discussions on the information being displayed.

5.9.6. Engaging Students Using PowerPoint

There are a couple of ways you can keep the students interested all through the lesson. These include:

- *You can have a slideshow running as the students walk into the classroom* – This helps to capture the visual interest of the students at an early stage. The teacher can also be displaying some truck questions that the students can enjoy and were as they wait for the other students to arrive.
- *Projecting and opening question* – This will help in keeping the students engaged, because they want to listen to the lesson so as to understand the answer that was given to the question that was before the lesson.
- *Using brainstorming techniques* – The teacher can have a slide that is dedicated to a brainstorming question during the lesson.

This helps to promote the thinking skills of the students, thus opening up curiosity and other aspects.

- *Providing a poll that the classroom can fill* – This will help in understanding what the students got during the lesson, as well as their opinion.

Chapter 6

Latest Trends in Information Technology

CONTENTS

6.1. INTRODUCTION

Information technology refers to the use of telecommunications and computers or the purpose of storing, retrieving and the sending of information. As we live in a world that revolves around technology, there are several advancements being made to the technological world to suit the current demands. This applies to information technology. Information technology is changing various aspects of the human existence by affecting the way humans live and work among other areas. One of the aspects of human living that technology has affected is human education. This is in the sense that the education sector is integrating the use of technology in the teaching process as well as the learning process.

All this is in a bid to make learning more efficient and productive in the long run. It is also a way of improving the quality of education that is being offered to the students. Technologies including networking and multimedia are among the technologies being used to revolutionize the education sector. They have been extensively applied to revolutionize the education by improving both teacher and learner experience. For instance, E-learning technologies have been used to allow students to access various information through the e-books, carry out the students' assessments and improve the communication within the learning process (D'Atri et al., 2011).

Figure 6.1. *Multimedia has been used by students to equip themselves with new knowledge and improve their learning styles helping them to improve and achieve their targets.*

Source: http://www.panworldeducation.com/2017/03/23/benefits-of-digital-learning-over-traditional-education-methods/.

The technologies are also being used by students to monitor their learning process and ensure that they are learning with the correct pace. Therefore, this unit entails the latest trends in information technology. They are the topics to be handled which include desktop publishing, multimedia, the internet, E-learning, and virtual learning, web-based learning, teleconferencing and video conferencing (D'Atri et al., 2011).

6.2. MULTIMEDIA

It is a term that can be used to reference two or more media in the sense of its definition. It entails the use of a computer in the creation of graphics, videos, and audio as well as the presentation and combination of text. It contains various tools that are useful to the user during the process of interaction and communication. In interactions, there are elements that are required to make it more effective and multimedia is one of the tools used in enhancing the user-based interactions. As it involves the use of digital media, it makes the process more efficient.

6.2.1. Nature of Multimedia Approach

- The multimedia approach involves the integration of media, techniques, and gadgets (devices) in the learning and teaching process.
- Multimedia approach entails the use of various media as well as techniques as a powerful mode of communication and interaction.
- It involves the analysis of various aspects required to aid in the careful selection of the media so that the selected media complements other media.
- It involves the use of media in the learning process to make it more effective and productive in the long run ensuring that the students get the best learning experience.
- The multimedia approach is an outcome of the research undertaken in order to improve both the teaching and learning process.
- It entails the extensive use of the required media in a bid to improve the teaching and learning process. It emphasizes on the use of using the required media so that it may economically suit the process.
- It involves the improving of the learning process by enabling students to get various information therefore use of multimedia gives the students access to such information.

- Multimedia approach embraces the use of various teaching styles as well as methodologies in order to improve the teaching-learning process.
- The multimedia approach improves the teaching process by giving teachers an opportunity to master teaching skills.

In summary, the multimedia approach seeks to show the different ways in which multimedia is being used in improving the learning process.

6.2.2. Interactive Media Components

Interactive media refers to a method of communication that entails the users is depended on in the program to produce the output. Basically, it shows how people share information and how they are able to effectively communicate to one another.

The interactive media sought out to improve the challenges of the non-interactive media by engaging and interacting with the user in ways that the non-interactive media could not. The traditional forms of interactive media were majorly passive. This includes media such as televisions and radios among others (Saeed et al., 2017).

This changed with the advancements in technology whereby most of the interactive media is active.

The user gets to interact with the given media. The advanced interactive media provides the user with various tools that the user can use for the interaction process. This has led to computers being a used in several households such that now it has become a household necessity.

The interactive media components include motion pictures and graphics, animation, digital texts, video and audio.

Motion pictures are a series of pictures that are projected on a screen at a set pace while graphics involves the use of various diagrams in calculations and design. Animation is a technique in photography whereby the position of drawings are used in the creation of illusive motion when a film is projected. While video is a recording of ever moving images that can be digitally made or are a recording on an ongoing activity. Audio is different from video as it lacks the visual aspect (Saeed et al., 2017).

6.2.3. Multimedia in Teaching-Learning

Figure 6.2. *Multimedia is one of the various approaches that education systems are taking up in order to improve the quality of education being offered to the students.*

Source: http://torcheduc.com/user/blog_post/1.

Various multimedia tools are being employed in teaching and learning process. The multimedia approach has a unique importance for education because it has revolutionized the way both teachers and students approach the education system. Teachers can improve their teaching by introducing a variety of strategies in the teaching process (Saeed et al., 2017).

Multimedia helped improve teaching methods and student-teacher interaction. The multimedia approach has involved the use of tools, such as videos, to make the content to be more interesting for the students. It also motivates them to learn more. The multimedia approach has enabled the teachers to be more creative when it comes to using various materials while teaching and also assessing the students. It has made the teaching process to be more interesting for the teachers.

The multimedia approach has made the learning system to be effective for many of the students. As the use of technology has brought about the learning process being learner-centered, the multimedia approach greatly focuses on meeting the learners' needs. By so doing it sought to avail a variety of learning resources for the learner to use during the learning process. As it involves the use of digital media, the multimedia approach has greatly been used to motivate the students. It has promoted learning by incorporating the use of pictures, posters, charts, and models among others (Saeed et al., 2017).

This makes learning to be more practical. The use of media has been used in the preparation and participation stages of the learning process. The various media that include the computer and video disks have been incorporated into the classroom so as to improve the learners' interests for the learning process. It has led to teachers even adopting smartphones as a resource in learning. In addition to that, the use of television media has played a key role in helping students to acquire more information. This helps the students to understand various concepts and supplements the knowledge they acquired in the classroom.

The use of visual media is very helpful for students. Not only does it improve their interests for the given subjects but it also helps them remember a variety of things. In the long run, it improves the learners' ability to retain information which makes the learning process to be effective. The multimedia approach is a useful resource in improving the learning and teaching environment. It encourages flexibility and gives room for individualized instruction. The multimedia approach has given room for innovation and creativity in the teaching and learning process thereby positively impacting the education system (Lakshmi, 2009).

6.2.4. Role of the Teacher in Multimedia Approach

The teacher plays a key role in the multimedia approach and will be determinant of whether it will be successful or not. In order to effectively incorporate the various media in teaching the teacher will be required to make some adjustments to facilitate its use. The teacher has the following roles to play:

- The teacher has to acquire mastery over the use of the various media that are available. The mastery should be in terms of the methods and strategies in teaching, mass instruction media, teaching and reading materials, auto instructions, media for gaining experiences and a-v aids among others. By so doing, they will be able to achieve the teaching goals with the aid of multimedia.
- The teacher has to acquire knowledge and skill in using and applying the different media. This will enable them to properly use the combination so as to meet the teaching and learning objectives in the given situation.
- The teacher has to make the learning process to be active. This entails actively engaging the students during the learning process to increase the student participation in class.

- The teacher has to play the role of the facilitator. This implies that the duty of the teacher to oversee all the classroom activities. This may involve them supervising students as they interact with the media in the classroom.
- The teacher should help the students to acquire independent and individualized learning. Therefore, the teacher should assist in making the learning process to be learner-oriented where the learner should actively look for information from various sources available. The teacher guides the student in identifying sources that will provide them with relevant information.
- The teacher has to have knowledge on the different media that is available. This requires them to know the availability of the media in catering for all the students in the classroom. If insufficient, the teacher should be able to know what media to use that will enable access for all the learners.
- The teacher should be skillful. This attribute will enable them on the basis of requirements to choose the media that is appropriate and competent enough to be incorporated into the learning environment.
- The teacher should have the ability to provide a learning experience for the students so that it is easy for the students to create a link between theory and practice. They should be able to integrate the two so that the learning process will be effective in the long run.
- The teacher is required to design a learning environment that will incorporate the use of the multimedia tools such as computers to make the teaching and learning process to be effective.
- The teacher is required to have a positive attitude towards the use of technology in the teaching and learning. This is important as it will greatly affect the use of the multimedia tools in the classroom and the use of other technologies in the classroom.

6.2.5. Educational Implications of Multimedia

The education implications refer to how multimedia has been applied in the education sector to improve the quality of education as well as improve the teacher and learner process. Some of the educational implications of multimedia include:

- The use of multimedia by students to represent information. This involves the use of the various media such the computer to present information. The students are able to use tools provided in the computer to represent information in forms that include the use of charts and diagrams among others. It also encourages creativity among the students as they come up with ways of representing the information.
- Multimedia presents different learning styles that can be employed by the students. Depending on the students' ability. They use the available multimedia to suit their abilities. For instance, some students learn by interpreting texts while some use graphical or aural representation to be able to effectively understand the given information. The teacher based on student evaluation the teacher will be able to choose the appropriate media to incorporate into the teaching process. This is why the teachers are required to have skills in choosing the appropriate media.
- The media enables the students to acquire high level of thinking skills. This is mostly through the use of various interactive media that include networking. The students will be required to apply thinking skills when using the interactive media. They then apply the skills in the learning process.
- For students to have a sense of focus or vision in their education, they need to know what they in tend to be in future. Multimedia has been used to enable the students to discover themselves. It is also used for self-placing. They enable the students to decide on the learning path that they are to take. This will give the students a sense of purpose in the learning process.
- Multimedia has facilitated unlimited access to information. This will enable to students to carry out the learning process at any place and at any time. This makes the learning process to be unlimited.
- Multimedia has been used by students in the creation and construction of knowledge. They are able to actively get involved in group discussions as well as projects and employ the use of their diverse senses in the learning process.
- Multimedia has been used to gain knowledge in the different disciplines. This involves them learning on the various concepts. The use the available media as a source of information. The media

may include televisions and computers among others. As they use the interactive media the students are able to acquire skills such as decision making, problem-solving skills and effective thinking.

- The use of the multimedia tools has been beneficial for the students in that they are able to acquire and apply interpersonal and group skills. This enables the students to improve their interactions by enhancing communication between the students.
- It has been used to develop a positive attitude among the learners towards the learning process. This will make the learning process to be effective as it motivates and creates an interest for learning among the students.
- Multimedia has enabled the effective application of the simulation technique in the learning process. This is through the use of videos and graphics during the learning process.
- It has been used in eradicating barriers in the learning process such as the language barrier which has been solved. Medias such as visuals and audios are useful in eradicating this barrier among other barriers.

6.2.6. Benefits of Multimedia in the Classroom for Learning

The use of multimedia in the classroom has been beneficial for both the teachers and the students in the classroom in various ways. They include:

- Improve the learner's ability to retain knowledge. This is through the use of video and audio which enable the students to easily recall the content that they were taught on.
- It supplements the learners' knowledge. The use of media such as television has enabled students to gain information that will supplement the information that they acquire in the classroom.
- It is a useful resource in preparing the students for their future. This is because it enables the students to learn better and also catch up with students from other countries that have already have the best quality of education offered to their students.
- It has enabled the teachers to improve the teaching process. This is because it has enabled them in preparing for the learning process, improving their teaching methodologies and strategies, improving teacher content and provide the materials that will be employed during the learning process.

- It has greatly motivated and created interest for learning among the students. This is because students have a spark for devices therefore its use in the education process has greatly motivated the students.
- It has made the teaching and learning process livelier. The use of multimedia has effectively made the teaching and learning process to be interactive making the process to be lively.
- It has enabled the students to understand complex concepts. This is mostly through the use of videos that elaborate on the concept allowing the students to easily understand the concept that was deemed to be difficult.
- It has enabled the learning process to be learner centered. Multimedia has promoted the importance of the students carrying out individualized learning.
- It has enabled the students to develop skills such as critical thinking and problem-solving skills. This are as a result of the students interacting with the different media.
- It has enabled better communication between the students. This is as a result of them interacting with tools such as emails and chat sessions. In the long run it has facilitated the collaboration between the teachers and the students.
- It is among the resources that are considered to be sources of information therefore the students are able to gain knowledge from it.

6.3. DESKTOP PUBLISHING

Figure 6.3. *Desktop publishing involves the production of printed documents or papers by the use of printers which are linked to a computer (mostly desktop computer) through the use of desktop publishing software.*

Source: https://www.star-group.net/en/services/desktop-publishing.html.

Desktop publishing involves the documents being easily produced with a given layout and a print that resembles the one of the typeset books. It is usually the desktop software that is used to generate layouts as well as producing typographic and good quality text and images. The initial desktop publishing software have undergone upgrading such in the current day the graphics designers use the software in transforming their latest ideas into a virtual presentation of a document. The document is essentially meant to be printed (Rocha et al., 2018).

With the advancements made in the desktop software, technology has been incorporated into its functioning so that in the current day, the documents don't have to be printed. Today it has been creatively used to offer services that include commercial printing as well as electronic distribution. An example of an electronic distribution is the electronic newsletter or newspapers among others. The advancements in desktop publishing are as a result of integrating communication and use of the internet in the working of the software.

This has made it suitable for use in various fields. The advancements have led to the creation of desktop publishing software that specialized for a given document. According to the tools available, it may be used to produce documents such as disc covers and business cards. The specialization of the software to the given document was made in order to improve the user experience. This is achieved by eliminating tools that may not be required for the specified type of project (Rocha et al., 2018).

There are various types of desktop publishing which include the Microsoft publisher which is a shareware, Adobe InDesign which is a proprietary license, Scribus which is a BSD license, QuarkXPress which is a proprietary software, the Libre Office writer which is a Mozilla public license and the Libre Office Draw among others. In this topic, we get to learn of the different features of desktop publishing

6.3.1. Features of Desktop Publishing

Here we are discussing the most basic and important features that a desktop publishing software should have to produce the required results. The importance of the feature is dependent on the type of print project that is being worked on. The features include:

Graphic tools: they are the tools that enable the user to edit images. Hence, the desktop publishing software should enable the user to edit various images. Editing involves resizing, cropping and compressing of images among others. For a good desktop publishing software, it should enable the user to edit multiple images. For some of the software, they have in built tools such as the image effects and filters to make work easier for the user. The software may contain various functions that will offer advanced drawing tools for the user.

Text tools: these tools facilitate the editing of texts. A good desktop publishing software should offer a wide variety of text editing tools. There has been recent advancement that enable the text to flow freely. This is made possible through the use of linked boxes. The linked boxes create a network between them and the flow of the text is usually between the networks between the boxes. This has greatly enhanced the text editing process by making it easier. The software has been improved by adding on to it applications that will make the adjusting of text properties that include the headers to be easier and less tedious. Examples of text tools include the circle text and artistic text effects among others.

Support for numerous projects: when purchasing a software, one of the elements considered it the number of users the software can accommodate. Same case applies to the desktop publishing software but in this case the aspect to consider is the number of projects the software can create and manage. The software should easily be able to create different projects. It is one of the aspects used to determine the flexibility of the desktop publishing software. For this to be possible, the software should be able to create various paper layouts as well as custom page layout with limited restrictions. Depending on the users' creativity, he or she will be able to come up with a variety of layouts.

Layout tools: layout refers to the arrangement of the document. Layout tools are the tools used in aligning and placing text or objects accurately. They include the adjustable and automatic guides that usually offers a point of reference when the user wants to place an object.

The rulers, the object snapping and object grouping tools. The multiple editing layers are used in creating and uncluttered workspace so that the user does not end up moving an unintended object. The object grouping tool is used to ensure that the objects in the document are positioned correctly and aligned in the required manner. In recent days the master pages' tool has been developed to enable the user to create a template that will be used throughout the document.

Printing and sharing: printing refers to using a device known as a printer to produce a hard copy of a document while sharing involves transfer of knowledge from one person to another. In the previous years when the desktop publishing software was not well developed, people would experience challenges when they had to print documents that had images as some printers would not promote this action.

It is only in the recent days that the printers can even print high resolution images. With the incorporation of communication in desktop publishing, there is easy sharing and receiving of the documents from one computer to another.

Fonts: it is another feature of desktop publishing. This basically deals with how the content is displayed with key emphasis on the shape and size of the letters in the context.

6.4. INTERNET

The internet refers to a worldwide system made up interconnected computer networks that links devices globally through the use of the internet protocol suit. It is mostly referred to as the networks of networks.

This is because it consists of private, public, business, government and academic networks. Basically, the networks range from the local to a global scale. These networks are linked by a broad array of wireless, optical and electronic technologies.

The internet has revolutionized the world today in so many ways. For instance, it has caused globalization where the world has been reduced to the size on a village in terms of human interactions. It has mostly improved the communication sector (Rocha et al., 2018).

It has been used to facilitate communication between people while removing the physical presence as a barrier.

This is through communication platforms such as social media and use of the electronic mail among others.

It has been used to modernize other traditional forms of communication such as use of newspapers whereby in the current day they are available in electronic format.

This brings about convenience. It has enabled easy access to information from even the remotest parts of the world through the use of search engines such as google and Yahoo among others (Rocha et al., 2018).

Figure 6.4. *Internet is a worldwide system made up of interconnected computer networks that links devices globally through the use of the internet protocol suit.*

Source: https://www.networkworld.com/article/3449217/as-the-internet-turns-50-experts-weigh-future-advances-and-emerging-issues.html.

6.4.1. Origin of the Internet

The internet was a concept developed when several computer science laboratories wanted to create a wide area network. It started off as the APARNET project which was basically funded by the US department of defense. The APARNET concepts were developed in 1963. In 1969, the first message was sent using the APARNET. The message was sent from one computer science professor to another in a different university. With the use of various communication protocols, parallel switching networks were developed. They included the merit network and the tele net among others. The packet switching was first demonstrated for research to kickoff and various tests to be carried out (Saeed et al., 2017).

After several experiments and tests, the APANET project advanced and led to the development of protocols. These protocols facilitated internetworking which involved the joining of several separate networks into a network of networks. The protocols involved the designs from the CYCLADES project. In 1969 the APARNET project carried its first packets. Later on, national supercomputing centers were established in different universities. The establishment was funded by the NSF which sought to provide interconnectivity within the NSFNET project.

This led to the creation of network access to the supercomputer sites within the United States. The supercomputers were mostly located in research and education institutions which were mostly universities. After it developed, it led to the emergence of commercial internet providers and afterwards the APARNET was decommissioned. This was followed by the decommissioning of the NFSNET to remove the restrictions on the use of the internet in carrying commercial traffic. In the 1980's research at CERN brought about the World Wide Web (Saeed et al., 2017).

This linked important documents (hypertext) in an information system. This information would be accessed by any node in the network. Since the mid-1990s there has been a constant revolutionization of the internet to the present day and it has impacted various aspects of human life such as their culture. It has also been used in revolutionizing the technology that is heavily depended on by the current generation. The research centers that were active in creation of the internet were the ones who came up with fiber-optic networks so as to transmit data at a higher speed.

6.4.2. Purpose of the Internet

In the current day and age, the internet plays a major role in people's day to day life. The internet can be used in the following ways:

- To facilitate the exchange of information between different parts of the world. For instance, one person can be in Africa and the other halfway across the world. The internet has been used to facilitate communication through the use of electronic mail which tends to be a cheaper method to use compared to other forms.
- To create a platform for interaction where people can discuss their views on various topics. This has been made possible through the use of social media platforms such as Facebook, Twitter, and Instagram. In these platforms, people have been able to give their opinions on various topics that cut across the different parts of the world.
- It has been used as a learning resource in the education system. Students use the internet to research on different topics to gain more knowledge. It also enables them access other reading material such as books that are available online. This includes the e-books. It has been used by teachers to get content on the given context as well as help them improve their teaching skills.

- It has been used by business owners to gain technical support. For instance, they are able to acquire knowledge on the type of products the users love to use so that they can produce them. It has also been useful for them when they market their product as it gives them a wide platform to advertise themselves.
- It has been used to make the shopping experience to be simpler and more convenient. It has brought about online shopping where people are able to buy different products at the comfort of their homes. Not only that, people are able to ask for services they would want to be offered to them with the comfort of their mobile phones.
- It has enabled people to be updated on the current news in different countries. This is made possible through the electronic aspect of the internet. This enables them to access breaking news and news updates at their convenience.
- It has given writers and musicians a platform where they can share their content with the public and be able to obtain feedback.

6.4.3. The Components of the Internet

Internet service provider: It is an organization that deals with the provision of dial-in internet account. The internet account can either be SLIP or PPP (point-to-point protocol) account. The SLIP account is not as complex as the PPP. This is because for the user to use the PPP account they are required to have a compatible program for it. The program enables the user to access the internet by dialing the phone with the use of a modem. This connects it to the ISP and logs in to the user's account. Once connected, the user is able to browse.

Computer address (IP): While connected to the internet, each computer has a unique number that people may refer to it as its identity. The number is called the Internet Protocol Address.

It follows a given format. The IP address is used to identify the computer while it is connected to the internet. It is usually allocated to the computer by the ISP. This enables the computer to communicate with and device that is available in the network.

Internet protocol: As the word protocol refers to a set of rules, the term internet protocol may be used to refer to a set of rules in using the internet. There are various types of internet protocols which include:

- Transmission Control Protocol
- File Transfer Protocol
- HyperText Transfer Protocol

The transmission control protocol is used to govern the way data is transmitted from one machine to the other. For the file transfer protocol, its role is to facilitate the transfer of files between two or more computers on the internet.

The hypertext transfer protocol plays a role of governing the transfer of hypertext between computers. It is the mode in which the World Wide Web shares its information.

Telenet: It is part of the internet service that grants access to remote computers beyond the area. The Telenet gives users access to databases and other public services.

Gopher: It is basically a distributed information service that makes collections of information that are hierarchical to be available on the internet for the users. The users access the information using a gopher server.

Wide area information service: It is an internet search engine that uses a given protocol for retrieval of information which is computer-computer based. It is a searching tool that can search for more than one database.

Uniform resource locator: It identifies the source of information on the internet and enables the user to access the information by indicating the exact source of information. The URL is unique for every resource available on the internet. It consists of numerical figures, letters, and punctuation.

World wide web (www): It contains collections of hypertext documents that are interlinked and reside in various places such as the web servers. It is what most users interact with when they use the internet. It is where all users get to access the various information they need through some information that is provided may be irrelevant.

Internet relay chat (IRC): It is a chat system that enables numerous numbers of users to communicate at the same time while on the internet. It is a platform where users get to meet other users and discuss on various topics.

Newsgroups: In newsgroups, each group has its own designated subject which the user can give input. This may be through the asking of questions and giving answers on the related topic. The people in such groups share the same interests. The information posted in such groups may not be private as it is sent to all parts of the world to every news server.

Usenet: Usenet bears a resemblance to social media platforms. It is where people meet and interact with friends or family, they get to know the latest trends in the field of computer or just share their day's experience.

Electronic mail (e-mail): It is the most extensively used tool more so in the business world as it seems to be more official compared to other forms of communication. It entails the sending and receiving of information electronically. It is composed of a letter written for someone, an email address, and the receiver. In this case, the number of receivers may be more than one. It depends on the targeted audience. The email address helps in directing the e-mail to the intended person or the intended destination.

Uses of the internet: Mobile commerce-this refers to the transactions that take place in the mobile internet. This is the use of the mobile phone by consumers in ordering and also payment of goods that were bought through the internet. This type of commerce is usually through the use of apps as well as the internet. An example is the Jumia app that enables the consumers' shop and purchase items online.

Entertainment: the internet has been greatly used for pleasure trough entertainment. Users are able to download movies or songs from the internet to enjoy. Some may stream the movies depending on the strength of the internet connectivity.

Mobile wallet: this is among the latest trends brought about by the internet. Rather than carrying cash around which may not be safe, users have opted to use the mobile wallet which enables them to keep money in their phones and they are able to pay for goods and services using the mobile wallet.

E-commerce: this is the latest trend among businessmen. They carry out all their trading activities while in the internet.

Chatting: it is the most commonly used software among several users. It enables the users to send and receive information while connected to the internet.

Online banking: this is whereby the consumers do not have to go to banks to deposit or withdraw money. They can still get those services online.

Communication: the internet has mostly been used in communication with the use of electronic mails.

The internet has also been used in collection of large volume of information and social networking among others.

6.5. E-LEARNING

With improvements being made to the education sector, there are changes being made to improve the quality of education. This has led to the introduction of technology into the learning system. This brought about e-learning. The students interact with knowledge using the computer. The computers are usually connected to the internet. It involves the students attending classes online as the computer or device provides the classes to the students. It has been useful in eliminating distance as a barrier to education as people who live in distant areas are able to attend the classes but it will not be physically (D'Atri et al., 2011).

6.5.1. Evolving E-Learning

In the previous days to develop an E-learning program, it would require a group of programmers to come together and work together in order to develop the E-learning programs. With recent advancements in technology, various tools have been employed whereby anyone can create E-learning programs. With the use of such tools, it is not a requirement that the person should have any programming skills. The advancement has facilitated other devices being used for e-learning. The devices include laptops, tablets, desktops and smartphones. The use of the mobile phones in learning has brought about the term m-learning.

6.5.2. Value of E-Learning

E-learning has been used to facilitate several activities and. Its special features include:

- *Cost-cutting*: organizations that use this type of tool for education purposes reduce their costs by saving money spent on instructors wages.
- *Global usage*: any individual in any part of the world is able to access e-learning provided that they have access to the internet. This is one of the ways in which people can pursue degrees and masters in distant universities without having to be physically present in the classroom.
- *Can be used by several devices*: the advances in technology has enabled E-learning to be offered in various devices. The courses offered can work in a variety of devices increasing the access to these devices by the students.

- *Time saving*: with the advances in technology, the computer scientists have been able to come up with a software that enables individuals to create the online courses within a short time. Therefore individuals are able to easily create, publish and share the created courses to several individuals. The shared course can easily be accessed by different and several users.
- *It is either synchronous or asynchronous in terms of activity*: synchronous refers to an activity being given an allocated time while asynchronous refers to an activity that does not have a given time limit. For quite a period of time, the e-learning process was asynchronous where people will take their free time to read. In the recent days the e-learning activity is synchronous. The users learn the course within a given period of time as they are required to give feedback within the allocated time.

The general value of E-learning is that it is both time and cost saving.

6.5.3. Common E-Learning Tools/Terms

There are various tools and terms in the field of E-learning. They include:

- Virtual learning environment: this is the use of digital media tools to provide and online space so that institutions can offer e-learning.
- Personal learning environment: this is whereby individuals make use of the available networks either personal or institutional to facilitate learning.
- Blackboard and Moodle: they are examples of virtual learning environments.
- Podcasts; audio or video: it is one of the ways used delivering information. It depends on the form in which the information is displayed for the user.
- Face-to-face teaching: it is one of the teaching and learning methods employed in the education process. It is used to create a clear distinction between a classroom environment and an online environment.
- Learning object: this entails the various objects used in the learning process. They may include audios or videos.
- Blended learning: it is a learning method that is made up of different learning methods. For instance, it may be made up of face-to-face and technology-based learning. It is generally a breed of the two.

- Blogs: a blog is a platform where people get to post on various topics of their choice. In education, these blogs provide students with information on different educational topics. Some blogs enable the user to give feedback on the given content.

These are but some of the terms/tools in E-learning. There are several others which include distance learning, web service, netbook, flash player and mobile learning among others.

6.5.4. Software Used for Creating E-Learning

Initially, programmers had to have high-level skills in order to create E-learning programs. It is a major leap in the current day as the individuals do not need to have programming skills. With the use of applications such as Microsoft PowerPoint, they have availed different tools so that individuals are easily able to create e-learning. Currently, the e-learning authoring tools are divided into two categories that include the form-based and the free-form authoring tools. For the form-based authoring tools, the user has access to e-learning parts that were already placed in the applications. These tools are mostly used by content developers who want to develop the e-learning course quickly. The free-form authoring tools require the individual to develop the e-learning course from scratch. It is the exact opposite of the form-based authoring tools.

6.5.5. Sharing of E-Learning

Once an individual develops and creates an e-learning course, it needs to reach the user. For this to happen he or she has to share it. There are two methods/ ways of sharing the courses which are formal distribution and informal distribution. Informal distribution deals with sharing of the content without any systematic procedure. The user can access the content through a link that was shared to him or her. Formal distribution involves the sharing of information through a systematic manner. It is the method that is mostly used in organization to make it more professional. It involves tracking and recording of the learners' results.

6.6. VIRTUAL LEARNING

Virtual learning to some individuals may be a branch of e-learning. It is part of the development that has been made in the learning process to increase the quality of education offered to the students. It is a learning platform that greatly utilizes the use of ICT systems thereby enabling the students and teachers to interact in order to develop various activities which may include curriculum activities. This brings about the term virtual learning environment. It refers to tools used in learning and teaching that sought to improve the students' learning experience. Tools used include computers and the internet (GAL-EZER & STEPHENSON, 2014).

The virtual learning environment was developed in order to improve the teaching and learning process through the use of technology. It has facilitated the option of students being able to carry out the learning process while at the comfort of their homes. This is beneficial as many students will be able to access the teaching services making the process to be widespread. For virtual learning to occur the virtual learning software has to be installed in the device used to facilitate learning. The internet is used to facilitate the entire process.

The teacher is usually present in the learning process but for those who want the learning process to be interactive they use video conferencing. Virtual learning is dependent on the internet for it to occur. It avails a variety of tools which include student and peer assessment, uploading of content and communication among others (GAL-EZER & STEPHENSON, 2014).

6.6.1. Features of Virtual Learning

- *Assignments*: the VL has functions that enable the students to get the assignments and also submit them once they are through.
- *Assessments*: the VL has distinct applications that enable the teachers to carry out student evaluations.
- *Quizzes and tests*: the virtual learning is designed in a manner that teachers are able to give quizzes and test to the students. It has advanced in that the students can be timed as they take the tests.
- *Interactions*: the virtual learning caters for students who treasure teacher-student interaction. This is made possible through the use of video conferencing where it is a form of face-to-face interactions,
- *Mobile access*: not all students are able to access computers. To cater for them, the virtual learning can be carried out through the use of mobile phones. It is convenient as almost every individual possesses a mobile phone.

- *Interactions*: this basically refers to discussion which is the basis of virtual learning. Discussions are made possible through the use of tools that include video conferencing which facilitates interaction between students and also with the instructors.
- *Browsing access*: the virtual learning is dependent on internet access. When an individual has internet access, they will be able to install applications that will facilitate virtual learning and also get the upgrades made on the applications.
- *Use of multimedia*: virtual learning embraces the use of multimedia in the teaching and learning process.

There are other features of virtual learning which include document management and synchronous among others.

6.6.2. Advantages of Virtual Learning

There are numerous benefits of having a virtual learning environment. They include:

- It enables the learning process to be learner centered. This is because it advocates for the students to carrying out individualized learning. This will enable them to maximize on their learning on an individual basis.
- It has facilitated to learning process being flexible. This is because the students are able to learn while at home or wherever they may be. The use of mobile learning (m-learning) has enabled learning to be carried out to the user's comfort.
- It has provided ways in which teachers can assess their students. Virtual learning has features that include assignments, quizzes and tests which can be used by teachers in evaluating their students. They also have assessment features. This enables the teachers to directly assess the students and monitor their progress.
- It has assisted in improving the learning process by improving the learning experience. It has employed the use of various multimedia tools by both the teachers and students making the learning experience to be fruitful for the students.
- It is available for all. This ensures that anybody can enroll to undertake the virtual learning training sessions.
- It enables students to get up-to-date knowledge. For virtual learning the programs are constantly updated so that the user gets to interact with the latest knowledge.

- It saves on time and money as one does not have to travel to and from a learning institution in order to learn. For the learning institution a lot of money is saved as they do not have to employ several teaching personnel.
- It has made the learning experience to be more interactive. This is through the use of video conferencing that enable the students to interact with their teachers.
- It teaches the students to have time management. As some of the virtual learning have asynchronous features, the students will be required to create time for them to learn hence they will learn the value of time management.
- It facilitates self-paced learning. Students will be able to learn according to the pace they can keep up with.

6.6.3. Different Forms of Virtual Learning

Online learning: this form of virtual learning takes place in the internet. It is composed of other forms of virtual learning instruction except the computer-based learning.

Computer-based learning: this form of learning works by having the software providing the instruction instead of the teacher. The instruction used to facilitate this form of learning is usually installed in a computer or server depending on the network layout available.

Internet-based: for this form of virtual learning the instruction is located in the web hence the name internet-based.

Remote teacher online: unlike the previous forms of virtual learning, for this form the instruction is provided by the teacher or instructor. It works in a way that the students interact with the teacher through the internet.

Blended learning: this type of virtual learning is made up of other forms of virtual learning.

6.7. WEB-BASED LEARNING

It refers to the form of learning that uses the internet as a medium in which students get to access instructions in order to carry out various learning activities. It came up as a result of advancements being made in technology. It has a form of relation to virtual learning. Web-based learning takes place in different ways but majorly there are two ways. The first one is learning purely online. The students get to learn what is in the curriculum online. They get to access all the content online. The students and the instructors don't get to interact with the students (Hazzan, Lapidot, & Ragonis, 2015).

Web-based learning is a hybrid that involves the students interacting with the instructors online or in the classroom. It depends on the requirement and needs of the implemented curriculum. It forms a basis on how time is divided so that the instructors get to interact with the students while in class and also online.

There are different forms of web-based learning which include wiki, webcasting, social bookmarking, social networking, microblogging, vodcasts, podcasts, blogs, RSS, synchronous conferencing, mail listings, E-mail, ADS and IRC among others. There are also web-based learning tools which include wikis, game, interactive videos and online word processing among others. For web-based learning to effectively occur, it requires the use of library resources. These resources are useful for students in gaining information. They include E-journals, E-books, databases, weblogs, digital library and library catalogs (Hazzan, Lapidot, & Ragonis, 2015).

In web-based learning, there are three major classifications. They include online discussion groups, tutorials, and virtual patients. The tutorials are majorly online and incorporate the use of various multimedia tools such as videos and audios. For the online discussions, they have no distinction to the physical group discussions.

6.7.1. Advantages of Web-Based Learning

It removes physical distance as a barrier to education. The instructions are provided online therefore students who are in different parts of the world are able to interact with teachers for the purpose of learning. This makes it a continent mode of learning. It also facilitates flexible scheduling. Through the use of synchronous features, the students are able to time the participation of the lesson. They are able to know when the lesson will start and when it will be ending. It is flexible for students as they can be able to access the tutorial at any time or day.

In modern learning trends, the learning process is learner-oriented. Web-based learning has been advantageous in the sense that it promotes a learner-oriented type of learning. This has been done by instilling in students the culture of individualized learning. Learners are able to use the available tools to improve on the areas in which they are weak. It has also facilitated student assessment and documentation. For the student assessment in web-based learning, it is carried out online bringing about the flexibility of it. It also carries out documentation of learning activities such as tests that have been completed (Singh, 2008).

6.7.2. Disadvantages of Web-Based Learning

- It is dependent on technology and if the technology in use has problems then the web-based learning process will encounter difficulties. Here the teacher may not be able to improvise so that the learning process may continue.
- It is expensive. Compared to the previous forms of teaching which involved the use of textbooks, on a large if web-based learning is used it may end up being expensive. For instance, institutions will have to pay for subscriptions for e-books so that their learners can access them.
- It leads to social isolation. This is because most of the time the student will be online accessing the tutorials and reading materials. The study session may involve only the student and the internet. Even though there are platforms for online discussion groups, the students will not be able to physically interact with other students.
- The web-based learning may not meet the individual needs of the learner. This is because the instruction set is usually generalized to accommodate all learner but does not look into the specific need of each learner.
- It requires more time for preparation. This more so applies for the teacher when they are preparing for each session. They have to know the concept to apply, the technology to use as well as the media to use when making the tutorial. This may be time-consuming for the teachers
- For the third world countries, this form of learning may not be available to all learners as some cannot access necessities such as electricity.

6.8. TELECONFERENCING

It is one of the latest trends in information technology. It entails people being in a meeting but some are not physically present but electronically present. The use various media such as live video to be present for the meeting. The teleconferencing happens in real-time where the participants that are not physically present use the available media to listen and contribute to the meetings. Teleconferencing has been incorporated in various fields more so in business. There are various types of teleconferencing currently available. They include video teleconferencing, audio teleconferencing, and computer teleconferencing.

Audio teleconferencing: Audio teleconferencing involves communication through the use of audio. Voice communication equipment is used to facilitate this kind of communication. For the communication process to occur, an audio link has to be established between locations of the people concerned so that the meeting can take place. The required systems have to be installed for it to work. It is the only type of teleconferencing that does not require a computer for it to work.

Video conferencing: This type of teleconferencing applies the use of both the audio and visual aspects of media. Therefore, the equipment to be used should provide sound and picture content. Video conferencing can occur in three different ways: one-way video and audio, one-way audio and two-way video or two-way video and audio.

Computer conferencing: A great example of this type of conferencing is e-mail. This type of conferencing is dependent on user of the system and content/subject matter.

Chapter 7 The Use of ICT in Teaching Computer Science

CONTENTS

7.1. INTRODUCTION

The term ICT refers to information and communications technology. Its role cannot be overstated as we live currently in the information age era. In a nutshell, ICT refers to communication technologies that provide access to information. It also refers to a combination of all technologies that enable people to interact digitally. As a result, we have been seeing a wide array of new communication innovations over the past several decades. Today people can communicate in real-time with others anywhere across the world using technologies such as telephone apps, video conferencing, instant messaging, voice over Internet protocol and so much more.

ICT is responsible for creating a global village whereby users from all over the world are able to be in contact and communicate with each other on a regular basis as if they lived next to each other. With ICT a company can operate with a flawless simplicity between clients, suppliers, distributors and other parties. It has a significant impact in our daily lives, for instance we can read our local newspaper online and be connected with our family, relatives or simply anyone else.

If we were to make a list of ICT components it would be exhaustive as ICT continues to grow. ICT encompasses internet-enabled, mobile-powered, wireless networks, antiquated technologies like radios and landlines, all of which are used simultaneously alongside new innovations such as artificial intelligence and robotics. We will broadly categorize them below.

7.2. COMPONENTS OF ICT

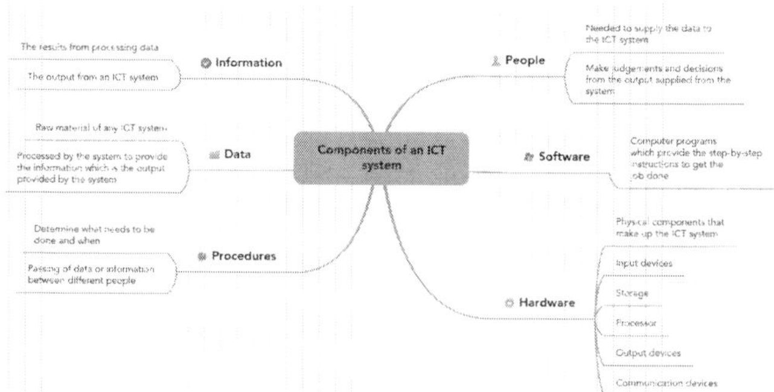

Figure 7.1. *Components of ICT.*

Source: https://www.mindmeister.com/14539822/components-of-an-ict-system.

Cloud computing refers to data hubs that are available to the masses over the internet today they operate as distributors over multiple locations from a central server.

A good example would be the largest public cloud that we have which is Amazon AWS (Woollard, 2007).

Software is defined as programs and operating information that a computer uses.

Applications, such as Facebook Skype, and other easily downloadable programs all count as software and they are technologies that enable us to communicate pieces of information in the way they are designed.

Hardware is the opposite of software in the sense that it describes physical aspects. It refers to physically tangible objects, such as a computer, a mobile device, a television, or a radio.

Digital transactions which are automated and often performed online save a lot of time and money. They are often very enhanced and minimize errors while increasing convenience.

Digital data allows us to store information in a machine language and communicate them using various technologies. The most commonly used machine language to store digital data is the binary system which uses, traditionally, a series of ones and zeros for on and off sequencing.

Internet access which is the ability to connect to a global computer network that provides a variety of information enables individuals and organizations to utilize services such as emails, etc.

There are several ways to gain Internet access like Dial-up, Hotspots, mobile connections and, etc.

7.3. ICT IN EDUCATION

Information and communications technology have become almost integral in teacher-student dynamics. Research has shown that ICT improves student learning define teaching methods.

More importantly, the results showed that are continuous exposure technology for students aids with knowledge presentation adeptness, innovative potential and problem-solving skills (Woollard, 2007).

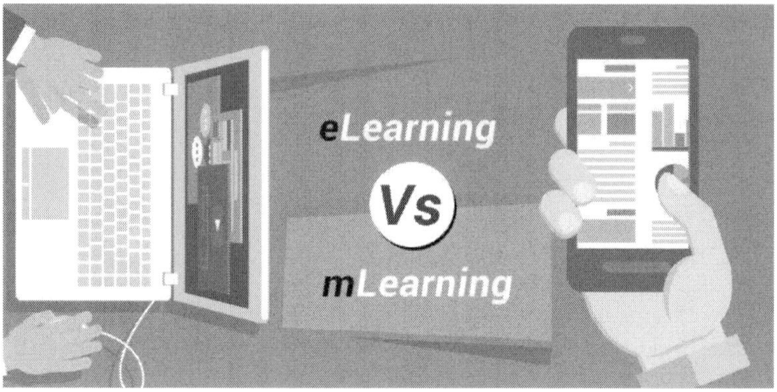

Figure 7.2. *ICT has taken education and given its mobility with the Invention of e-learning and m-learning.*

Source: https://knowzieslearning.com/5-differences-between-mlearning-and-elearning/.

Students are able to access information anytime they want and the number tertiary institutions that provide these technological tools continue to grow. This came almost naturally because of the fact that education institutions will always try to increase their reach and target a larger number or clients. It has become almost a symbiotic relationship where there is an increasing demand for out-of-class learning and institutions have to get highly creative using a diverse range of ICT equipment to communicate, disseminate, store and manage information (Woollard, 2007).

One example of how this is done is with the new concept of the flipped classroom. The flipped classroom is an idea which takes away from the conventional and customary classroom environment highlighting the students teaching themselves at their own pace the basic conceptual knowledge (Barton, 2004). Instead of lectures going on for hours solely delivering information, the content is covered online to students beforehand and the classroom is used for higher-level discussions, experiments, applications, projects, and student interactions.

Techniques such as these where education and ICT are used hand in hand also prepares the student for real-life and workplace scenarios where these communication technologies do not change much. Together with the fact that learning also takes place without time constraints the benefits only continue to grow. The main objective of this paper is to dive deeper into the uses of ICT in education and more specifically in Computer Studies.

7.4. COMPUTER SCIENCE

Computer science which falls under the discipline of computing is the study of the processes of both hardware and software of a computer. It is a broad topic covering everything from algorithm building to artificial intelligence and digital design. It has strong undertones in mathematics and engineering but has applications across all vocations. As a discipline on its own computer science was born in the early 60s with most computer users working either in scientific research Laboratories or in large corporations. However, today you may find computer science being taught in middle schools and even some elementary schools. Most education systems around the world have computer science as one of the mandatory subjects to study at some point. It has become so foundational that many believe it should be taught just as physics or geography is.

The 10 Fastest-Growing Industries In The U.S.

	Industry (NAICS code)	Sales Change (%) (1/1/2016-12/31/2016)
1	Computer Systems Design and Related Services (5415)	18%
2	Services to Buildings and Dwellings (5617)	14%
3	Building Finishing Contractors (2383)	14%
4	Residential Building Construction (2361)	14%
5	Foundation, Structure, and Building Exterior Contractors (2381)	13%
6	Other Professional, Scientific, and Technical Services (5419)	13%
7	Building Equipment Contractors (2382)	13%
8	Other Specialty Trade Contractors (2389)	13%
9	Nonresidential Building Construction (2362)	13%
10	Other Heavy and Civil Engineering Construction (2379)	13%

sageworks

Figure 7.3. *Forbes List of Fastest Growing Industries.*

Figure: https://www.forbes.com/sites/sageworks/2017/04/09/the-10-fastest-growing-industries-in-the-u-s/#4676f5cc1ef2.

The field is offers of the fastest-growing and highest-earning careers they are out there. In fact, extensive studies show that where computer science is not taught it is largely due to limited exposure to technology and resources and even though opportunities are not universally accessible this is beginning to change quickly (Barton, 2004).

7.4.1. Teaching Computer Science

Teaching computer science came with the birth of the first personal computers. The first computer science exams were held in the 1984 where students were required to learn a single programming language in affluent schools with well-off families in the United States.

In the 90s, High School institutions we are ready and willing to teach these college-level classes but many were deficient the computer science backcloth. This means that they had to solely rely on very dense collegiate textbooks to design the syllabus. These heavily articulated and dense textbooks meant and even more difficult curriculum (Kadijevich, Angeli, & Schulte, 2013).

This period brought a bad reputation for computer science where most people opted out of taking it as a course because it is perceived as being so hard. In fact, today, exposure still remains as the biggest hurdle in computer science.

Many tech leaders went on to be very successful simply because they had early exposure and education. Mark Zuckerberg, for example, launched the first version of Facebook from his dorm room at Harvard University. However, prior to attending Harvard, he attended a prestigious private school where computer science was a mandatory course and was also tutored weekly by a computer scientist.

In this way, today studying integrated computer science early on even from Elementary school has developed popularity. It may be difficult to imagine that at such a young age computer science can be taught but the K-12 system has computer science frameworks that fit from kindergarten to grade 12 (Barton, 2004).

A computer science teacher usually must hold a bachelor's degree in computer science and some teaching qualifications as well although you do not need a bachelor's degree in education. Clearly one must have a doctoral degree to teach at the post-secondary level. Diplomas in computer teacher training available and focuses on computing for both teaching and training.

You will find that the most successful computer science teachers are those who genuinely love the subject, keep up to date on current affairs, are highly critical and create an enthusiastic environment where the students are highly motivated. The next session will focus on teaching framework employed by K-12 computer science by grade.

7.4.2. Teaching Computer Science in Elementary Schools

As mentioned earlier, it may appear that elementary school is an ideal period to introduce computer science to children because it foster creativity and teachers critical thinking skills. Interactive demonstrations can include robots' games buttons keys and dials and other interactive hardware and software suitable for young age. Writing and designing algorithms may not be taught at this level but simple tasks, such as automation or following specific sequences, can be taught at this age (Leask & Meadows, 2000).

Understanding computing systems hardware and software create need-finding and problem-solving processes. Other ideas which should be introduced early include law and ethics. The need to use computers responsibly and ethically cannot be overstated. The conceptualization of data analysis is also taught at this level. Simple notions, for example, that pictures can be stored on a cell phone or a computer and viewed later redeem can be saved and continued after sometime are covered broadly.

In grades 3, 4, and 5 students begin to understand more about computing systems and how they work together with devices, for example, they learn that a smartphone can be connected to wireless headphones but the headphones are useless without the information source. When troubleshooting they will begin to learn straight forward things like checking connections, replacing a working part for a defective one. With information storage it will become apparent the different types of files required different amount of storage and a video file is ordinarily larger than an image file for example. All in all very basic computing system functions and behavior are taught at this age (Leask & Meadows, 2000).

7.4.3. Teaching Computer Science in Middle Schools

At this level, further abstractions should be taught. Students begin to see that all interactions pose advantages and disadvantages. For example, enabling your GPS on your phone will give you directions but can also track your position in order to sell this data to other parties. Selecting a faster computer with more memory means sacrificing cost (Unesco, 2011).

The fact that advancements in technology change our everyday lives, and that user-centered designs create solutions that have great community effect will be some of the things that become apparent as well. Understanding algorithms require input that reflect results, for example, what recommendations one may get on the YouTube channel is dependent on past searches, is gathered. Programming language such as python present themselves at this stage with the syllabus becoming more programming and algorithm oriented. Python is a text-based programming language that is the most widely used at tertiary levels.

7.4.4. Teaching Computer Science in High School

By 2013, more than half of Google's engineering employees were admitted having taken computer science in some form in high school. Carnegie Mellon University known for its world-class computing, engineering, and interdisciplinary programs in 2019 list of free online curriculum for high school students with highly engaging graphics that teaches programming skills (D'Atri et al., 2011).

By the end of grade 12 institutions teaching computer science will have students will understand data can be collected from millions of people even when they are unaware they are engaging and data collection. Social media another account online can have one raise privacy concerns. The scope of computing devices continues to grow with applications in medical, agricultural, and industrial applications. Some of the popular key skills being taught (D'Atri et al., 2011).

7.4.5. Teaching Computer Science at Collegiate Level

A computer science degree will typically focus on software and software systems. Subjects including computer systems, database systems, network systems, and bioinformatics will be studied in a systematic structured process.

Entry requirements for a bachelor's degree draw on mathematical or prior computer science background. Core computer science courses include:

- Theories of computation and information
- Fundamentals of programming
- Software systems development
- Algorithm and data systems
- Computer architecture and design
- Discrete mathematics
- Database management
- Computer network and communication systems
- Programming language theory
- Computer graphics

- Human-computer interactions
- Artificial intelligence
- Algorithm and data structures

The top universities in the world offering computer science degrees are Stanford University, University of Oxford, Harvard University, and Massachusetts Institute of Technology. These universities are consistently placing amongst the top universities worldwide.

7.5. ICT TOOLS USED BY COMPUTER SCIENCE TEACHERS

It is imperative to list the various ICT tools that can be used for teaching, more especially teaching computer science. Below is an exhaustive list of the general ICT equipment used for teaching and learning. All ICT tools can be broadly categorized into two major sections hardware and software. As already discussed, hardware consists of the physical, tangible equipment and tools used for information processing and the software consists of the programs that organize the tasks to be performed.

7.5.1. Hardware

Desktop Computer: The desktop computer remains popular even with the growing implementation of bring your room device policies. In computer science, this is a tool that one cannot operate without.

Laptop Computer: Laptop computers have brought a feature of flexibility and portability designed to be taken place to place they are great for working anywhere anytime. This is also another two that a computer scientist cannot survive without. Laptops help teachers especially with reaching technology-based materials.

Tablets: Tablets are simplified mobile computers without touch screen instead of a mouse they lie somewhere between a smartphone and a laptop in size comparison they are small convenient and very portable in comparison to laptops and desktops. With growing wireless technology, a tablet is one of the best ICT tools that a teacher can use.

Projectors: Chalkboards have almost become obsolete because of projectors which receive an electronic signal and display a video onto a screen. Rather than writing on the board teachers can now save time and effort by simply showing films videos and graphics. In computer science they can be extremely useful demonstrating programming algorithms and math manipulative.

Smart Board: A Smart Board is generally a larger computer tablet that sometimes is operated by Touch. Smart board or now what will temple jacket is obsolete just like projectors turned chalkboards obsolete.

Interactive smart boards can turn a lesson into right learning environment. With constant developments in technology there are some smart both these days that do not even require a projector. White boards are also very versatile and can be used with an array of attachment tools.

Smartphones: More than half of the global population owns a mobile phone some was better capabilities than others. At first smartphones would be the biggest distractions teachers would have to deal with, however, smartphones have now become part of the classroom experience.

Radio: Educational radio has been used in very many countries with varying effects. In the past the power of the radio has proven to educate listeners, improving writing, listening and speaking skills.

Television: Television has been used as a learning tool because of its combination of sensory stimulus. Students can see historical events as they happened, explore the world and sometimes, TV has served inadvertently to learn and teach without even knowing with its escapism character.

7.5.2. Software

Authoring System: An authoring system is software that has pre-programmed designs for the creation of multimedia.

Watering systems allow our teacher to make their own instructional software they can develop contents like speech lessons, tutorials and other multimedia applications. The types of authoring systems include:

- Digital audio
- Music editing
- Image graphics editing
- Animation and gamification
- Multimedia authoring

Some examples of authoring tools include Adobe Captivate Adobe Presenter Brain Shark Presentations, Cameo, Course Avenue Studio, Flash Point and Code Baby.

Desktop Publishing: Teachers can use this software usually to prepare reports Canada's most commonly what is used to present information to parents and students about general activities and events. Desktop publishing sweets such as Microsoft Office and Adobe Creative suit are some of the most familiar software that one can come across. Examples include Adobe PageMaker Express publisher Microsoft Publisher, Lucid Press, Scribus, etc. They are ordinarily used by professional graphic designers.

Reference Software: Teachers use reference software to access large amounts of information that would ordinarily be found in an encyclopedia or an atlas for example. Reference software most commonly used today includes Britannica, Google Earth, Stardict and Encarta. Reference software is constantly expanded upon print references and uses hyperlinks.

Figure 7.4. *Britannica.*

https://www.britannica.com/technology/technology.

Drill and Practice Software: Drill and practice software or programs designed to test skill and make ready them for exams. The most common drill and practice software include Quizlet, PowerPrep, SAT, PSAT, and Flashcard Machine.

Tutorial Software: Tutorial Software is similar to drill and practice software in that some are also built to test aptitude and skill levels. They allow the student to develop their own pace to learn and can also be used to teach new information and allow it to be practiced upon. It is an interactive learning tool where step by step comprehension of concepts is structured. It can be useful for example when teaching how to create a basic web page when teaching web design. The tutorial can further explain how to add features that are progressively more difficult. Examples include iSpring Suite Open Broadcaster, Panopto, Debut Video Capture, Camtasia, and WM Capture.

Educational Games: Game software has become one of the most popular ways to import knowledge. It is especially effective because of the high level of motivation that it gives especially young children. It has become very popular in recent years because it serves the advantage of teaching many children with many different personalities without losing the audience. It has also psychologically proved to back up retention longer than other teaching and learning methods. In a sense, all games are learning processes and as most games are usually casual it makes the learning process more entertaining. One way usually is for learners manipulate this game software to create their own games. The second way then would be for the trainers to design their own games from scratch according to the student's levels using the same game software. The third approach would be to amalgamate already commercially available education software into the classroom for effective learning. The list of Educational gaming software is endless especially for children and that includes Cluefinders Gold Geries, KidPix, Reader Rabbit Zoombinis, Edmark, Museum Madness, etc.

Simulation Software: Simulation software creates a virtual reality that enables students to learn through actual experience. Experience of flying a plane can be through flight simulation software just like experience of racing an F1 car has its own software simulators. Allowing the user to observe operations without actually performing them in real-life. It is a very powerful technique used for education. In computer science specifically as we will tackle later on circulation can be used for systems representations and knowledge encapsulation. Examples of Simulation software include Any Logic, MATLAB, Sim Scale, Simulaing Arena, etc.

Others: Other software includes spelling software that helps kids learn how to spell, speed reading vocabulary, special needs software and math problem-solving software are also becoming very popular in education.

7.6. ICT IN COMPUTER SCIENCE

In computer science, ICT hardware and software naturally constitute majority of the job requirements. Considering hardware first of all, ICT and computer science are actually synonymous and go hand in both teaching and learning. A computer science student and teacher are virtually and literally crippled they do not have either a laptop computer or a desktop computer. Laptops, as stated earlier, have become more popular and affordable overtime and policies like bring-your-own-device (BYOD) employed in many institutions (Woollard, 2007).

7.6.1. Computers and Laptops for Computer Science Teachers

Computer science teachers understand that just like any other educationalists it is vital to have the right tools for the job. A desktop computer and laptop computer are precious to these trainers. When choosing desktop computer brand names like Apple HP and Acer are a good start and provide high levels of functionality depending on the objectives that need to be met. Many institutions would offer desktops in their computer laboratory and some would offer laptops as well for both the student and lecturer (Woollard, 2007). The software on these tools would be what determines what is chosen but generally a strong processor able to hold many software packages and laptops with great battery and portability are of vital importance.

Other priorities to be considered include plenty of storage where many computer scientists prefer having a Steady State Drive (SSD) compared to a Hard Disk Drive (HHD). A computer with plenty of RAM for running plenty of programs at the same time and one with great display 1080p or better is also attractive.

7.6.2. Tablets and Smartphone's for Computer Science Teachers

Capabilities of tablets and smartphones have exponentially grown over the last couple of decades. These types of hardware tools are examples of portability. Radio and television take a backstage as tools for computer science educators. On the other hand, the small and portable tablets and smartphones have become particularly important in quickly retrieving scholarly articles recording notes and planning lectures.

7.6.3. Smart Boards and Projectors for Computer Science Teachers

Smartboards and projectors especially interactive ones have propelled us further than simple chalk-and-talk in the classroom. They allow for more efficient note-taking especially for difficult students who have trouble concentrating and listening they keep the students engaged and allow you to teach with a wide range of mediums. In computer science they become especially important when using graphic software simulation software where display is an important factor of the lesson plan. When it comes to teaching, smart boards and projectors display is usually the primary factor and finding one that is suitable for the task at hand is fairly straight forward. Examples include the Smart Board M600, The Nierby HC40 Interactive Projector and the GoTouch Basic 3.0 which all come with additional devices such as touch pens or laser pens (Barton, 2004).

7.6.4. ICT Software for Computer Science Teachers

Software between ICT and computer science have also shown as symbiotic relationship in the sense that majority of the ICT software produced are actually made by computer programmers and computer scientists. When it comes to teaching and learning computer science all types of software are used in one way or another.

When it comes to ICT software and teaching computer science, the two concepts go hand in hand . A computer scientist can write or create software and make computers perform new, abstract, and problem-solving tasks. Hence a computer scientist can work together with software engineers and software developers to create these programs (Barton, 2004).

7.6.5. Authoring Software Systems in Computer Science

As an ICT tool, authoring software systems are used often in computer science because they provide plenty of graphics and multimedia interactions manipulation tools in software form. Three components that are inclusive of authoring systems are content manipulation content delivery and assessments.

Authoring tools have become very popular in augmented reality and designing software in various areas such as education marketing and entertainment advertising, etc. Authoring programs allow users to create their own processes especially in multimedia and training and so it is no surprise that computer scientists' trainers use it.

Learning how to build your website, for example, would require you to learn a domain-specific language which is a type of authoring language. This is now most commonly used in high schools that offer computer science courses. Most schools normally us authoring systems or packages that generally provide these powerful tools such as HTML for creating Web pages. You will find the authoring systems a father used to produce other software such as tutorial software computer-based training courses and other interactive computer programs. All three languages that are most popular used by computer scientists and engineers are Doc book, DITA, PILOT, and TUTOR.

Computer scientist can create programs that non-programmers can use by tweaking some of the features. These features are normally pre-existing and because of this the user does not necessarily need to know how to program to use the software. Teaching computer science authoring systems can go well beyond just teaching students but also can be used in teaching-related self-assessments (Barton, 2004).

7.6.6. Desktop Publishing Software in Teaching Computer Science

Desktop publishing software also known as DTP produces documents meant to be printed. Desktop publishing software essentially took over producing typed content over the typewriter. The non-printable materials produced by desktop publishing software or websites and content that is easy to disseminate like PDF files and in this sense, they mainly refer to digital typography. The technology is mainly used in businesses or organizations' or self-publishing a wide variety of contents.

Basic high school and college-level computer science classes would teach the finer controls over the materials that many desktop publishing software used beyond just word processing. Continue to become more and more complex with systems allowing you to create, embed and edit illustration within the program with a wide range of printing options (Barton, 2004).

In the corporate world, it is probably the most utilized kind of software for sending PowerPoint presentations, producing books newspapers and magazines, and the element of web design and user interface design may be involved. Xerox with the first produce and develop a desktop publishing software and Apple Macintosh although initially lacking in capabilities became a strong market contender shortly after and continue to dominate with Microsoft. When correlating computer science and mass production, desktop publishing software has become extremely popular for creating both printed and electronic materials (Barton, 2004).

7.6.7. Reference Software Used for Computer Science

Because of the nature of reference management software, it is used across all disciplines when teaching and learning computer science. One can access an array of information from reference management systems that are based on the internet. This is software that can be used by scholars and authors as well for recording as well as managing information. They are built on databases in which verifiable content, articles and journals can be entered. Reference software is studied in computer science under Information Management (Woollard, 2007).

7.6.8. Drill and Practice Software Used in Computer Science

In the past, drill and practice software were the most popular sometimes because teachers were not entirely sure how else computers could be used. This actually gave birth to the commonly used computer-assisted instructions and computer-based learning. Drill and practice software arms beginner students with conceptual understanding and provide exercises to further develop creativity and aptitude by the end of learning database and information systems (Woollard, 2007). Computer-based systems, for example, provide lessons tests and immediate feedback to the student who is learning with very little or no involvement from the teacher.

Not only do direct teacher-centered teaching methods become passive and boring, but using student-centered learning models with drill and practice software can allow computer science teachers to take time to correct specific student problems interact with them individually as well as in small groups. Normally this drill and practice and tutorial software or used when teaching chapters that require emphasis on conceptual understanding and deep practice to exposed unstructured cases these include topics like database systems (Woollard, 2007).

They are also beneficial to use because they prompt participation and turns the computer into a research center for the computer students.

7.6.9. Tutorial Software in Teaching Computer Science

Together with drill and practice software, tutorial software is a great way to teach new concepts that require practice.

When it comes to teaching complex ideas like abstractions algorithms and programming, tutorials are a great way to narrow down information and dictate the learning pace. With the general growth of ICT and technology tutorials are available everywhere online for even the most basic computer fundamentals and also for the most complex like coding and programming (D'Atri et al., 2011).

Tutorials like Kid Ware software produce age appropriate programming tutorials for elementary schools and come together with computer science teacher keep and self-study tutorials.

In Middle School, there are plenty of tutorials for students who are gifted in high-level coding and programming. Various tutorials specifically for example introduction to JavaScript introduction to HTML and CSS are available as well.

Tutorials have been prepared for beginners and advanced learners alike and they can be very useful not only for computer science students but engineering, administration, management sciences and others. In reality the industry has become so well integrated with the use of ICT and education the one can literally teach themselves computer science using these tools.

7.6.10. Educational Game Software for Computer Science

Game software has become its own industry today not only for entertainment purposes but for education as well. For kids, it is a great way to interact with concepts of computer science and as adults there are actual degrees in computer science with game technology where one develops technical game building skills with an overall computer science education. With gaming software students actually learn computer science in formally even before they first attend school and so a growing number of teachers relish at the idea of incorporating educational games especially when teaching programming. Prospective computer scientists who can't even code a single line can use game making software to build their own games. When closely analyzing game software, it is a great innovation in computer science subsets like network protocol design, compiler construction and operating system configurations. Computer science has indirectly benefited from gaming software with an increasing number of students interested solely in game software.

7.6.11. Simulation Software for Computer Science

Simulation systems and problem-solving software target higher-order thinking skills. Computer simulations aura powerful technique especially for systems representation because has a precise knowledge encapsulation factor.

In computer science and software engineering many simulation tools have been developed to help both students and teachers in areas of software project management. Simulations in computer science not only come in the software version but also hardware simulation is available where students are required to conceptualize computer organization and architecture effectively. Most textbooks available are soft and dense and traditional experiments may not be enough to provide adequate experience. Hardware simulations give a deeper insight into functions of specific parts. (D'Atri et al., 2011)

Software engineering simulations builds the student software engineering skills and concepts through real-world software projects. Most universities today have small project groups where undergraduate software engineering students are taught using simulations that present Concepts and methodologies.

In learning and teaching computer network protocols, design and applications, large specialized laboratories, which are most commonly found in universities, are needed and without simulations it would be hardly possible for students to understand and apply the concepts. There are many emerging Technologies that are very handy in teaching practical computer networks the most commonly used being the network modeling and simulation technology (NMS) it creates virtual Laboratories where a student can experiment with computer networks.

Network modeling simulations provide virtual network components that are even sometimes more effectual than the actual physical devices that they are modeled after and they provide a detailed understanding an in-depth look of each component in building complex networks.

Some simulations are specifically built to provide graphical interfaces and graphical presentations. Simulators range also in complexity but even the very simplest enable a user to work with a network topology and use nodes to specify the network. Some examples of great software simulators used in computer science are listed below

- *OPNET:* OPNET products given all round understanding of networking technologies and their applications. It works great with modeling and simulating communications networks and protocols and uses object-oriented modeling with graphical representations.
- *"ns":* Also referred to as the open-source network simulation, it supports a myriad of network protocols and can be used to simulate routing and multicast protocols as well.
- *CNET simulation tool;* This network simulation tool allows the students to play around with data link layer is network layers routing and other protocols it was developed in Australia specifically to cater for university students and is used world over. It is a flexible tool that is able to detect a wide variety of areas that are made undergraduate students when developing their own networks.
- *GTNets:* The Georgia Tech Network simulator was designed to allow researchers and students to monitor the behavior of very large-scale networks.

- *JiST:* Java in simulation time there's also another network simulator that is credited with high-performance discrete event simulation. It can be built to form completely wireless networks and run network applications over the simulated networks.

ICT has been used by trainer teachers and lecturers over the past several decades with great success. Although teachers continue to remain central in the learning processes, the ever-increasing utilization of ICT has converted trainers into facilitators and also promoted the self-teaching culture. From a teaching perspective, many ICT tools have been used for routine administrative tasks rather than for computer-assisted instruction.

7.7. TEACHING ALGORITHMS AND COMPLEXITY USING ICT

Complexity is referred to measures of time and space and general computing resources that a specific algorithm consumes when it is functional. Computational complexity of an algorithm can be calculated by computer scientist in reasonable amount of time in relation to input size and it essentially is a measure of how efficient an algorithm is. ICT tools are used later on when teaching algorithmic complexity because it is mainly a theoretical topic with concepts like the notional computer. When it comes to measuring efficiently, the step from the theoretical representations to the actual implementation has to take place, which already is so difficult because a real computer is and imperfect complexity. ICT tools are used to teach in both the software and tangible forms (Barton, 2004).

It must be apparent that theory of computation is a difficult study in computer science. A good example when teaching algorithms with ICT is when it comes to the implementation and sorting algorithms where there are several developed interactive simulations that make the subject easier to instruct. These simulations create exercises where learning and sorting objects is the introductory element and develop into manipulating conceptual visualizations of data structures in order to observe the functions of an algorithm.

Teaching algorithms using this tool allows the users to work their own values and attempt random numeric values and sort them to the tools and algorithm so that they understand the design paradigm (Barton, 2004). The teacher can allow the students develop new algorithms very easily by adding them in the simulation environment on top of already what has been developed.

Several studies have been carried out to see the relation between using ICT tools and students' performance. The results consistently show the grades of the students who used the simulation of algorithms performed significantly better than those who took the course previously without using such ICT learning software. It must also be noted that algorithm simulation differs widely in objectives and complexity (Barton, 2004). While some may use the drag-and-drop method others use some more advanced algorithm programming language.

7.8. TEACHING COMPUTER ARCHITECTURE AND ORGANIZATION USING ICT

Computer architecture encompasses how computers are designed and data storage devices and all the networking components which contain and run the programs. This subject requires more hardware information and communications technology because you learn about the tangible objects of a computer that make a computer what it is. A computer is comprised of a control unit, a memory unit input, and output devices and an arithmetic logic unit (building blocks of a CPU).

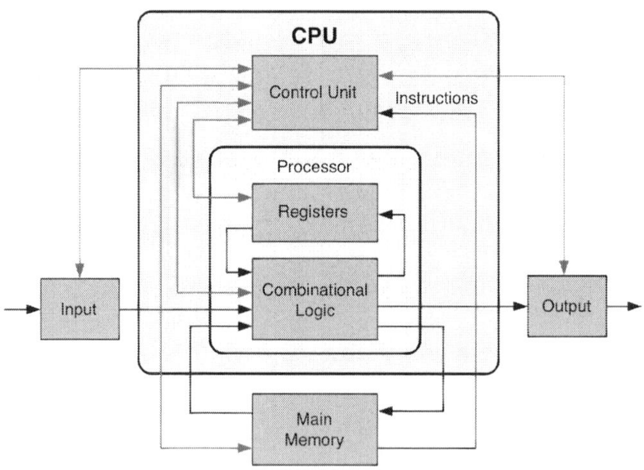

Figure 7.5. *Block diagram of a basic computer.*

Source: https://en.wikipedia.org/wiki/Computer_architecture#Design_goals.

There are visual simulators, drill and practice software and tutorial software available for architecture and computer organization learning. Evidently, different concepts and technologies present different complexities that will be applied in computer systems. When a computer science architects begin designing, they have many considerations like power performance size and weight cost expandability memory capacity and many more features to consider, therefore, the ICT tools are designed as well along the same parameters.

There are many computer systems simulators that help teachers and students through the course of computer architecture and organization and it is important to note that they are built upon the intended features of the specific computer systems course to be taught.

These include simulators like simple CPU and the DXL view. Some teaching tools allow the user to first build a whole computer system and then run the simulation with various ways of analyzing the results. Examples include HASE. These tools count as drill and practice software as well as simulations (Barton, 2004).

7.9. ICT TOOLS USED TO TEACH COMPUTATIONAL SCIENCE

Computational science is the study of solving complex scientific problems with the use of computing capabilities and design implementation and mathematical models. Computational thinking is a subject that is now commonly taught in high schools and equips students to solve problems with a methodical approach. Teaching computational science used to be a taxing job both financially and logistically but with the use of computational tools has become easier.

7.10. TEACHING GRAPHICS AND VISUAL COMPUTING USING ICT TOOLS

The ICT tools of desktop publishing and graphic design are used interchangeably. Although there are some correlations, they are distinct differences. Computer graphics design and visualization deals with the manipulation of information on a computer screen whereas desktop publishing is using pre-existing programs already on a computer system to present information. In reality desktop publishing design can be thought as a byproduct of computer graphics and visualization (Leask & Meadows, 2000).

Computer graphics consists of four major computational tasks:

- Rendering
- Modeling
- Animation
- Visualization

Like computational science graphics, visual computing has crossed over into other disciplines and now covers data visualization, medical imaging, animation, and computer games. Visualization technologies like MRI and x-rays were born from graphics computing.

Because of the use of various techniques like modeling 2D and 3D objects and realistic rendering, ICT tools used in graphics and visual computing are endless in terms of both hardware and software versions. Most if not all simulations that are produced even to teach other computer scientists using the well-designed graphics and simulations, were developed by computer graphics and visualization specialists.

The field continues to be an ever-evolving discipline with virtual reality computer-simulated holograms and many more concepts waiting in store for the future. Specialized computer graphics hardware now is also built to keep up with the ever-growing complex graphics algorithms.

7.11. TEACHING HUMAN-COMPUTER INTERACTION USING ICT

Human-computer interaction is the study of the relation between users and computers. The main goal of this discipline is to make the relationship between humans and computers more seamless, efficient and effective. In actual sense the concept of interactions between a computer and a user being like that of an interaction between two humans has become highly popularized. Due to its very definition, information and communication technologies is highly correlated in the field and one would not exist without the other. With the growing development of our technologies, deeper academic investigation into human-computer interactions will take place and make both fields more symbiotic. Because human-computer interaction is not only theoretical but practical, students must continuously interact with the computer which in many cases the interaction being observed and tested is built as an ICT tool (Woollard, 2007).

7.12. TEACHING INFORMATION MANAGEMENT USING ICT TOOLS

Information management in computer science refers to proper data management and generally the storage and retrieval of specific data for processing. What information management systems specialist do is manipulate large amounts of information by creating algorithms that make databases that are very efficient installing retrieving updating and deleting of specific data (Woollard, 2007).

Reference software is a program that is revised and added upon when print forms of information come out, examples include encyclopedias yellow pages and dictionaries. They are in themselves information communication technology tools. Algorithms have to be designed to perform functions, for example, placing the dictionary in alphabetical order.

7.13. TEACHING INTELLIGENT SYSTEMS INSTRUCTION USING ICT

Intelligent systems have become synonymous with artificial intelligence and it is an area of research that dates back to the crib of computer science. Intelligent systems respond to the world around them and are perceived as computers able to perform with human-like intelligence. This propelled invention of robots and later autonomous systems.Teaching intelligence systems means that one has to be familiar with various subject areas. For students, it tops the list as one of the most difficult subjects under computer science. This is because it requires a cross-disciplinary approach and time-consuming. In a physical world that is ever dynamic.

Figure 7.6. *Students in laboratory in Distributed Intelligent Systems Department in Saint Petersburg State Polytechnic University.*

Source:https://commons.wikimedia.org/wiki/File:Distributed_Intelligent_Systems_Department_laboratory.jpg.

The real-world applications are endless including.

- Character recognition
- Visual surveillance
- Medical care
- Education (e.g., intelligent tutoring system)
- Military applications
- Factory automation

Ordinarily, teachers instructing students on intelligence systems have little to no time for information and communication technologies for the purposes of training only unless it already serves the purpose of simulation and experimentation mainly on theoretical levels.

7.14. COMPUTER NETWORKING AND COMMUNICATION INSTRUCTION USING ICT

Networking and communication in computer science entail the study of networks that link computers together and how they communicate. These networks or digital communication paths run as local area networks, wide area networks, mobile networks just to name a few. Computer scientists study the design analysis creation and implementation of these networks.

The internet which is by far the most useful information and communication technology tool across all disciplines is in itself a network and makes it possible for almost all the computers across the globe to communicate. Networks like most computer components have software components and hardware components.

Similar to most of the sub-topics in computer science, computer networking has tutorials online but even high school concepts of linear algebra statistics and probability numerical analysis and differential equations are useful. Programming, and more specifically distributed programming is important skills to have. There are basic level simulations drill and test software and tutorials that can allow a student to practice their computer network programming skills (Singh, 2008).

Networking and communication have also further propelled the industry of information and communications technology especially in the digital world. Share data and transmission of media is now effortless and serves as a good example at how prolific network and communications specialist are in the computer science world.

7.15. TEACHING OPERATING SYSTEMS USING ICT

In computer science, operating system is software that manages the relationship between the computer hardware and the software applications that the user normally interacts with.

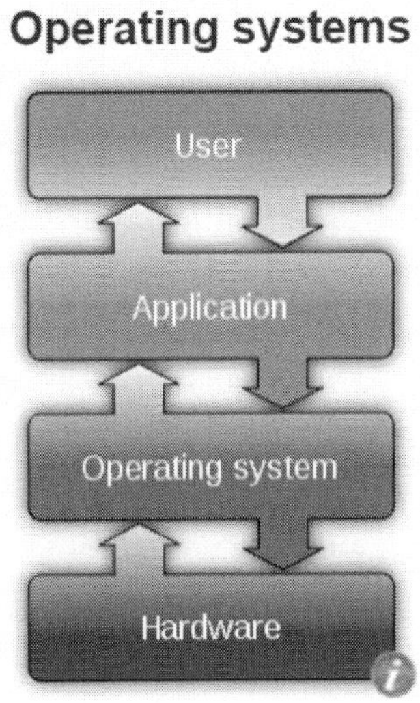

Figure 7.7. *Operating System.*

https://en.wikipedia.org/wiki/Operating_system.

Some of the applications of operating systems include managing important activities, such as security supervision, system performance, error detection, and coordination between applications and users.

When teaching operating software, which is required in computer science, one of the main challenges is that it is difficult to sequence lesson plans based simply on different topics, hence the use of ICT tools is of great usefulness (Singh, 2008).

When teaching operating systems in computer science, one information and communications technology tool that has been used is educational operating systems such as MiniX and Xinu which allow students to play with the source code and provide a practical framework (Damon et al., 2016). Operating systems classes is taught in the conventional teacher presentation fashion can turn the lecture into a boring and abstract class and ICT software used for this class have allowed better illustration of concepts also allowing higher interaction between the student and object of study.

7.16. USING ICT TO TEACH PROGRAMMING LANGUAGE IN COMPUTER SCIENCE

A computer program is sometimes called a piece of code and writing a program is sometimes referred to as coding. Teaching programming with or without ICT as a supporting tool is a difficult task. Programming language is used by a programmer to write computer software. They are very many languages used for programming each with their advantages and disadvantages. This makes it one of the most abstract studies.

When learning how to program, learners do a lot more work on their own. With their teachers, creating a goal-oriented project like building a 2D simple game allows the student to figure out their programming style.

There are very many ways to teach programming code some are listed below:

- Statement oriented where the language is written as a bunch of statements with individual elements.
- Using language tools and software technology.
- Task-oriented where new programming languages taught and problems to be solved create themselves.
- Sample task-based.
- Action-oriented.

7.17. TEACHING PARALLEL AND DISTRIBUTED COMPUTING USING ICT

Parallel distributed systems programming skills are mandatory in the field of computer science with the rise of the big data era. In the past, it proves difficult to bring it into school curriculums but it is necessary nowadays even the other topics like operating systems algorithm classes.

A class in itself begins with a kick-start in programming using software like the PBS cluster or UNIX systems normally in C or C++ programming language. Supporting ICT tools are then later going to be used for assignments in solving problems like reduction, integration, merge sort, prefix sum. The trainer, however, has to be particular especially in picking the correct models and using appropriate teaching tools together with the ICT tools (Singh, 2008).

7.18. THE USE OF ICT IN TEACHING SOFTWARE ENGINEERING

Software engineering is a field that follows the application of all the learned knowledge and theories putting them to practice to satisfy customers and client's computer requirements. They make sure that the software that is already running works flawlessly with the hardware that is in place as efficiently as possible for the desired objective.

Drill and practice ICT tools come most handy in this discipline of computer science. Drill and practice computer instructional techniques provide a series of systematic problems and exercises with which immediate feedback to the student is given. Drill and practice software are available at all levels for children and novice learners to experienced computer scientists. As a computer science teacher, drill and practice software must be carefully considered when selecting. The trainer must have good control over the rate of learning and it must contain appropriate feedback for correct and incorrect answers (Unesco, 2011).

7.19. ADVANTAGES OF ICT USAGE BY TEACHERS IN COMPUTER SCIENCE

The 21st century classroom has evolved into a very dynamic learning environment where instruction techniques are endless to promote student success. ICT usage by teachers in computer science has had major effects on the discipline itself. Some of the advantages include:

- ICT technology motivates children and makes computer science attractive.
- ICT tools encourage communication between the students, teachers, parents, and administration.
- ICT tools for computer science encourage and support different teaching techniques and this way a variety of students learn.
- ICT tools can be built to provide instant feedback on work completed by students.
- ICT tools are versatile and some can also be designed to encourage collaborative work while some allow students to work at their own pace.
- ICT tools prepare students and teachers with real-life application potential.

- ICT tools take learning outside of the classroom.
- ICT minimizes costs, and provides trouble-free student management.
- These advantages come with some drawbacks some of which are listed below:
- Some ICT tools can be extremely expensive especially in the computer science world where the latest technology is what is needed. These tools are not only expensive to buy but expensive to maintain. This counts for both hardware and software tools.
- Introduction of ICT to children is still a topic of debate.
- Some ICT tools provide misguiding and misleading information and it can be difficult for some students and teachers to know the difference between reliable and unreliable ICT resources.
- Issues of privacy, safety, and plagiarism are also major concerns.

Chapter

8 Evaluation of Computer Science

CONTENTS

8.1. INTRODUCTION

Evaluation is the well-articulated interpretation that provides meaning to the assumed or factual effect of a proposition or a result. It analyses the original goal and how its corresponding result was fulfilled. This chapter is going to discuss the concept, tools, and techniques of evaluation, formative and summative evaluation, grading pattern, computer-aided evaluation, online examination, and e-assessment.

Generally, evaluation enables one to make a judgment about how desirable something is. In an academic setting, it is a new term which was introduced to give meaning to a concept of measurement which is not emphasized in normal tests and examination.

The main aim of evaluation is based on changes in personality and other vital objectives and the academic program thus, it not only involves achievements obtained but also ways of thinking, idea, attitude, work habits, and personal and social adaptability. The use of evaluation is not only about testing since there are many different techniques that lead to the evaluation program becoming a full package. Therefore, evaluation is any continuous procedure that is systematic and is used in determining.

- The level at which a particular academic objective which was earlier identified and has a definition will be attained.
- How effective are the learning experiences are being administered in the classroom
- How proper the objective of academics have been accomplished and achieved.

It is with this that evaluation is incorporated with the whole process of education and its aim is to advance and grow instructions and not just measuring its achievements. It plays a big role in the student habits of studying and teachers' methods of instructions.

Due to this, it not only aids in the measuring of academic achievements but also how to improve it. Evaluation technique is important for evidence collection pertaining students' growth in the desired direction.

At its highest level, evaluation brings out elements that are inherent in pupils' development like proper attitude, courtesy and decorum, manipulative skills, appreciation and comprehension and furthermore to the conventional acquiring of knowledge (Movaghar, 2012).

8.2. PURPOSE OF EVALUATION

The main reason a program evaluation is undertaken can be to "determine the quality of a program by formulating a judgment" Marthe Hurteau, Sylvain Houle, Stéphanie Mongiat came up with that definition in 2009.

Another definition is that "projects, evaluators, and other stakeholders which also involves financers will all have potentially different ideas about how best to evaluate a project since each may have a different definition of 'merit.' The main challenge finding the definition of value. From the perspective of value, evaluators describe evaluation as the research and assessment of a program. Others define evaluation to be synonymous to applied research.

According to the evaluation purpose, evaluation has two purposes.

- *Formative evaluation*: in this form of evaluation it provides information on the improvement and modification of a commodity or procedure.
- *Summative evaluation*: in this form of evaluation, it provides information regarding how effective adopting a product or a process will be short term and its effect in a long-term horizon.

Other purposes of evaluation are to serve as a monitoring function more than a measuring function or evaluation function.

8.3. STEPS INVOLVED IN EVALUATING

Clarification of what needs to be evaluated: the aim of this is to develop an assessment that has evaluability and which has a well-defined objective, strategy, activity, output, and an outcome. The parties involved checks if the process of evaluation can be carried out using the given information and the present situation. One should give a clear description of what is to be evaluated. In our case computer science in order for it to be shared. Create a framework that shows goals, activities, outputs, and objectives.

Involve stakeholders: this enables building support to aid in the evaluation process. In this process, the appropriate stakeholders are identified by having knowledge of what they expect and what they are interested in. This is done by giving them a summary of objectives so as to develop questions to be used in evaluation.

Assess resources and evaluability: the aim of this is to check if the available resources can be utilized and if the program is evaluation worthy. Since evaluation is time consuming and costly, to a thorough assessment so as to avoid incurring expenses later. Resources include money, approval procedures like ethical acceptance, time and time for implementation and completion. During evaluability assessment, make sure the program has properly been clarified and reasons as to why the evaluation should take place as it will help in its management and will help in proper utilization of resources and time. Once the all the information has been obtained, use it to check if the evaluation process will be feasible.

Determination of evaluation questions: this is to help in the identification and determination of questions in order to meet your evaluation objectives. During this process, ensure that stakeholders have been involved in order to make sure their needs have been catered for. Factors such as logic framework contents, stage of development, evaluations already completed, decisions need, needs of stakeholders and resources should be considered. The type of evaluation should be considered. In development and planning of strategies, formative evaluation is commonly used. Process evaluation mostly discusses the extent to which an intervention is implemented. A program's success in achieving its objectives is evaluated using outcome type of evaluation.

Determination of the effective procedures of measurement and processes: the aim of this is in the identification of the most necessary and feasible method to be used and how data is going to be collected. During determination, you should consider reason for evaluation, questions to be asked during evaluation, feasibility of accessing data, how reliable the data is, who will use data, the expectation of stakeholders and what is already being captured. Your data collection plan should be developed in a way that it includes; indicators that will be measured, when the data will be collected, how the data will be collected and finally where the data will be collected. Issue of integrity and ethics should also be considered, e.g., confidentiality and consent issues.

Come up with a plan that will be used during evaluation: this aids the identification of particular evaluation activities, roles, allocation of resources and when is the evaluation is due. The plan outlines how the policies of the program will be monitored, how the findings will be utilized and at the same time ensuring there is transparency to everyone involved. A data collection matrix can be part of your evaluation plan as it provides data collected from earlier processes like evaluation questions, indicators, procedures, sources of data, work allocation, timeline and how information will be analyzed though this is optional. A dissemination plan will then be developed and added to the other plan once everything is done.

Collection of data: here, credible and accurate data is collected to act as evidence during answering of the evaluation questions. The data should be credible as recommendation of the evaluation depends on the quality of the data collected. Data collectors should have and utilize appropriate data collection tools like use of questionnaires and survey. The use of incentives is appropriate in order to improve the quality of data collection. To make sure there is validity, pilot test tools, and processes and closely monitor the data collected. In the case of an issue occurring, one can modify the process of data collection. Use of technology that is computers should be taken advantage of as it will aid in analysis.

Process the data and analyze the result: the purpose of this is to input information, analyze its quality and consistency of its entry and scrutinize the data so as to check your evaluation results. Strategize o how you are going to review your data during and after collection of data. During the process of collecting data, check on the first attempt of responses and how the participants are actively engaging in the process. Once data collection has been completed, input the data and check on its quality and how consistent it is during entry. Check factors like low and high values and also check missing values. You should also check on the content through reviewing data entered (qualitative). Put data in organized manner to enable summarization and interpretation of data. The data is then analyzed by performing statistical analysis of quantitative data and in qualitative data, you should identify themes. Expert support is critical at this point as the process gets more technical. This sets the phase for interpreting data.

Interpretation of results: the aim of this step is to interpret and share your research findings. Stakeholders get involved in this stage as they aid in formulating recommendations. Pivot the interpretation of the findings to your initial evaluation questions. From your recommendations, make a list of what needs to be done on the output and from this information, make tools to communicate your output. During presenting the findings, the outcome can be presented in the form of either a report or a slide show presentation using PowerPoint. The use of visual aids can help during the communication of results. After the presentation, the results should be made available to the parties involved that is stakeholders and participants. Modify the results so as to suit their particular interests and how they intend to utilize the results.

Application of the evaluation findings: the parties utilize the evaluation results. With the help of stakeholders, the recommendations are reviewed to identify actionable outcomes and also what has been picked from the process of evaluation plus how to integrate the results. Come up with action plans as a groupmate-evaluation is also conducted (Movaghar, 2012).

8.4. TYPES OF EVALUATION

- *Context Evaluation/Situational Evaluation*: This type of evaluation gives a logical reasoning of determining goals and setting priorities. It gives a definition of the relevance of a given environment and describes the conditions and suitability of the environment that makes it desirable. At the same time, it aids in the identification of unseen needs and opportunities that the environment has to offer.
- *Cluster Evaluation*: This type of evaluation aims to show the effects a group of related projects have on a community in general. It analyzes a set of projects so as to aid in the identification of challenges and difficulties that impact an area of a specific program. It was designed by W.K Kellog foundation so as to investigate how effective making of grants is to a certain area.
- *Empowerment Evaluation*: This type of evaluation utilizes concepts of evaluation, techniques of evaluation and its results to enhance determination of self and improvement of self. In empowerment evaluation, the participants of the program are the ones who control the process of evaluation. External Evaluators work hand in hand with the participants to assist them to utilize their results to advocate for their programs by empowering them.
- *Formative Evaluation*: Formative Evaluation is the type of evaluation which is carried out during the process of implementation and development of the program whose main objective giving information used for program improvement.
- *Implementation Evaluation*: This form of evaluation is used to document how a project has evolved and give indications of what takes place within a project and why so. Project directors alter present activities with the use of information. Implementation evaluation requires close monitoring of program delivery.

- *Participatory Evaluation*: In this evaluation, the thoughts of the evaluator have equal weight to that of other parties especially the stakeholders. The results of the evaluation are vital to the stakeholders for their own future actions. This type of evaluation tends to be more practical, useful have a big insight to stakeholders and actively engage all stakeholders in the process of evaluation.
- *Performance Evaluation*: This type of evaluation analyses a specific program achievement in terms of its outcome and process.
- *Policy Evaluation*: This type of evaluation analyzes policies, plans, and proposals for use by policymakers and or societies trying to influence policy change.
- *Program Evaluation*: This analyzes the structure of particular interventions so as to check whether it can impact positively the wellbeing of people, societies, and organizations.
- *Self-Evaluation*: This form of evaluation can be done individually. One self-accesses his or herself on a certain program and its outcomes by either yourself or those parties involved.
- *Stakeholder Evaluation*: In these, stakeholders analyze and evaluate the design, conduct, and interpretation of already carried out program.
- *Summative Evaluation*: This type of evaluation is carried out when a particular phase of a program has come to an end so as to gauge how effective and worth it is.
- *Utilization-Focused Evaluation*: This type of evaluation puts on emphasis on the style and implementation used by the audience. The evaluator engages the audience and lets them become the judge of the evaluation as he or she is the moderator.

8.5. TOOLS AND TECHNIQUES OF EVALUATION

In academics, the word tool is defined as an instrument that collects the achievement done by a student. The main tools of evaluation include questionnaires, cumulative and anecdotal records, achievement test, rating scale, and checklist to mention but a few.

8.5.1. Achievement Test

In education, achievement test is the most commonly used tool. Achievement is mainly related to the objectives if the evaluation program which is translated into changes in behavior. The learning point being achieved might have been learnt at different levels by the student and the tutor is particularly concerned is comprehending what the student has achieved at every learning point and an evaluation is performed in accordance to the instructional objectives that has been preset by the teacher. The test performed for the purpose shown above is the achievement test (Movaghar, 2012).

8.5.2. Anecdotal Record

This is findings regarding a student and it is normally informal in nature in terms of observation. A Teacher will seize a chance to observe a student so a to pick up some of their personality and attitude without their awareness. This can be undertaken anywhere either in class or outside class. The teacher then records what has been observed immediately after the occurrence. Accurate and objective observations are recorded. Normally, the teacher creates two columns on the sheet where he or she describes what was observed on one column and the other column is for interpretation purposes of the incident.

8.5.3. Cumulative Record

The pattern of development and growth of each student is recorded in a cumulative manner occasionally so as to monitor their progress. This is done in a comprehensive manner. It records a variety of information regarding the student. Some of the details that is recorded can include health condition of the pupil, degree of achievement in certain subjects, etc.

8.5.4. Check List

Normally a checklist is simple to construct and use. It comprises of list of items that are prepared to be used. It is two dimensional in that is provides two options that is one for the behaviors observed and the other for the identification or names of the pupils being examined. Results are usually recorded by ticking on the item.

8.5.6. Rating Scale

This is an advanced form of a checklist. Here, a specific variable is recorded. There is no limit to how much that specific variable will be observed. For this issue to be solved, a convenient point can be used to indicate the score which will represent a specific level for example fair, poor or very good in the case of a three-point scale.

8.5.7. Questionnaire

This is a versatile equipment that is used to mainly collect quantitative information. It has the ability to cater for various aspects of a large challenge across the questionnaire. It is simple to give out to people and also it is easy to pick responses. Though it has some limitations like inadequate coverage of the topic study, questions might not be well interpreted and biasness of responses.

8.6. EVALUATION TECHNIQUES

The common techniques used in academic evaluation is sociometry, case study, Testing, Observation, Interview, and Projective Techniques. Testing is the most common among them.

8.6.1. Observation

Here, the teacher makes a continuous and meticulous observation on a particular student. The teacher measures various dimensions of the student in terms of character which has relevance to the teachers' instructional objective. If the teacher observes a behavior that has relevance to him or her, it is then recorded and it should always be objective and not subjective. Observations are of two categories:

- controlled and uncontrolled
- participatory and non-participatory.

The teacher directly observes the student's character and information gathered through word of mouth. The teacher and the student communicate with each other using a language they both understand. Interviews can be of different types, such as:

- Survey interview which are used to collect data, diagnostic interview which is used to comprehend a student's challenge
- Therapeutic interview which is used to plan appropriate therapy
- Counseling interviews which is used in problem-solving

8.6.2. Case Study

If a teacher wants to monitor a student as a whole, the use of case study will give the best outcome as the teacher is able to collect data about the students in totality.

Normally, data is collected from several sources and the data is synthesized and interpreted.

8.6.3. Sociometry

From the name it shows that this technique was designed to assess social relationships from members is a specific group depending of the circumstance of meeting. This technique can enable a teacher to identify celebrities, loners, and cliques. Celebrities are the people who are chooses by the majority of people whereas loners are students who are not chosen by any and cliques are the people who exclusively have a close bond among themselves. A socio graph is a graphical representation of a sociometric.

8.6.4. Projective Techniques

There are rare cases where students' behavior is governed by their subconscious part of the brain. For such a behavior to be projected to enable evaluation, certain stimulus in the mind of the student is triggered. Then these responses may be interpreted. Some examples of such projective techniques include; Rorscharch Ink Blot Test, Thematic Apperception Test (TAT).

8.6.5. Qualities of a Good Test

Objectivity: For one to know if a question is objective, we check on the answer given. The response has to be definite from the answer that was expected. This can be done by identifying a particular behavior which is being investigating and from that, an expected response is formulated and a scoring procedure is created for the test. From this procedure, the questions are then re-examined.

Objective Basis: Before coming up with a test meant to measure a certain achievement of a student, the teacher should look at the objectives of the study and from that create a measuring point that will coincide with the objectives. This will enable the test to be objective based.

Comprehensiveness: The test should be able to touch on all the points across the syllabus. Ensure that the objectives have well been outlined in the test cover the whole syllabus. Due importance should be given to all the relevant learning materials.

Validity: Validity of a test is checked when it measures what it was meant to measure and does not deviate to other things that are not relevant at the moment. There are different types of validity as shown below.

- Content Validity: the content being presented in the test should come from the scope of the study or the course and should be relevant to the instructional objectives.

- Predictive Validity: this can be achieved by ensuring that the test has some relevance and relation to already established external criteria. The external criteria have to be proven by the right authorities. The co-relation of the two can be statistically determined as the test scores will have a relation with the external criteria.
- Concurrent validity: other measures that have the same characteristics are compared with the results of the test to obtain a co-relation that is simultaneous between the two. If there is a mismatch, then the test has concurrent validity.
- Construct Validity: the examiner will develop of the construct of his or her accord that has traits and the traits from the test should have a relation to the traits of the construct. The test is meticulously scrutinized to see if its traits correspond to the construct and from this, the construct validity will be determined.

Reliability: A test is considered reliable if it is consistent with the measures it is required to perform. If there is reliability in a test then this is an indicator that there is validity though, reliability is not enough to ensure there is full validity in the test. Reliability and validity, therefore, are directly proportional.

Reliability of a test can be determined using various methods such as;

- *Test-retest method*: here, a test is given twice to a similar group of people with a very short interval in between the tests. The test scores are then recorded and co-relation between the two is tabulated. If it is high, then this means there is more reliability.
- Parallel or equaled form method: here two tests that are equal in all manner is administered and a comparison is done so as to determine their co-relation.
- Split half method: here, the underlying assumption is that the two scores are comparable and therefore scores of the odd and even particulars are recorded and the co-relation between the two sets of scores are checked. The reliability of the half test is determined by the use of sphere man. The reliability of the full test is then determined using the Brown Prophecy formula.

Discriminating Power: A good test has the ability to categorize students in terms of their strengths towards the subject matter for instance low performing, average and high performing.

Practicability: A test setter should enhance practicability by planning about the time and the funds required for the test to be a success.

Comparability: A test is said to be comparable if the sources of the test questions can be well understood from a common base that naturally has an accepted definition. Two methods are used to check for comparability and it involves making available equivalent forms of a test and making available adequate norms.

Utility: If a test has the conditions to which it will provide realization of a point then it has utility. This is usually the last criteria that is checked. To achieve this, the test should be designed in a way that its purpose and interpretation is well perceived by the person doing the test.

Computer-aided assessment: Computer-assisted assessment is used to describe all assessment criteria. It can be summative or formative and its delivery is aided by computers. Assessment can be done either online or on a localized network. Optical Mark Reading (OMR) are also applied.

Computer-assisted assessment can also be seen in various ways in that homework can be done and investigated online. The most often used form e-learning is online tests and examinations. Such examinations are executed and marked online since all their responses have already been inputted in the system. Online examinations are simply set up due to the availability of systems that easily incorporates content online in the system. Computer-aided assessment has the ability to support certain goals using pictures, filling in of blank spaces and by the use of true or false nature of questions. In the modern world, there has been a lot of technological advancements which enables assessment to be done subjectively in the evaluation process by the user. The model is able to analyze theoretical answers provided by the user.

It has been noted that computer-based formative assessment will be vital in the learning process. With the heightened use of pile of questions items for building of dynamic on demand assessment. This has been projected on systems such as SQA's solar project.

Through positive feedback from students and the overall improvement of student performance, the effectiveness of these assessments has been frequently demonstrated.

Chapter 9

Computer Science Education in Developing Countries

CONTENTS

9.1. INTRODUCTION

The aim of teaching computing subjects in developing countries is fulfilling the manpower requirements of this field, which ensures quick economic development in the country for popularizing the usage of processors as an essential component of engineering design. Stakeholder also seeks to promote self-sufficiency in app development across the emerging economies, while further ensuring that CS plays a vital role in various fields of science and development.

Figure 9.1. *Children from developing nations need computer literacy skills in order to be competitive in the digital world.*

Source: https://www.brookings.edu/research/how-ed-tech-can-help-leapfrog-progress-in-education/.

To meet these goals, a wide-range computer science training would be needed (Unesco, 2011). The educational courses may be grouped into the following general categories:

- Professional courses in computer sciences;
- Continual education courses for practicing managers, teachers, and researchers;
- Diffusion of computing subjects into other fields;
- Training of computer design specialist and maintainers.

The vital role of this technology in fast-tracking industrial expansion in developing countries might be achieved in part through setting up local computing centers and attributing them to respectable colleges.

Largely, educational technology reform courses which have been fruitful, such as the one implemented in Chile, have allocated only a small part of their resources to buying and installation of equipment. Through establishing and researching model programs, together with funding for training development and community participation, it is possible to recognize and develop support for the application of technology in various substitute educational techniques and structures which might go contrary to conventional methods and points of power (Damon et al., 2016).Nevertheless, in developing countries, oftentimes computer infrastructure must be developed from scratch. Examples include setting up appropriate classrooms, telephones, electricity, and lavatories. Likewise, operational costs might be substantial. For example, network connection costs in many of these countries rise sky-high or the salary of competent IT personnel may be higher than those of industrialized countries.

Schools must consider all these factors in their learning modes before providing any computing subjects. Class sizes can differ from small to large, plus one should appreciate the various situational dynamics of different class sizes. Likewise, appropriate review of communication trends among learners and teachers is central for successful development of a computer learning environment (Damon et al., 2016).

9.2. TEACHING CODING KNOWLEDGE IN DEVELOPING COUNTRIES

To promote a high course completion rate in coding subjects, two key elements are emphasized which are commitment and collaboration (Nagao, Rogan, & Magno, 2007). Among the more challenging features of learning how to program is the readiness to put in enough time to achieve proficiency. During the process of learning to code, it is possible for a student to feel disheartened and reject a potential profession in coding when struggling to grasp key ideas, or attempting and failing to remove a bug for long periods-particularly if one lacks a stable support system that can help them persevere.

In a certain computer teaching program, during the initial two weeks of the course, 9 students left or were requested to drop out of the program since they didn't display the amount of commitment needed for the course. Trimming down the classroom to only those that were ready to invest their time and effort to the program, allowed the remaining learners to enjoy an environment which encouraged positive outcomes, further permitting the teachers to derive the most from their limited resources.

Additionally, students are encouraged to cooperate by assisting each other on projects plus by developing a virtual chart forum to share material and collaborate. Most students in developing countries are unused to working in teams, but computer training can help them quickly come to understand the benefits of working collaboratively since it leads to faster progressing through the content (Nagao, Rogan, & Magno, 2007).

Computer science teachers must work hard to understand and adapt to each learner's particular needs. From student interviews in some developing countries, it was noticed that many pupils lacked the basic infrastructure at home for finishing homework by themselves. Thus, sufficient time should be provided during the session so that they can work on their class assignments.

Taking into consideration slow or intermittent internet connection, teachers can prepare their computer classes beforehand. This includes downloading the necessary lecture videos, setting up appropriate files in time, and translating certain common terms so that pupils who aren't native English speakers can understand. The greatest challenge, nevertheless, is something far less obvious. Many students from developing states lack the motivation and confidence for even believing they can become successful developers. Teachers sometimes don't recognize that for many individuals, minorities particularly, the greatest barrier to achievement is lack of belief that they, also, can succeed in various computing fields professionally (Nagao, Rogan, & Magno, 2007).

Throughout the years, many minority group students have never had privilege to access great quality learning materials. It is also unlikely that they have met or heard about a successful computer professional, coming from a background that's same as their own.

Due to these reasons, they seldom follow these types of career prospects even when they're seen as promising professions. In places like Haiti, computer science isn't yet a renowned career path, plus there aren't many noticeable role models in this industry.

Therefore, teachers should spend more time on one-on-one lessons with their students. They can share their personal story, including those of other successful professionals who can inspire the students to embrace a discipline which otherwise feels so remote and unachievable to them.

Knowing that there are other individuals like them who've gone through the same process can help promote the idea that they too can endure through the most difficult parts of the program and find success.

Regrettably, most coding courses still fail to tackle these problems for minorities plus, consequently, both registration and completion rates aren't where they should be for those underprivileged groups. During the final stages of the computer teaching program, a demo day can be organized where the pupils' family and friends plus respectable members of the local community, including prospective employers.

Typically, the levels of excitement for such events are unparalleled. A number of native organizations that require computer developers may even approach the school, in order to discuss internship prospects. Though the pupils may eventually develop a strong understanding of coding, as may be shown in exhibitions, this experience is just the initial step in a longer road ahead of them (Unesco, 2011).

There is a great need to assist students in their programming skills by providing them with continual access to computing infrastructure, such as internet, laptops and Android devices—coaching as well as practical opportunities for working in the field. Teachers should also envisage scaling up their program, so as to reach more pupils in the developing regions, plus one day seek to launch empowerment programs in other underprivileged countries as well.Through such teaching programs, the experience of computer science instructors can further be concretized. They will understand the significance of leveraging the web to empower all individuals, not just a tiny fraction of those with access to digital resources.

It is one matter to 'connect' the globe with the internet, though it's a totally different one to provide everybody with the instruments they require to contribute to the worldwide internet ecosystem. Various tech businesses have invested resources towards growing their reach, though they are yet to provide people across the globe the tools required to address their own issues and to become active participants in the rapidly shifting technological world (Unesco, 2011).

9.3. COMPUTER SCIENCE LEARNING TOPICS

Most computer science (CS) topics address the theoretical aspects of IT and computation, covering both scientific and practical aspects of computation and its uses. Computation is described as any form of calculation or application of computing technology which follows well-defined systems (such as protocol and algorithms) in the application of information processing (that's in turn described as the application of these systems to transform information in computers).

CS is regarded by many of its users as a foundational science – which essentially makes other types of knowledge and accomplishments possible. Studies on computer science entail systematically studying methodical procedures so as to help in processes such as acquisition, processing, representation, communication, storage, and even access to information.

All this is done through analyzing the practicality, structure, manifestation, and automation of these processes, including how they are relevant to the availed information. For computer science, the word 'information' refers typically to information that's encrypted in bytes and bits within the computer memory.

For many schools, the entry requirements for students who want to pursue computer science is some background in math, with some centers asking for some experience in physics.

Furthermore, some understanding of sociology or psychology can offer an added advantage to your studies, since you shall have gained insight on how people process information, whereas other natural sciences can also be helpful (Singh, 2008).

For high school students, applications for undergraduate computer science courses normally won't be required to have officially studied the subject before university.

Nevertheless, it's advisable that you choose a coding language to understand what is involved. Although generally accepted novice languages include, Haskell, Java, C++, Python, and Pascal, there are other languages that you might come across in your studies.

Furthermore, you may realize that some schools discourage learners from studying coding beforehand to avoid pupils learning 'bad' coding habits early on. There are also various institutions that provide joint programs, in which computing is studied together with topics like mathematics and engineering.

Additionally, some higher education centers may apply computer science as a cover for different specialist and professional degrees involving computers and technology.

Likewise, you may notice the word computer science can be used to denote to information technology as well, even though many learning centers now differentiate between the two (precisely how and where the line is drawn varies) (Singh, 2008).

9.4. THE THREE STAGES OF COMPUTER SCIENCE

Figure 9.2. *A child playing a coding game from his tablet computer.*

Source: https://www.makeuseof.com/tag/best-coding-apps-kids-learn-programming/.

Most highly successful computer scientists advance through three consecutive stages. It should be noted that some people never progress past the first phase, while others don't go past the second. Basically, only the highly successful computing experts reach the final phase.

These three stages are:

- Coder;
- Programmer;
- The Computer Scientist.

It is vital to mention that the classification is based on observations made from students living in developing countries.

9.4.1. Coder

Every computer scientist starts his profession as a coder. It can occur from a rather young age. Also, you don't need a college qualification to become a coder. A coder can be described as somebody who understands how to talk the language of machines.

When presented with a particular issue, the coder comprehends how to subdivide that problem into guidelines that the machine easily understands, so as to arrive at a solution. The coding stage is virtually the easiest stage of the Computer Science career. In case you make it in coding, then well and good! You may actually have a promising career as a computing expert (Singh, 2008).

Regrettably, many software developers remain in this stage for their entire careers. In case you're only a coder, then your payment may not be that great since your talents are easily replaceable. Plus, if you remain as just a coder, it means your promotions may be considerably limited. During this phase, you shouldn't even anticipate to get any entry-level job from big tech firms. As a student, you must progress at a minimum to the next level for this to occur. You should be a programmer (Singh, 2008).

9.4.2. Programmer

After you master the essentials of about two programming languages, possibly one statically-typed while the one dynamically-typed, then you could become a good coder. The question hence is how a person promotes their talent to reach the programmer status. The programmer is basically a more skilled coder. Writing code which involves the actual practice is mostly what coders do, though writing an effective code is what most programmers aim for. There are various skills that you must have as an established programmer. First, you must understand the basics of how a code finally becomes something which a hardware chip can easily understand and implement (Woollard, 2007).

You must further understand that any network has finite computing, storage, and communication resources, plus your software must utilize these resources resourcefully. Also, understand how to use information systems and algorithms for writing efficient codes, including what makes a particular code effective and what doesn't.

While there are many coders in the market, there aren't as much solid programmers. Meaning if you really grasp this technology, you can effortlessly get a job at some big tech firm like Google, Amazon, and Facebook, among others. As a matter of fact, majority of the interviews done at these institutions test how proficient a programmer is, not how great of a coder a person is. Furthermore, you must recognize that quality is crucial and that testing the code equally is crucial. But programming stage is not the end because there is still a long road ahead on your career journey (Singh, 2008).

9.4.3. Computer Scientist

Generally, learning doesn't stop after grasping the programming stage. In fact, it really starts from here! Once you reach the computer scientist stage, you're fundamentally a developer who looks at the wider picture mostly instead of the nitty-gritty particulars. You gain a strong understanding of developing large distributed structures, besides you understand how to create scalable systems which can handle big loads and endure failures. Computer scientists also don't stop learning, plus they always try to stay updated with the newest developments in technology.

During this stage, you'll most probably be responsible for big projects, plus you shall also be supervising a whole team, consisting of solid programmers and coders. You may further need to collaborate closely with other teams. These skills need impeccable social and leadership abilities. There are also certain technical skills which you need so as to become a coder, programmer, and ultimately a computer scientist (Singh, 2008).

9.5. PROMOTING COMPUTER SCIENCE IN RURAL SETTINGS

If CS is to become an essential part of modern century education, stakeholders must address the issue of how to provide competent schooling. First, they need to offer greater access. In comparison to urban or suburban settings, rural schools are not likely to provide computer science programs. With millions of students living in rural areas around the globe, considerable numbers of young individuals are denied the chance to participate in computer science subjects in school (Unesco, 2011).

The next phase, as identified by researchers, is transforming the computer-science classroom culture and education format. The need for change is clear when checking the current issues: including gender gap, threat of racial/gender stereotypes, plus the learning requirements of students with special needs.

For purposes of addressing both availability and equity, stakeholders must campaign for rural educators to learn CS as well. If this isn't done, the expanding access gaps between the rural pupils and their urban counterparts will continue perpetuating the already unfair equity gaps in CS education (Unesco, 2011).

Rural schools in developing countries face multiple challenges. However, they provide opportunities for educators who seek to be part of the local community and nurture significant long-term connections with their students.

Many teachers in rural communities serve in small schools. In some institutions, school districts have less than 200 pupils and this is regarded as "frontier" regions. However, small rural schools provide what many educators want: the opportunity to know learners well, establish connections in the local community, and also customize learning in multi-age perspectives.

Upon visiting a single-room schoolhouse in a developing country, researchers observed a closer interaction between teachers and learners, where the instructors were able to meet each of their requirements (Unesco, 2011).

Close community ties allow rural tutors to advocate for the learners needs, and encourage change in their specific schools. In a recent study, some rural STEM instructors identified how they took advantage of local community to make real-life connections to content. A particular teacher pointed out that, rural schools are surrounded by farming fields, windmill farms and wind turbines which allow kids to make real-life connections besides only the algorithms which they do in class.

Instructors in rural schools may develop the methods and relationships to achieve curriculum objectives, while customizing the school experience for their pupils. They perform this with their field of expertise —humanities or STEM—plus may do this with CS which is a field that currently affects rural life, with progresses in agriculture, manufacturing, and other popular economic drivers based in rural areas. Having that said, CS is hardly rural teachers' main subject area. They must learn it before attempting to teach it (Unesco, 2011).

9.5.1. How Rural Tutors Develop New Knowledge

Despite having strong community ties as well as close associations with their students, rural instructors may feel isolated from specialized learning opportunities due to distance, focus, or practicality.

One answer for this type of isolation is building hybrid certified learning communities. In a study, rural teachers partook in a one-year skills development that comprised of both in-person and virtual participation. Relating to the topic—incorporating computers in the class—instructors developed application projects which they taught in class. For post-project interviews, learners (particularly female students) reported improved application and futures in operating computers (Unesco, 2011).

Other hybrid teacher improvement initiatives are online resources. They foster an online setting where computer science teachers can exchange project ideas, ask questions, and participate in other common activities. They can also attend and present their ideas at teacher gatherings. Instructors usually report improvements in learners using computers, cooperating with each other, plus asking questions which reach beyond the standard course material.

Rural CS teachers from developing countries mentioned that the network enhanced isolation and availed resources, plus offered a unique form of support compared to what they went through at their individual schools. In particular, one teacher said that, digital learning's potential for superseding the boundaries of location is particularly essential for rural teachers. It opens the world for them and provides resources which may otherwise be inaccessible to schools in these regions.

While studies on rural tutor networks are scarce, among the most recent is a multi-year expert development network of the rural CS teachers by American scholars. It reinforced the significance of partnership and relationship-building in continuing, hybrid professional development. Furthermore, their study established how technology access was differentiated in rural contexts, occasionally even acting as an engagement barrier (Unesco, 2011).

Learning with other people certainly requires time and commitment. Furthermore, the advantages of networked PLC's offer rural teachers an ongoing, mutual, reflective, comprehensive, and learning-based community. Essentially, these networks affect both tutors and their students.

9.6. IMPROVING ACCESS TO CS PROFESSIONAL DEVELOPMENT

A number of studies with instructors in developing nations provide some insight, regarding ways of addressing the inequities which CS education must tackle. The findings include:

- Offering professional development as well as support, which is a crucial component of increasing capacity for CS teaching. Apart from a creative curriculum, teachers should have broad content knowledge including practice with pedagogy which engages students.
- Tutors act as vital mediators of learners' participation in computing courses, plus. In addition, instructors' roles as computer science learners, within a system of learning and mental reflection, affects how they eventually teach their students.
- Courses must regularly and proactively assess recruitment, growth, and equity. In CS, scaling up can easily slide backwards and reflect the field's present racial and gender gaps.
- Long term online learning programs sustained around CS professional development caused teachers to report that their

pedagogy improved, plus the ongoing collaboration that this platform provides breaks isolation. Another finding highlighted that this project takes time.

All these findings denote the importance of tutors as learners. Equally, they strengthen their ability to teach computing by participating in all-encompassing, critical communities. Going forward, the question is how these findings determine rural tutor professional development. Including how their learning affects pupils' computer science learning.

How rural teachers influence the evolving nature of computer science to provide equitable learning opportunities and access for their pupils?

Rural STEM tutors are typically the only official mediators of their pupils' developing computational skills, while acting as advocates for sidelined students. In terms of equity, research also shows a way forward that involves supporting well-resourced, solid networks of tutors sharing practice to enhance educational prospects for their students. If developing countries are serious about offering computer science to every learner, they must first offer it to the teachers (Unesco, 2011).

9.7. EDUCATION ACTIVITIES FOR COMPUTER SCIENCE TEACHING

Schools in developing regions need equipment including screens, mice, and keyboards that can be used to educate. They also need word processing tools, such as MS Word and Excel, which are essential in the digital world that they live in. Later on, the students can be taught how to program basic guessing games such as Python. They will learn about how the computer "thinks" including how to subdivide an activity down into lesser parts (Singh et al., 2019).

Among the main teaching methods in this context is the jam-sandwich comparison. This is where the instructor pretends to be a programmed robot, which follows commands just like a computer does. This teaches children that they not only can instruct a robot to prepare a jam sandwich, unless the device has been fine-tuned to do so. During class, students have to go down up to the most basic level, showing how to handle the knife and even opening the butter before spreading the bread. The period of realization is when the tutor acts like they can't get a piece of bread, since they hadn't yet opened the bag. Following this, the pupils can understand the programmer's mindset and structuring a project for programming.

The teacher can then go through a guessing game together with them and allow them to practice, before asking them to demonstrate how to operate the game similarly as is done in the jam-sandwich analogy. Through this simple demonstration, the teacher can introduce pseudo code to students, while actively using this pseudocode in the clarification and walk-by of the code.

In areas where the code reprocessed a concept showed in previous lines, the teacher can ask their students what they believe shall be ideal for this line. Most of them will recognize that they have already coded a similar program before, and may even begin coding the line prior to telling them exactly what to write (Singh, 2008).

Essentially, this reassures the teacher that students were indeed learning, not just copying content that had already been inscribed on the board. By the end, everyone will understand why their code is working. Relying on feedback from previous participants, student enjoy these learning actitivities and are surprised at the range of possibilities regarding working with computers.

9.8. TRAINING TEACHERS IN DEVELOPING COUNTRIES

Apart from students, workshops can further be arranged for adult teachers in disadvantaged communities. Even instructors from external learning organizations who make their way to the venue should be allowed to participate in the training.

Typically, the adults have a much more instinctive understanding of the jam-sandwich example described above, plus may come up with details and snags which the instructor hadn't thought of themselves. Nevertheless, a good number of these adults aren't computer literate. For them, the teacher may have to explain certain concepts like Caps vs Shift Lock or, even using a mouse. This may not be something that's anticipated, but in extremely rural areas of developing countries, some people have never used a computer before. Irrespective, with proper training everyone can get their code working in no time, and it's believed that most people actually find this useful and can even understand programming concepts that will be useful for their day to day activities (Barton, 2004).

The goal of training more CS teachers is to try and reach more pupils than a single teacher could teach at any given time. While there's no particular measure to determine the impact of these programs, they can help spark an interest in doing further research and allowing the adult to be in a position to teach programming topics in the future. Nevertheless, to fully enable CS teachers to start giving lessons in their individual capacity, developing countries must run multiple workshops meant for different skill levels so as to promote knowledge acquisition and deliver further material for teaching.

In some situations, both students and learners may already have some background in programs like Scratch, but may not have learnt this from an intuitive capacity yet. For such groups, teaching the jam-sandwich analogy can be pretty quick since they already have some basic background on computing (Barton, 2004).

Python language is relatively new to most students compared to Scratch. However, with proper guidance it can still be learnt by the students quite fast. The pupils may even be able to present across most of what they have learnt through actual presentations.

9.9. SUSTAINABLE TEACHING PLANS

Figure 9.3. *A teacher showing her students how to program.*

Source: https://www.tshwifi.com/2019/08/16/google-to-teach-south-african-learners-computer-science-fundamentals/.

While teaching the children in developing countries, many teachers realize they are genuinely interested in programming. To equip this group of teachers to train their students effectively, the governments are organizing educational workshops. This is based upon the assumption that instructors should master the content before teaching it to others.

Unfortunately, this assumption isn't always correct. If you can teach other tutors, then far more students will be reached indirectly compared to those that are benefiting directly. Governments can arrange for empowerment programs that focus primarily on educators – plus run workshops intended at preparing them to teach coding from the surface up. The other matter that educators must face is politics, which may not be favorable in developing nations. In some developing countries, resistance movements prevent access of computer training materials to certain regions where they are needed the most by locals (Yoldere & Adamu, 2014).

Teaching CS can be an enriching experience for both the children and teachers. Instructors will really love the kids' genuine reactions to learning new concepts, including how they handle or apply the information in class. Most learners are extremely grateful for the teaching experience, sometimes even being hungry to grasp more.

This is where the kits eventually come in – they permit students to continue grow their knowledge and skills.

9.9.1. Computer Literacy Volunteer Programs

There is only very little you can perform without a computer nowadays. Just stop to think about the number of tech equipment that you own. Processors are convenient and assume boring admin tasks on your behalf, without putting in too much effort.

In most developing states, technology hasn't infused as deeply and locals lack the basic understanding that could provide extra skills and revenue-generation prospects (Unesco, 2011).

Even though smartphone permeation rates are comparatively high all around the globe, still many individuals in poor and rural zones still don't understand how to operate a computer. For volunteers teaching computer science abroad, they can help to impart basic skills which make a big difference.

In industrialized regions, many people can't imagine themselves lives without personal computers, plus they seem to do almost everything with assistance of these computing devices, however, there are nations where that isn't a reality. In case you have hardware or software skills, then you can volunteer in developing countries and put your expertise to work for improvement of local communities across various destinations (Unesco, 2011).

9.9.2. Teaching Basic Computer Operation Skills

The communities a volunteer will be helping via this form of programming may have never experienced much contact with processors before. In this case, you will basically be helping them to learn basic techniques like internet browsing and word processing. You don't require advanced computer science knowledge for this kind of volunteer work, however, you should show interest in teaching CS in under-resourced locations.

9.9.3. Helping with Specific Tasks

Nowadays, business skills and computing skills follow each other hand-in-hand. For budding business owners in developing markets, extra skills and technical resources for supervising things like staff working hours, credit card payments and stock management, are extremely helpful. You may also assist community organizations or schools learn to develop a simple website, or come up with a couple of databases for financial management. The uses of technology are limitless in the 21st century.

9.9.4. Developing Infrastructure

This kind of program may have a major influence on the community's self-sustainability. Determining how to develop a computer network, or connecting to a Wi-Fi router by themselves not only means prospective job openings for native citizens, but further allows emerging businesses to be self-reliant in terms of their IT needs.

9.9.5. Coding

While relying increasingly on technology, coding shall be among the most significant job skills needed in the future. Considering that there are various online courses which anybody can register for remotely, coding programs aren't yet available worldwide. Teaching native students to create something as basic as stationary web pages, while sharing your knowledge in CSS and HTML is an especially rewarding experience plus highly beneficial for them.

In Ghana, for example, economic growth in the West African nation has been substantial, however, the opportunity gaps that exist between South and North, women and men, plus rich and deprived still run deep. For instance, joining volunteer courses in Ghana which empower ladies with technology skills can stimulate a constructive ripple-effect which can fast-track their economic development and independence. Training basic computer proficiency means Ghanaian girls and women will enjoy better prospects of getting jobs, thus minimizing the rates of teenage pregnancy and childhood marriages (Unesco, 2011).

Thailand is yet another budding region where CS literacy is needed. While it isn't the primary country which comes to the mind when thinking about computing literacy volunteer programs, there are some remote places in the country where computer teaching is still required.

Thailand boasts of an advanced economy, where Bangkok serves as among the largest trading and manufacturing centers in the region. Nevertheless, the rural places still lag behind. Case in point, if you have some basic understanding of stock administration or accounting, there's possibility for assisting local businesses – particularly those experiencing significant growth coming from the region's tourism boom –to better manage their operations. All these processes need some basic understanding of computers, which can be achieved through training programs (Unesco, 2011).

Through computer literacy programs, the gap between wealthy and poor families can be bridged. Women in particular will be greatly advantaged by learning computers, since it will help them compete at an equal level with men who are generally more tech-savvy.

9.10. COMPUTER SCIENCE TEACHING IN AFRICA

Figure 9.4. *Young students working with laptops in a computer lab.*

Source: https://worldcomputerexchange.org/computers-for-girls/.

Africa is, from the Western point of view, an unfamiliar place. It has a diverse culture which borrows profoundly from customs of the native tribes and the European cultures which previously held the African continent as a colony. In many countries, people value teamwork, elders' authority and tradition, however, their academic system has many unpleasant aspects as well. One of them is the so-called "African time," or a tendency of most African people to not respect timekeeping as much as their European counterparts. This can affect computer science learning since pupils won't be able to attend classes in time and may ultimately miss out on important topics.

Another common issue that troubles CS teachers is that despite English language being the official communication channel in many institutions, some students still have no proficient understanding of this language whatsoever, only nodding "yes, yes" in agreement whenever the teacher says anything, since they've been trained to respond so since childhood. Yet another big issue is that in some African schools a large number of lectures are abruptly canceled, due to factors like low attendance levels or teachers skipping class without being penalized in whichever way (Unesco, 2011).

Not learning anything during a course isn't a problem either in some countries, cases have been reported where students that pay their tuition are provided with easier examinations until they pass, basically making such learning institutions certificate mills.

It's baffling that students themselves accept or tolerate such an academic culture. In the West, one can't even imagine fully paying for education but then only getting some certificate for going through the course, without having proper education.

Such institutions feed on the learners' tuition fees or grants, but deliver only worthless computer science certificates and some falsified sense of learning. Indeed, there are many instructors who are honestly concerned about the education of their students, however, they are quite far and apart in some African countries. The issue is further intensified by brain leak were skilled, hardworking and authentic teachers are at high demand and get higher wages in other bigger schools, leaving smaller learning institutions with the least qualified CS teachers.

To counter some of these problems, schools must develop strong rules and regulations on CS that both teachers and students should follow. The learning material needs to be comprehensive, and cover a broad array of topics right from the basic ones to item-oriented programming, plus other useful algorithms such as selection sort and binary search among others.

This is what computer science students, even the ones without any prior programming skills typically learn in the primary stages of their programming courses. Comparatively, some students in Africa spend a good part of their programming course having a hang on basic concepts, despite the fact that majority of the course's main topics are similar as those from certain developed nations. For computer science training to be effective in Africa, the educational system must be restructured right from its foundations: so long as the learners don't know the formal English teaching language, are trained to not ask relevant questions and lessons provided by individuals who don't understand what's going on, computer education won't be effective no matter how much effort is put towards teaching (Unesco, 2011).

9.11. THE CS TEACHING EXPERIENCE IN DEVELOPING COUNTRIES

Potential tutors may ask if it is practical to teach computing subjects in developing regions. Within the last years, nevertheless, a nearly exponential increase in overall quantity of mobile devices in Sub-Saharan Africa has grown over the recent years. Moreover, within the countries, there are various network operating companies which exist and fresh jobs for individuals in IT have also been created. This has made computer subjects to become interesting to students once more (Seendani, 2014).

Some of the computer courses offered in developing countries target pupils who already have some background knowledge in the programming language, like C++, Pascal or Java, plus some have carried out projects of around 500 programming lines. Out of most applications who come from the immediate community, most students are chosen to begin the original part of the program (which is introduction to Java). The rest are typically permitted to follow the subsequent portion of the course, which involves Java Imagery and Interface.

During the first sections of the course, learners will be taught Java as well as object-oriented programming among other subjects. Later on, focus can be shifted to interface elements or lessons useful for script editing and picture manipulation, involving more complex functions such as mouse interaction, text areas, menus, buttons, image buffers, sliders and mouse interaction. Some of the tasks that students can be given include; putting together interface widgets and creating an interactive editor used for extracting or pasting image tiles (Seendani, 2014).

There are institutions which are quite selective in choosing pupils to learn CS in their classes. The student may be required to take an entrance exam to show their ability before being allowed to study computer science. These learners may register in different institutions such as private schools, or even high level training institutes depending on the type of skills they want to acquire.

During some classes, the lessons may be organized in conjunction with experts from the computer science field such as university lecturers, PhD pupils and master pupils who would want to follow this discipline up to the highest levels. They can motivate other lower level students to develop an interest in CS from the earliest stages of school. Some subjects of interest that can be asked include; client-server systems, Web interfaces and applets, as well as Java for integrated systems like mobile phones (Seendani, 2014).

9.12. DEVELOPING DIGITAL SKILLS IN YOUR CLASSROOM

Figure 9.5. *Learners actively participating in a computer lesson.*

Source: https://www.futurelearn.com/courses/digital-transformation-class-room.

It is not surprising that computers are essential to daily life, therefore it's no wonder that digital skills are necessary for modern day students. Certain skills, like working cooperatively online, or being in a position to securely and efficiently use an internet browser and resources like search engines and email, may seem easy, but in fact they can unlock various possibilities. These virtual skills are also vital in schools. Learning how to read and write involves a procedure of learning basic skills that would be needed daily, for your entire life; but digital skills are a bit different since they evolve from time to time based on the prevailing technology (Rocha et al., 2018).

In developing nations, digital skills are increasingly becoming a vital requirement for youngsters to thrive in a digitized society. These skills are not just required for most types of jobs, but are also a necessity and right of citizens, for them to be functional members of the society. Learning institutions and teachers thus need support to correlate with their pupils to develop a vast range of virtual skills, which ensure youngsters leaving school get the skills needed by the labor industry, and by a progressively digitized society.

The learning program can be organized around certain thematic fields of digital skills which are relevant at different levels of both primary and secondary education. In context, it explores the meaning and role of virtual skills generally, while also looking at specific skill sets and ways of addressing them in the class setting. The focus of computer science modules should be on how various skill areas can be taught pedagogically, including tools which are available for helping the teachers and learners (Rocha et al., 2018).

Teachers also need to learn relevant skills for developing a range of virtual skills and introducing these to the resources which are accessible to them. By the end of such a program, teachers must be able to develop lessons which concentrate on a variety of digital skills, be able to use innovative tools in aiding their own work and the pupils' role in the learning process.

Since there are very few jobs to which people won't require digital skills, computer science has become a 'foundational literacy,' together with literacy and numeracy. Digital learning is something which should occur, and indeed, should be a possibility, all through the person's lifetime. However, the seeds of computer learning interest are sowed in school. Regrettably, for the greater part, digital abilities haven't been the top priority they should be. Virtual skills remain astonishingly low in most cases.

Only 7% of 15–29-yearr-old pupils in some developing countries have functional computer skills, based on studies carried out by education stakeholders. A common reaction for the need to build young peoples' virtual skills is throwing technology at almost every problem. Massive investments in computer appliances for classrooms, plus e-learning solutions allow for the unleashing of a cohort of 'digital natives.' But, buying lots of class-room technology is just not sufficient on its own; fostering the digital abilities of instructors and learners is an essential step in really benefiting from workstations in education. Students who regularly use computers in schools develop a higher interest in science and mathematics subjects (Unesco, 2011).

These findings suggest that nations should consider investing more in technology within schools, so that a greater number of students can be exposed to technology. There are multiple ways that computers are able to open up prospects for education and learning, in case they're used effectively. Even when schools are fitted with computers, the technique for teaching must be adapted. Meaning, learners must be taught practical skills on how to utilize digital technologies efficiently and productively. Education stakeholders believe technology is the best way to drastically increase access to knowledge. For purposes of delivering on the possibilities technology holds, nations must invest more efficiently and ensure that tutors are at the frontline of designing and executing this change.

There's research which promotes the need for instructors to have solid skills in utilizing technology in the class setting. One study done by European Commission discovered that only 25 percent of pupils in some countries are taught by technically confident and supportive tutors, whereas another study conducted by OECD established that 56% of educators say that they have "medium to high development requirements" in matters of using technology within the workplace. Therefore, while digital abilities are vital for pupils to make the best of computers, similarly they're vital for teachers, allowing them to wholly benefit from technology in the classroom, plus to avoid the possible risks of low ICT use (Unesco, 2011).

While there's a lot still that needs to be done throughout the globe, there are inspiring initiatives to encourage the use of digital skills in the syllabus in several developing countries. In some education systems, reforms on the computing syllabus can make virtual literacy a central component of learning. A number of schools are currently using ECDL programme for building the essential ICT skills which their students require. In some countries, ECDL even forms a part of the concluding school exams.

Developing nations should put in place a digital literacy system which recognizes the significance of core digital abilities in a structured manner. Some education foundations have also been launching ICT empowerment programs in schools, which have been validated in test trials with instructors in conjunction with stakeholders. Using certification, such as ECDL, schools can be able to ensure that their pupils meet a globally approved standard of virtual literacy.

It's at the core of technology that it's always evolving. Workstations are becoming increasingly commonplace in our day-to-day activities; from smartphones to laptops and tablets, the whole idea of a workstation being a static and bulky machine is, in most ways, declining. At the center of things, digital abilities are necessary for competently using a computer, no matter what shape it may take (Unesco, 2011).

Digital literacy is an essential skills for work, life, and learning. Without virtual competences, youngsters have minimal chance of profiting from the improvements in technology which are restructuring the workplace and redesigning the way people live their lives. Just as learning centers have a major role to play in equipping learners with literacy and numerical competence skills, similarly they have a crucial role to play in giving their pupils the skills to use workstations effectively and safely.

9.13. HELPING CHILDREN DEVELOP THE DIGITAL ABILITIES FOR THEIR FUTURES

Today, programs such as Applied Digital Skills—which is a new virtual literacy program that is part of Grow with Google project—helps schools in developing regions address a couple of the challenges which learners face. The syllabus uses video-based courses to help students develop projects with virtual applications and absolutely is free for everybody. As children build tasks, they actively practice the fresh skills they'll need for future careers, including other real-world skills like financial literacy, critical thinking, communication and cooperation. The course includes well over 100 hours of lessons which can be applied in the library or classroom, individually or in groups.

Another effective learning program is If-Then Adventure Stories module, which allows learners to create interactive tasks both solely and in teams. While learners cooperate in sharing documents, they eventually collaborate in solving problems and motivating one another to keep on track. In some Elementary schools, projects like Research and Build a Topic unit for helping scholars conduct research more efficiently. One 7th grade Elementary teacher mentioned how "students have a difficult time determining what's crucial and should be added, and what's not. They get a tough time interpreting the study into their unique words…" For the unit, students identify credible sources, assess bias of virtual information, give report about their research, plus get feedback (Connell et al., 2014).

Some schools also use Applied Digital Skills in constructing the curriculum to support learners in developing resumes, searching for jobs, planning events and exploring local history.

Devising real world situations which are appropriate to the students while also being capable of teaching them particular skills is often tasking, but through programs like Applied Digital Skills this can be made much easier.

The format of lessons has been simplified, so that students can follow the guidelines and instructional videos at their unique pace. These are some of the few examples showing how educators can use programs like Applied Digital Skills syllabus to provide learners of different ages free, integrating lessons which teach the vital digital skills they'll require for their futures. Any school is free to use Google's Applied Digital Skills Starter Guide, even those based in developing countries (Woollard, 2007).

9.13.1. Why Learn Computer Science?

Nearly every job nowadays involves a variety of digital skills, though employers report a deficiency in skillful new starters. These training programs will enable students to develop computing skills for effective employment in the modern-day society, plus to progress in the workplace. As a teacher, through practical case studies, resources as well as support you'll eventually be able to assist your learners to manage their virtual identity and digital data needed for day to day operation.

Instructors can learn how to help learners create digital content, plus may be provided with effective tools for communicating effectually and working cooperatively.

By acquiring the digital abilities relevant in the workplace, learners will be able to manage their personal online identity, manage digital information, create digital content and use modern tools and techniques needed for working collaboratively.

Furthermore, the technology allows students to collaborate on various models for imparting digital skills in practice. Training also supports teachers in the computer science field to build their digital prowess.

9.14. IMPACT OF ICT EMPOWERMENT IN UNDER-PRIVILEGED COMMUNITIES

Figure 9.6. *Students learning computing skills which are relevant to the 21st century.*

Source: https://www.cfr.org/report/investing-girls-stem-education-developing-countries.

ICT role out in developing-country schools can help improve education standards, and interest in science among the students. Equally, among other matters the curriculum can promote implementation of an all-inclusive education system, enhancing quality and significance of computer science education, evaluation of qualified teachers' deployment and situations of service, including reviewing the instruction policy language among other functions (Rocha et al., 2018).

Through these programs, it means that teaching of ICTs plus computer studies would be common in the community, both in government and private schools. However, the big question that remains unanswered following the implementation of these new measures is what procedures have been put in place for ensuring that they initiate successful instructive strategies to utilize ICTs for training and learning. Even though ICTs introduction is welcome plus being taught in most schools, still ICT teaching remains to be a daunting task in the rural schools as well as community schools. In some countries, both rural and community institutions don't have sufficient infrastructure or equipment to utilize for subjects such as ICT's or computer studies. Yet pupils in these underprivileged schools are needed to understand the technology subjects. Typically, community schools make up the final resort for those children who can't afford state or private school education in developing countries. Since the kids are mostly enrolled free of charge in these schools.

Community learning institutions also provide uncovered demand for school positions among the poor, including other marginalized societies. These schools are affordable, close to home plus less demanding in regards to entry requirements. The amount of licensed community schools registered within developing countries has increased manifold since the 1990. Furthermore, these institutions can supplement state efforts in regards to educating youngsters in the country. The growth in total number of schools continues increasing, plus is another substitute path to get basic education for the part of kids (Unesco, 2011).

Likewise, in most scenarios, no training, credentials, or resources are needed for those who want to join these community schools. But there's need for businesses to help community-based schools, particularly with the modification of curriculum so that they also can be at the same point of learning ICT such as their counterparts in Government schools. Most community schools are managed by the local community itself, thus the requirement for cooperates and businesses to get concerned so that they can assist them to advance at the same stride with both private and government schools.

Although the curriculum may be implemented, it is typically examinable for grade 9 learners who already learned business studies and ICT. Normally, ICT isn't examinable from grades 1 to 8 and this means that the syllabus won't affect majority of the community-based schools which don't move up to the 7th grade. The education quality in these schools may not be at par with State and private schools because of lack of adequate resources and training of teachers, but they can still fill the gap for computer science education in countries.

The introduction of computer education in developing schools hasn't been simple, particularly considering that some students have never physically placed their hands-on any computer before. In some regions there is not even sufficient electricity to run the computers that students need to learn. Pupils in poor communities may struggle with computers compared to their more privileged counterparts, since their parents might not be privileged enough to own them within their homes. Community ICT schools provide creative options for pupils to learn technology and become exposed to new trends in the digital world, no matter their sociocultural background (Unesco, 2011).

Still, Community School instructors work on a volunteer basis and get little remuneration for their efforts, which usually comes from community support. It's for such reasons that most Private Schools in developing regions only accommodate a tiny percentage of kids in these regions, due to high costs which are associated with running an ICT facility among other expenses such as books, school fees, and uniforms. Community technology empowerment programs are open to everyone, but particularly aimed at individuals who are in Vocational Education or Training sectors, such as: skills training, further education, vocational education, job place learning, and lifetime learning or adult training. Typically, the computer science activities have defined timeframes, plus there are various resources that teachers can explore more if they'd wish to discover a particular topic further (Unesco, 2011).

9.15 CHALLENGES FACING COMPUTER EDUCATION IN SCHOOLS

Whereas ICT continues advancing in most western countries, those in some parts of Africa and Asia are still experiencing lags in implementation, which continues to extend the digital gap and heighten virtual literacy challenges. Within a recent study, it was observed that the access to ICT resources is a key challenge facing many African nations, with a quotient of one workstation to 150 learners against a rate of 1:15 pupils in the developed regions.

While results show that ICT has infiltrated many sectors such as banking, communications, transportation and medical services, still the educational system in developing regions continues lagging behind. Furthermore, recent reports by education organizations show that computer usage in classrooms still remain to be in its preliminary phases, plus that the perceptions, as well as experiences of educators and administrators, continue to play a significant role in utilization of computers within the classroom setting (GAL-EZER & STEPHENSON, 2014).

Among the major challenges is lack of experienced teachers to coach ICT in schools. There's been high demand for technology learning in developing regions, though the number of qualified teachers who are qualified to teach ICT can't meet the demand. Generally, there are more pupils ready to be taught computer skills compared to instructors who are available to transfer the knowledge. Another common issue is lack of computers. These machines are still quite costly and in spite of spirited efforts by state agencies, corporate organizations, NGOs and persons to donate workstations to as many learning institutions as possible, still there remains a huge percentage of schools which are unable to buy computers for day to day use by their students.

This is further compounded by lack of electricity. A great deal of schools in developing regions are still not fully connected to electricity. In most of these countries, the state hasn't been able to link all regions of the nation to the main electricity grid. Accordingly, those schools which fall under such zones are left handicapped, whereby they can't possibly offer computer studies to their students. Computers also are quite costly in marginalized regions which have a low GDP ratio, meaning majority of people and schools can't afford buying a computer, and instead take it to be a luxury item which is costlier than a TV. Even though 2nd hand workstations cost as low as $150, while branded new computers may be bought at $500 or much higher (Yoldere & Adamu, 2014).

Broken down computers are an issue of concern a well. Even though a considerable number of learning centers have profited from donated used workstations, they haven't been sufficiently equipped with similar resources on maintenance and repairs, therefore its rather common to see an institution's computer lab packed with broken down computers, whereby some repairable and others not. This has really been a major concern, besides the state has now put stringent measures on any individual, NGO or corporate entities willing to contribute second-hand computers. In places like Africa, old or broken down computers are usually given away or dumped as a way of e-waste management by some industrialized countries.

Burglary, especially in low income areas, further threatens the supply of computers for learning purposes. The fact that these machines are still quite costly in Kenya means they are a potential target for burglars, who typically have readymade markets to other dealers at a much lower rate. This has made most schools to incur increased costs seeking to burglar-proof the workstation rooms. This additional expense makes some learning institutions shy away from buying computers for their learners (Yoldere & Adamu, 2014).

Another issue is unnecessary fear by school administration; there's still a widespread perception particularly by the much older generation that workstations require very skilled staff members to operate them, even though this may actually not be the situation. Some school principals also distress that their pupils may be exposed to various undesired sites, by having access to the internet. There's also fear that virus infection to their computers may lead to data loss. While this might be accurate to some point, adequate education on the proper usage of computers can help to lessen some of these fears.

Similarly, the tutor may panic being rendered irrelevant due to the incorporation of computers in their classrooms. The 'perception' that the tutor still remains a key authority or a 'know-it-all' in the classroom is something which most trainers value, and anything which goes otherwise is considered a foreign influence. Moreover, lack of sufficient internet or low connectivity is a major challenge. Many schools lack adequate internet access because of the high rates involved in connectivity. Generally, it costs around $120 monthly to connect to around 15 computers operating on a bandwidth level of 128/64kbps. The figure is considered quite costly, despite the internet running at rather slow speeds (Yoldere & Adamu, 2014).

Chapter

10 Role of Government in Computer and Technological Education

CONTENTS

10.1. INTRODUCTION

The government is a group of people in a country or state who are given the mandate and authority to govern the country. The government is a very important sector in the country for it is responsible for making the rules of the country, legislating and executing these rules. The government has three arms which is the legislature, executive and judiciary. When it comes to its involvement in education these three arms work together to get involved and to come up with solutions to any problems that may be facing the education sector.

Computer and technological education is the study of computer and the technologies that revolve around the computer. Computers are commonly used in the present world as there is technological revolution which make computers to be the main tools that are being used to perform many tasks today. Most schools are incorporating the study of computer through means such as adding computer science to their school curriculum and adding computers in the classrooms. Technologies that are present that revolve around computer and the knowledge of computers include the calculators, mobile devices, tablets and speakers or television. Computer and technological education therefore involve the study of all these devices.

There is great importance in the study of computer and technology because the use of computers in the current world is vast and people cannot run away from it (Barton, 2004). Individuals who lack the knowledge of the computer may be disadvantaged to the extent of lacking jobs. Most employers will give jobs to individuals who have the knowledge of the computer because they will be sure that these individuals will fit in well and will be able to operate the computers. A person who lacks computer knowledge and skills is also outdated and can be easily conned as they fail to understand what is revolving. They can also be hacked and their information was stolen which may result to them losing a lot of information or resources like money.

The advantage of computer and technological information in schools include; students acquire skills which are important to them in future life and in acquiring employment. The skills which are acquired from computer science education include analytical skills, problem-solving skills, creativity, and resilience. These skills are important since they are required by employers before they give employment to the interviewees. They are also essential in the general life of the individual as it enables them to correlate well with the people around them. Another advantage is that computer scientists acquire knowledge of the computer and the technologies that revolve around the computer knowledge therefore they can use any computer and this makes their processes easier and faster. They are also advantaged because they can acquire employment when they are done with their studies. Individuals who learn computer can acquire employment such as IT specialist, software engineer or computer lecturer. It is therefore more important to ensure all students acquire the knowledge of the computers and related technologies (Barton, 2004).

The government is involved in education for several reasons. Its involvement in education has seen the education sector grow and a lot of disadvantages that were present in the past have been eliminated. By government involvement in computer education we mean that the government is incorporated in the affairs of computer education such that it can make rules that favor or limit the learning and teaching of computer education. There is great importance of understanding how the government is involved in computer education not only to understand the role of the government and appreciate it but to also know how the computer sector has increased on account of the government being involved.

The ways in which the government gets involved in the computer and technological education include; subsidizing education, providing equality in education, provision of free computer and technology education and other ways.

10.2. SUBSIDIZING COMPUTER AND TECHNOLOGY EDUCATION

Figure 10.1. *The government offers subsidies to schools for educational purposes.*

Source:-https://islandfreepress.org/news-and-business-briefs/community-grants-available-for-area-nonprofits/.

Subsidizing education is the process where the government offers a certain amount of money to be used in the education sector for student's aid or for grants for educational institutions. The aim of subsidizing education is to help students by transferring wealth from taxpayers to academic institutions.

School fees for low income students: Many students lack school fees as they come from poor backgrounds. There are also others who cannot afford to access education due to the high standards of living so they end up choosing to meet the most required needs other than education. For some of these students, they are not able to get sponsors who can help them pay for their fees. The government can assist these students by setting aside some funds which can be distributed to the various schools in the country to facilitate the education for these students. By subsidizing the money given to the schools by the government is used to eliminate some costs thus the fees are lowered hence parents of the less fortunate students can be able to raise the fees. For the very poor children or those who are offered and cannot raise the fees the subsidies can be used to raise money for their education so as to ensure they too receive education. When school fees for low income students are provided it will definitely lead to students accessing computer and technological education since they will be able to access all the services offered by the school.

Offering of computer and technological education textbooks: According to the government policies legislated recently the government is given the obligation to provide books to schools as a way of subsidizing education. These government subsidies can be used to buy textbooks for the schools such that the schools will not have to ask the students to buy their own textbooks which may be expensive and disadvantageous. The government has also associated with textbooks publishers like the longhorn and mountain publishers to publish books that are used in schools. These books are offered free of charge to every school according to the number of students in the schools. These textbooks are not to be sold and hence the school fees in schools is reduced since the books are already available and the parents will not be required to pay for book fund. By the government offering books instead of money to buy the books to schools it prevents the probability of the schools engaging in corruption where the schools may use the money for their own needs and benefits and fail to buy books for their students. It also ensures that the books bought cannot be sold as they are indicated not for sale hence ensures that these books are used only for students benefit and not to generate income. This has been of great benefit to the students since they are able to access textbooks that will enable their learning of computer and technological education no matter their location.

Offering government bursaries: Another way that the government has been used to provide subsidies is by offering government bursaries to the less advantaged students. The government identifies the students from the less advantaged backgrounds and they work in association with the schools to pick the students who cannot afford fees and they are bright and they offer them bursaries to aid them in the paying of fees. These bursaries may be full to take them through their education until their completion of education or they can be half to take them for a certain period. The process of acquiring a bursary also includes the government giving notices of the availability of a bursary. The student then signs up for the bursary with the correct and require information to ascertain they are from poor backgrounds. The government goes through the student's applications and they choose suitable people who have qualified for the bursary then they offer the bursary to these students. For example, in Kenya, the government offers help which is a bursary offered to university students who may fail to be able to raise the required amount needed by the universities and also for their upkeep in schools. When students are offered bursaries, they can also pay for their computer and technological studies.

Figure 10.2. *The government may get involved in education by offering government bursaries.*

Source: https://www.slideshare.net/BiancaBartucciotto/t317-scholarships-and-bursaries-guide432x289reworked.

Lowering school fees for computer and technological education: The government plays a key role in the lowering of school fees for computer and technological education. Initially, the government processed bills in the parliament so that the ministry of education gets to decide the amount of money that will be set as school fees. The members of the ministry hold meetings to decide on what will be the school fees. In the meetings they look at the various factors such as the student enrolment they are expected to have. Since the ministry champions for all students to be able to access the learning facilities therefore having high numbers of student enrolment, the ministry will have to make the fee to be affordable for all the students. For example, in Kenya the ministry of education under the government sets the fee for all the levels of education. There is a certain amount for primary education which is different for the secondary education. The ministry makes a fee range for all the students. The school heads then set the school fees within the range provided by the government. In order to cater for the students from poor backgrounds, they set the fees in a range that they can be able to afford. Lowering the school fees leads to a definite decrease in the cost of computer and technological education offered in the schools.

Set policies that prevent schools from having high school fees for computer and technological education: In public schools the government is responsible for knowing and determining the amount of school fees that is payable to the institution. This is advantageous because they keep in mind people in all works of life hence the fees are favorable to all students from any background. These policies prevent malicious school heads from increasing the school fees for their own benefits. The government ensures that all the country members are aware of the limit of school fees that is payable to any government school at any time.

10.3. PROVIDING EQUALITY IN EDUCATION

Institutions that provide education are divided into public institutions and private institutions. Private institutions are self-sponsored but public institutions are sponsored by the government. It is known that public institutions offer lower quality of education as compared to private institutions because private institutions have more educational equipment and they are less congested therefore the teachers can concentrate on all the students. Due to these factors many parents prefer to send their students to private schools but because of the high school fees in the high school fees most parents may fail to raise the fee hence send their kids to public schools.

The government is involved in ensuring there is equality between the public schools and private schools by improving the conditions in the public schools. If they improve these conditions then parents will start investing in public schools as much as private schools therefore, they will take the students to public schools since the education being offered will be quality education in both public and private sectors (Unesco, 2011).

It should also be noted that most public schools may fail to offer computer and technological education due to the factors like high number of students such that the students cannot access the required resources or lack of qualified teachers but the government works to reduce these factors so as to promote equality.The following are some of the ways the government is involved in providing this equality between the public and private schools. They include building more public schools, employing well trained teachers, government being involved in the private schools and improving the quality of education in public schools.

10.3.1. Building More Public Schools

Figure 10.3. *Public schools are built by the government which offer cheaper education.*

Source: https://www.studyinternational.com/news/why-the-us-government-should-increase-funding-for-public-schools/.

Most public schools are very congested to the extent that some students lacking seating spaces. Since education in public schools is cheap and easily available many students find their way into public schools. The result is that the schools register a lot of students. The disadvantage of having a lot of students in a class is that the teacher may fail to concentrate on each student hence they only pay close attention to the bright students hence they register a lot of poor grades (Odera, 2011).

When the government builds more public schools the number of students will be distributed in these schools making one public school to have a manageable number of students. It will also reduce the amount of work which is given to the teachers hence the teachers will not be overworked and it will enable them to concentrate on each student and teach each of them at their own level of understanding. Building more public schools will also enable more students to access education hence increase the number of learned individuals in the country.

When the government builds more schools, it will also encourage the schools to take up and add some subjects to the curriculum like computer and technological education because they can easily teach this subject not only physically but also practically. They will have the opportunity of having a computer laboratory that the students may access because their number is limited and each child may have access to a computer (Odera, 2011).

10.3.2. Resources and Books in Public Schools

Figure 10.4. *Government provides books and resources to public schools.*

Source:-https://www.usaid.gov/philippines/press-releases/dec-13-2017-us-government-provides-million-books-public-schools.

The government works to increase the number of books and resources in the public schools. In the private schools there are enough books and resources such that each student owns their own book but in the public schools they have very few resources due to their high number of students most students fail to have the opportunity of having their own books. This disadvantage the students in public schools since they lack enough information for study and they may fail to get enough information causing them to lag behind as compared to students in the private schools.

The government is trying to solve this problem by increasing the number of books in public schools and resources like the computers for learning computer science.

The lack of computers may prevent the students from learning computer science practically but when the government buys computers for the public schools' students can access these computers and they can use them to boost their computer language. The government has gone to the extent of buying tablets for these children to learn using them and also offering laptops at very cheap and affordable prices (Odera, 2011).

10.3.3. Employing Well-Trained Teachers with the Required Skills for Teaching Computer and Technological Education

The government does not pay close attention when interviewing the teachers who teach in public schools. They ignore the fact that teachers are the key determiners of the quality of education the students receive. In private schools they pay close attention to teachers they employ so as to ensure they get the best so that they offer quality education to the students. So as to ensure equality in the public and private schools the government should ensure that the teachers, they employ have the required skills too and they are qualified in their area.

Teachers who teach computer and technological education should have the skills in how to use the computer and they should know how to pass this information to their students.

Since computer and technological education requires a lot of practice the teachers should be keen enough to direct each student and they should involve all the students so that they ensure that all students understand what they are teaching.

If the government makes this possible then it will easily close the gap between the public schools and private schools (Odera, 2011).

10.3.4. Government Involvement in the Private Schools

In spite of there being very little involvement of the government in the private schools it is still involved in areas like ensuring the syllabus is the same by preparing the syllabus. The government dictates what should be taught and what should be in the syllabus. It therefore sets the computer and technological education syllabus that is used in the whole country in both private and public schools. By making the syllabus it has ensured equality because students learn the same things and hence, they acquire the same knowledge (Bulman & Fairlie, 2015).

The government also gets involved in the private schools by seating the school calendar so that it ensures both private and public schools have the same time for study to ensure equality. This helps teachers to plan their teaching time appropriately so they compete their studies.

Lastly, the government also gets involved by setting a common exam that is undertaken by both students in the public and private schools. The computer and technological education main exam that is undertaken by students in the public schools is the same as that undertaken by the private schools. This ensures equality since the students prepare for the same exams hence it promotes equality (Odera, 2011).

10.3.5. Provision of Free Education

The government has taken a step in providing free education which has been of great help in the growth of computer and technological education. When the government offers free education it means that the subjects such as computer and technological education will also be offered free of charge and many students from all walks of life including the poor and the students who cannot access education that they have to pay for it will be able to access this education. By providing free education the government creates awareness to the country to ensures that the citizens of that country take full advantage of this opportunity and utilize it.

The advantages that come with the provision of free education include; the needy will have an opportunity to access computer and technological study, all students will have the opportunity to study, literacy level in the country will increase gradually, school dropouts will decrease because of the lack of school fees and the economy of the country will increase because employers will have the required skills to take the economy at a higher level (Bulman & Fairlie, 2015).

Other ways that the government gets involved in computer and technological education include; ensuring accessibility of the institutions that offer computer and technological education, funding competitions that concern computer and technological education, increasing job opportunities for those who study and complete computer and technological education, funding a revolution, creating awareness of the computer and technological education and its importance and creating eligibility for the people. These are ways in which the government gets involved in computer and technological education to ensure that many students take up the learning of this course as it makes it advantageous and the students are motivated to learn computer and technological education. These factors are discussed further to increase understanding.

10.3.6. Ensuring Accessibility of Institutions That Offer Computer and Technological Education

Figure 10.5. *Students learning computer and technological education in an institution that offers computer and technological education.*

Source: https://edtechreview.in/trends-insights/insights/1230-what-educational-technology-challenges-do-schools-face.

As the computer revolution increases, the need for many institutions that offer computer and technological institutions increases gradually. This is because there is a need for people to know how to use a computer as most duties are now performed using the computer. The computer revolution has therefore brought a need to the government to ensure accessibility of institutions that offer computer and technological education. The government is involved in this process through the following ways: building institutions that offer computer and technological education, creating awareness, providing funds to people or groups that want to start institutions that offer computer and technological institutions, ensuring the school fee of this institutions is favorable to all students and funding students who may fail to have the ability to raise the required fee (Farrell, 2007).

Building institutions that offer computer and technological education: Since computer study is very important it is the initiative of the government to ensure all its citizens have access to this education. In the current world, anyone who lacks the knowledge of computer and technological education is disadvantaged in many ways. The government has therefore carried out its statistics of areas that do not have the access to this education and since it is the role of the government to ensure equality in the country, they have to ensure that these areas access this education. The government has built several schools and educational institutions that offer computer and technological education.

When the government builds these institutions, it will ensure that students from all over the country can access computer studies, therefore, they will be able to get the advantages that come along with the study of computer and technological education (Farrell, 2007).

Creating awareness: Creating awareness is the informing of the availability of something that the people being informed had no idea about. The government creates awareness of the availability and accessibility of institutions that offer computer and technological education. They also create an awareness of how important it is that everyone takes the initiative to study this course. The government does this in several ways which include; using the mass media, during political campaigns or their general meetings with the citizens. When they are talking to their citizens, they inform them of how important it is for them to learn computers and its advantages to their lives in future.

Providing funds to people or groups that want to start institutions that offer computer and technological education: The government also provides funds to individuals who want to start schools that teach technological and computer education but lack the required funds or resources. This enables creating accessibility of institutions that offer this course because they will increase in number. These funds are given to the individuals as loans such that they are required to pay back once the institution begins to bring profit with a certain amount of interest included.

Ensuring the school fee of these institutions is favorable to all students and funding students who may fail to have the ability to raise the required fee: The government also provides accessibility of the institutions that offer computer and technological education by ensuring that the fees that these institutions are favorable to people of all walks of life. When the fee is favorable it means that students who come from disadvantaged or poor backgrounds can also access this education as much as the rich can also access it. It is important because they will be equality in the education sector and it will lead to growth in economic stability in the country.

10.3.7. Funding Competitions That Concern Computer and Technological Education

Figure 10.6. *Students presenting a computer and technological project.*

Source: http://www.uwindsor.ca/dailynews/2018-12-05/students-showcase-projects-computer-science-demo-day.

Some competitions assist students to acquire certain skills in their area of study. For example, the national science and technology fair is a Kenyan national competition that assists students to acquire skills in science and technology. The students acquire these skills when they are conducting research and during presentations that enable them to succeed in the subject. Likewise, some competitions involve students who study computer and technical education that enables students to acquire skills that improve their performance.

The advantages of these competitions include; the students can improve their skills since the students get more information about this subject as they conduct their research. They may come across several things that they had not been taught in class so they will be ahead of their teachers. Students also can interact with other schools and as they promote social interactions, they also learn new things from them that they can include in their studies. Lastly, when students are presenting their project to the judges, the judges correct any false information that the students may pass to them hence the students can correct any misconceptions they had and therefore they are will avoid passing this to their studies (Farrell, 2007).

The organizing of these competitions is very expensive since a lot of funds are required to organize the whole process and pay the judges. Due to this, there may be a lack of these competitions but since government understands the importance of these competitions, they may sponsor them with the funds that may be required. The government may also sponsor the winners of the competition or award them so that more students may be motivated to take part in the next competition that would be held (Farrell, 2007).

10.3.8. Increasing Job Opportunities for Those Who Study and Complete Computer and Technological Education.

Many students take up a course because they are assured that they will not lack to obtain employment. The government needs to increase the jobs that are offered to computer and technological education students so that it may encourage and motivate other students to take up the course too. The government has looked for ways to increase job opportunities to these students which include; ensuring the use of computers in all government institutions, creating a new job sector which includes software engineering and also employing teachers to teach computer studies in schools (Bulman & Fairlie, 2015).

Ensuring the use of computers in all government institutions: The government has ensured that all its institutions use computers to carry out their daily duties. The use of computers in government institutions is advantageous for the following reasons; the government can save a lot of information without it getting lost or tampered with. In the past, the information was stored in files and written in papers. Thy documents could easily get lost or stolen and hence the need for the use of the computer arouse. The documents in the computer can also be secured with a password hence information cannot fall on the wrong hands easily and retrieving of the information is easy than having to look through documents to find a file. Another advantage of the computer is that it enables processes to be carried out faster. A good example of a government institution that the computers have helped speed up processes is the hospitals because since they started using computers, more patients have been able to see the doctor unlike in the past. The processes of computers are very fast because they involve giving the needed information to the computer and sending them automatically. Another advantage is that the information that the computer provides is normally accurate and correct. When the computer is used for example to perform some calculations, the result is always accurate that is if the information fed to it is accurate. This enables the prevention of error-free information therefore the information can be trusted. Lastly, computers enable easy retrieval of information. One can retrieve information which is dated as far as 2000 years ago through simply requesting it from the computer. This is efficient and enables saving of a lot of time that could be wasted searching for information (Unesco, 2011).

When the government ensures that all government institutions use the computers to carry out their duties it enables increase in job opportunities for computer students since they are the ones who will be able to perform these functions, This, therefore, encourages students to study computer since it will lead to them securing a job upon completion of the course. It will also assist the government to carry out its processes fastest, efficiently and avoid errors in their performance. It should also be noted that computers can also lead to people losing their jobs because the duties that could be performed by people are now taken by the computers, therefore, the government should find alternative ways to add job opportunities for students who study computer and technological education (Unesco, 2011).

Creating a new job sector which includes software engineering: The government has also increased job opportunities for those that study computer and technological education by creating a completely new job sector for them. In the past jobs like software engineering were not present but with the introduction of computer and technological education, the gradual effect is some new careers are introduced, for example, software engineering. Software engineering is set up to ensure these engineers research ways they can make new software for the computers that will assist in the computer working. They are also other job opportunities, for example, those who work to come up with more computers or carry out its repairs. Others work to improve the versions of the computer. When there are diverse jobs that computer and technological education when they complete their studies then the students will be motivated to continue with their studies and also new students will develop an interest in learning this course. An increase in job opportunities will also lead to an increase in the country's economy significantly.

Employing teachers who teach computer and technological education: This affects technological and computer education in two different ways. When the government employees' teachers to teach computer and technological education, it increases the job opportunities that this course can offer. Students are therefore assured that they will not lack jobs when they complete their education. Teachers who teach computer and technological education must have also studied the course to ensure they have what it takes to pass the information to their students. The government, therefore, employees them in the public institutions to ensure the students also receive knowledge of the computer too.

Another way in which employing teachers who teach computer and technological education assists this sector is the students who are taught can receive these skills which they can pass to other people or use them for their benefit. For there to be education going on there is a need for teachers to be present. The government should carefully select teachers who will deliver skills in the required way and who can interact with their students effectively to promote better understanding. These teachers must also be dedicated to their work such that they offer only the best and nothing else.

10.3.9. Funding a Revolution

The computer revolution is the digital revolution that is the shift from mechanical and analog electronic technology to digital electronics which began in the late 1950s to the late 1970s. It involves adoption and proliferation of digital computers and digital record keeping that continues to the present. The computer and the digital revolution are expensive.

Computer revolution is deeply embedded in computer and technological education. It is typically associated with the onset of new technologies or devices. An example may include the invention of a tablet, which is cheaper than a computer. This has significant benefits in terms of wide adoption because all students can own their tablet because it is easy and cheap to purchase. This wouldn't be possible with a computer, which is typically more expensive than the tablet, hence making it out of reach for most students. Also, the computer revolution enables students to get more digitalized studying materials that are associated with computer. As a result, the students can study more effectively with plenty of material they need. The computer revolution, therefore, makes the study of computer and technical education more interesting, fun, efficient and increases the opportunity of each student to access a computer device or have contact with one (Farrell, 2007).

The government, therefore, needs to fund these computer revolutions since it is expensive and it may be difficult for an individual may fail to do it on their own. An example of the computer revolution that occurred and how the government aided the process is in Kenya when they were transiting from analog to digital the government offered free digital televisions to the people in the poor communities so that they can abandon the analog televisions. In the sector of education, the government helped in the computer revolution by offering students in the classroom tablets to enable students to have access to technology that will aid technological and computer studies (Farrell, 2007).

10.3.10. Creating Awareness of the Computer and Technological Education

Many people do not know that computer and technological education exists and what its advantages are. This has caused many individuals to lack jobs despite being learned because they lack the necessary skills required to operate the computer. People more in rural areas do not know how to operate a computer since most of them have never encountered or even used a computer.

The government has to ensure that all its citizens know what a computer is and how it is used. The only way is by them going to an educational center that offers computer and technological education and being taught how it is used but since this people do not know if it exists or even its advantages in their lives, the government is obligated to create awareness to them such that they do not remain outdated. The government may involve many ways to ensure students in all part of the country receive knowledge of this subject and its importance and they work to receive the education (Farrell, 2007).

These include using the mass media where they may advertise the course and its benefits through the television, radio, ads in the computers and mobile phones. The government can also spread and create awareness about it during the public speaking example national holiday celebrations, they can introduce to the individuals the importance of studying computer and technological education and explain to the people about technological and computer revolution and its effects. Since there is an increase in computer and technological revolution students and people must be made aware of this to prevent any misunderstandings that may arise in the future (Odera, 2011).

10.3.11. Creating Eligibility for the People

Eligibility is the state of having the right to do or obtain something through the satisfaction of the appropriate conditions. The government should create eligibility of its citizens to enable them to acquire computer and technological education in ways that include; ensuring laws that revolve around this sector of education is favorable such that it does not hinder any individual from obtaining this education, ensuring that all citizens have equal rights to obtaining computer and technological education, reducing tax that is payable to the government which is associated with the study of computer and technical education and making the fee that computer and technology education is offered with favorable (Odera, 2011).

By ensuring laws that revolve around this sector of computer and technical education is favorable it means that the laws that the government enacts to regulate the computer and technological education are favorable such that it does not hinder any students from acquiring this education. If the laws set are favorable more students will be able to acquire it. Some laws which may be set for example computer and technological education will only be received if the students have learned to a level of degree may disadvantage the children who may fail to reach that level but if it states that any student can receive this education as early as elementary level then it will be eligible enough.

The government creates eligibility by ensuring that all citizens have equal rights to obtaining computer and technological education. Since the government is responsible for making and enacting laws it should make laws that favor all students and not favor only a specific group of individuals. The example of making rules that the students who can obtain a computer and technological education are only those who are learned above the degree level is also applicable in such a situation. If the government makes such a law then it will disadvantage the less fortunate students hence eligibility reduces (Odera, 2011).

Another way in which computer and technological education may be made eligible by the government is reducing the tax that is payable to the government which is associated with the study of computer and technical education. If the tax that is payable to the government is reduced, then there will be a gradual decrease in the fees that the students undertaking this course are paying will also decrease. If the tax that the institution that offers computer and technological education is increased, then it means that they will have to increase their fee too so that they may acquire profit for the services they are offering but if tax reduces then they too will decrease their fee.

When the government follows these ways there will be an increase in technological and computer education and more students will acquire the required skills to operate a computer therefore, they will fit appropriately to the society. It is therefore important that the government gets involved in the study of computer and technological education (Odera, 2011).

10.4. ADVANTAGES OF GOVERNMENT INVOLVEMENT IN COMPUTER AND TECHNOLOGICAL EDUCATION

As we have noticed above, the government is highly involved in the study of computer and technological educations. Due to this involvement, several advantages and disadvantages arise which may promote more students to learn computer and technological education and bring the success of this field. The advantages that arise as a result of the government getting involved in computer and technological education is mainly shown by the advantages of technology in the classroom since the government enables technology to be incorporated in the classrooms. These advantages include;

10.4.1. Helps Children to Stay Motivated During the Learning Process, Encourages More Communication between Teachers and Parents

Technology options in the classroom are very affordable, creates new ways to learn for today's student, technology allows us to give students access to data from a single location,

It gives us better access to behavioral data on students, technology helps to prepare students for their future world, allows for the teaching of needed vocational skills, technology in the classroom encourages collaboration, encourages students to stay engaged with their learning environment and teachers have more credibility when they use technology in the classroom (Odera, 2011).

10.4.2. Helps Children to Stay Motivated During the Learning Process

Figure 10.7. *A teacher motivating students to study by observing their progress.*

Source: http://blog.spaweek.com/2013/05/06/teacher-appreciation-day/.

When the government gets involved in computer and technological education, it helps students get motivated during their study because they are assured of getting employment after they complete their study.

Majority of the student does not enjoy going to school if they lack a purpose of attending it therefore, they need to have reasons that will enable them and motivate them to attend lectures. When there is technology allowed in the classroom, it allows students to work at their own pace without having to interfere with the work of other students. Teachers therefore only have to ensure these students are performing the work needed and in the appropriate way. Learning with a computer is way fun than writing on paper with a pen therefore students are motivated to learn. Students can research about what they will be learning that day to gain knowledge about the topic before the teachers teach them, play educational games that will enable them to understand their lessons better or work on advanced material using a program which is created for their use for example earn (Farrell, 2007).

Most of the technology options that are used by students enable them to see how well they are doing compared to the average of all users an example being the application Grammarly that rates the students writing. This enables students to rate themselves and this encourages them to study as it motivates them. Also, programs that enable or facilitate the learning of students give them awards or certificates that encourages students to study and motivates them more because they feel appreciate more.

When the government gets involved in computer and technological education it provides these computers or tablets to the students which have study pieces of equipment that enable students of all walks of life to have access to computers including those in the disadvantaged areas. Therefore, students from all walks of life get motivated to study as they have resources already given to them by the government to study computer and technological education (Farrell, 2007).

10.4.3. It Encourages More Communication between Teachers and Parents

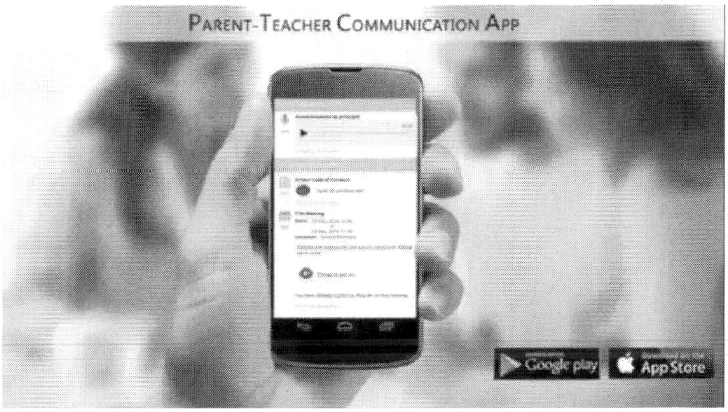

Figure 10.8. *Communication between teachers and parents using a technological device.*

Source: https://www.gurutechnolabs.com/wp-content/uploads/2018/09/schoolapp.png.

Communication is transmission of information from one person to another. Technology aids with communication using devices that speed up and facilitate information exchange. Students who learn the computer and technological education can invent devices that facilitate communication. These devices aid in teachers and parents' communication in several ways. Teachers can communicate the students' progress to the parents and parents can communicate conditions that the students may be facing that the teacher should take note of in the classroom. The teacher can also communicate with the parent or require the parent to attend the school session or the conference. It is better than the traditional methods since traditionally they would send the students home with letters and the students could fail to deliver them. Also, the processes were very slow as compared to this era that they include computers and other technological devices (Odera, 2011).

This, therefore, means that when technology is incorporated in the classroom, then there are more opportunities for parents and teachers to connect.

Parents can easily see their children in the class using a particular blog, therefore, they can ensure their children attend lectures and they can supervise their child's behaviors when in class which helps them to understand their children better. They can also know the homework the child is given so that they can help them work on it when they are at home and they can supervise and rate how the teachers deliver their message to see if it is effective to plan for the future of their child.

Apps and software options allow teachers to instantly report on a child's behavior to let parents know in real-time what is happening throughout the day.

Teachers can also chat with the parents or send messages to the parents in case of a meeting. If the parents are many, teachers can easily send messages to all of them due to technologies help therefore they can broadcast information easily (Odera, 2011).

There is also the email that is used for communication of very important information. The email is mainly used by the schools when communicating very important information that requires the whole school to be aware of.

The technology was mainly integrated into the classroom around 1990s and it has been used since then. It created more reliability in communication between teachers and parents should there be a need to communicate.

Government involvement in computer and technical education, it enables more students to know how to utilize these technological devices. It also assists parents to be aware of these technological devices and how to use them. Many schools can acquire these technological devices due to the help of the government and hence they can promote communication between the teachers and parents. Lastly, the laws that are enacted promote the use of these technological devices in the schools for communication (Odera, 2011).

10.4.4. Technology Options in the Classroom Are Very Affordable

Figure 10.9. *Students in work with technological options.*

Source: https://edtechmagazine.com/k12/article/2019/11/how-leverage-your-classroom-tech-project-based-learning.

Earlier technology was very expensive hence it could not be introduced in the classrooms. As other technological options were invented, they became gradually cheaper and more accessible. These technological options include tablets and mobile phones. Schools can easily purchase tablets for each student. Therefore, despite the cost of having technology in the classroom, tablets and class essentials are cheaper due to buying them in bulk.

The government has enabled students to access technological options, for example, giving and distributing free laptops in the schools. This enables schools to get technological material at a cheap price and an affordable one.

For example, most student computers cost less than $200 each, and there are several grants available at the local, state, and national levels to offset these costs.

The internet can make a good education result since the printing press and, in doing so, make the cost-benefit analysis much easier for most students. "It could allow American schools to serve twice as many students as they do now, and in ways that are both effective and cost-effective." as stated by a great philosopher (Farrell, 2007).

10.4.5. It helps Creates New Ways to Learn for Students Today

The incorporation of technology in the classroom enables students to learn in different languages and it creates new ways for students to learn. A child is either emotionally intelligent, creatively intelligent, or instructional intelligent. Earlier education was mainly instructional based such that it mainly focused on the child following the instruction given to them. With the incorporation of technology, it has enabled lectures to focus on all the three forms of intelligence. It can affect their emotional intelligence. It also requires them to be creative and it enhances their creativity and it gives the children instructions that should be followed.

Standardized tests and similar ranking tools do the same. When children have access to today's technology, then those who excel outside of the standard learning can still be successful and achieve their fullest potential.

The use of technology enables children to use their creative intelligence in multiple ways such as the children can try out new things without having to fear that they might get embarrassed or ashamed since it enables them to remain anonymous and no one will know who did what using the computers and technological options. This process allows kids to work to try new things that they have never done before and that they lack knowledge of the outcome, to see if a different strategy helps them to learn more effectively.

The government involvement in computer and technological education enables students to be able to access computers and technological options and it helps them incorporate them in the classrooms and hence children to have many ways they can use to study instead of one way that could easily prove boring to the students and demotivate them from studying.

10.4.6. Technology Allows Us to Give Students Access to Data from a Single Location

Instead of students having to take a lot of time while they are conducting their research, technology enables students to access a lot of information way faster than having to visit the library to conduct their research where they will have to search for 4 or 5 books and have to read through them to find the information that they require hence they save on time and they can do extensive research that is more accurate than using their knowledge. The use of technology saves children the stress of having to go to the library and go through an encyclopedia to enable them to find information for their assignment or to enable them to complete their project.

Technology allows a student to access every item they need for a project from a central resource. Instead of spending all of that time searching for something specific or waiting for your library to order it, you can run a few queries on Google and find what you need and also you will find other resources that are identical that can help you to find alternative ways to complete the assignment or project.

The government involvement in technology enables educational research to be carried out using the computer which is beneficial as it breeds good performance.

10.4.7. It Gives Us Better Access to Behavioral Data on Students

There are several software or apps that track the student's behavior, if they attend lectures, how they behave and how they react to certain situations. These apps enable parents and teachers to track the student's behavior to ensure they are following the rules that they should follow and know how to react if the student does not follow rules appropriately. The teachers or parents create a school profile for their children where they can track their kids to ensure they follow rules and this enables the teachers, schools, and parents can work together to identify places where additional learning may be necessary. Technology can even help a school district find their highly capable students to keep pushing them toward more challenging work so that they remain engaged with the learning environment and they can avoid being idly minded at any given time (Bulman & Fairlie, 2015).

Government involvement in technological and computer education still ensures computers are incorporated into the classrooms and ensure that this software aid in the general study of the children.

10.4.8. Technology Helps to Prepare Students for Their Future World

The world changes every year and every decade. New things are introduced daily and there is a need for every individual to keep up with the changing environment.

Medical providers give a specific time that a person should be exposed to a screen that is applied in the classroom to the students through the modern educational system demands that students must be technologically exposed such that they keep up with the change in technology and they become aware of new things that are introduced so that they can be prepared for their future lives as adults.

Technology will continue to evolve and new things will continue to be introduced daily. If students are not made familiar with the current technology, they may fail to understand the new technology and they may struggle with it before they adopt to it but in case, they have the information they are therefore enabled to adopt efficiently as required.

Traditional systems might fail to be as important to teach as a means for some teachers or students. For example, is it more important to have a student learn how to write in cursive or know how to type without using the two-finger chicken-pecking method? Is coding more of an important skill to be taught than learning how to cook? Should kids know how to put a chair together in the woodshop or have the ability to put together their computer?

These are some of the questions the facilitators of education should be able to ask themselves when they want to note the advantage and disadvantages of the use and incorporation of technology in the classroom.

The government involvement in computer and technological education enables students to apply these concepts of using technology in the classrooms to achieve a prepared nation in future that is ready for any form of technology that may be introduced (Bulman & Fairlie, 2015).

10.4.9. The Introduction of Technology Allows for the Teaching of Needed Vocational Skills

Technology allows students to be taught the needed vocational skills. Despite the high price of computers and the high level of poverty in the states, most homes have at least internet connection and home compares or can access online resources. Despite this, many students have their own mobile devices which are way cheaper therefore vocational skills can be instilled in the children during their holidays.

By introducing technology to students from an early age, we can teach them the critical vocational skills that are necessary for success in the digital world. Writing continuously remains a major vocational skill that is instilled in the children since they are continuously typing and therefore these skills can boost their grades and even assist them in their future (Bulman & Fairlie, 2015).

By the government getting involved in computer and technological education many students have had the opportunity of acquiring their computers or technological equipment therefore it has enabled vocational skills to be instilled in the students.

10.4.10. Technology in the Classroom Encourages Collaboration

Classroom collaboration is the ability of students and teachers to be able to collaborate during the lessons to ensure that the students understand what they are being taught fully and they do not misunderstand or misinterpret any piece of information during the lesson. When a teacher uses a textbook to teach, students understand very little and they can retain very minimal information. When the teacher uses an interactive lesson such that they write on the blackboard or whiteboard, the students can grab some little more information up to about 20% of what the teachers are teaching them. If the use of group discussions is added up then students understanding is improved and the percentage of understanding increases by a certain percent since the students can debate the facts that they may not have understood and they come into cohesion over one thing (Odera, 2011).

Technology gives us an easy way to develop collaboration skills for students using online tools that encourage them to work together in safe ways. If kids can then practice what they were taught immediately, there is very little that they will forget.

Therefore, the use of technology enables students to obtain much more information that they understand and they can retain this information. The use of government involvement in the computer and technical education enables students to understand and retain more information since the government ensures the students get involved in the study of computer and technological education.

10.4.11. It Encourages Students to Stay Engaged in Their Learning Environment

It is boring to attend a class that you are already aware of what will be taught just like it is boring to watch a movie that you had already watched before.

Some children will transform into mentors or leaders in this situation to help their fellow students, but there are many more who disengage because they lack stimulation. The introducing of technology in studies is advantageous because it reduces the chances of students learning what they had been taught before. It enables teachers to use different tactics to approach a topic that the child will view as a completely different way hence it will become interesting and more engaging. Teachers can also find the opportunity of introducing new subjects, try new teaching techniques, or use different projects to encourage ongoing learning, which creates more overall engagement and eliminates boredom in the classroom (Odera, 2011).

Figure 10.10. *Government involvement in computer and technological education assists students to find studies interesting and captivating therefore keeping them engaged.*

Source: https://www.brookings.edu/research/how-ed-tech-can-help-leapfrog-progress-in-education/.

10.4.12. Teachers Have More Credibility When They Use Technology in the Classroom

Teachers thought they may become hesitant when introducing or using technology in the classroom because they may dread the end result of integrating it, they come to learn that it is actually a good idea to use it. They can easily assign assignments to the students that they are required to perform when they are at home using the computers and from this, they may save a lot of time and prevent wastage of time by the students.

The parents may also be afraid of giving students technological devices thinking that they will use it to perform a lot of unnecessary things but they actually find it beneficial eventually since it enables the students to learn more than they would without these devices. When you can introduce these elements to the classroom and have children learn there, then you can overcome the socioeconomic barriers that are sometimes in place for low-income families (Odera, 2011).

Therefore, the use of the government in technological education is very beneficial as it assists the growth of the students in general

References

1. Alessandro, D'Atri, Maria, F., Joey, F. G., & Paolo, S., (2011). Information Technology and Innovation Trends in Organizations: ItAIS: The Italian Association for Information Systems (pp. 1–99). Berlin: Springer Science & Business Media.
2. Álvaro, R., Hojjat A., Luís, P. R., & Sandra, C., (2018). Trends and Advances in Information Systems and Technologies (vol. 1, pp. 3–92). Berlin: Springer.
3. Amy, D., Paul, G., Suzanne, W., & Bixuan, S., (2016). Education in Developing Countries – What Policies and Programmes Affect Learning and Time in School? (p. 214). Sweden: Stockholm.
4. Andrew, C., Anthony, E., Alison, H., Gavin, R., & Neil, S., (2014). A Practical Guide to Teaching Computing and ICT in the Secondary School (p. 154). London: Routledge.
5. Barton, R., (2004). Teaching Secondary Science With ICT. (pp. 3–69). London: McGraw-Hill Education (UK).
6. Djordje, M. K., Charoula, A., & Carsten, S., (2013). Improving Computer Science Education (pp. 50–99). London: Routledge.
7. Elisa, R., & Andreas, B., (2017). Managing the Quality of Teaching in Computer Science Education (pp. 1–10). CSERC.
8. Faisal, S., Nadhmi, G., Srikanta, P., Ali, S. S. B., & Fathey, M., (2017). Recent Trends in Information and Communication Technology: Proceedings of the 2nd International Conference of Reliable Information and Communication Technology (IRICT 2017) (pp. 3–100) Berlin: Springer.

9. Farrell, G., (2007). Survey of ICT and Education in Africa: Kenya Country Report (p. 14). ICT in Education in Kenya.
10. Fu Lee, W., Joseph, F., Liming, Z., & Victor, K. S. L., (2009). Hybrid Learning and Education: Second International Conference, ICHL 2009, Macau, China, August 25–27, 2009, Proceedings (pp. 1–89). Berlin: Springer Science & Business Media.
11. George, B., & Robert, W. F., (2015). Technology and education: Computers, software, and the internet. IZA Discussion Paper No. 9432 (p. 67).
12. Hamidu, M. Y., & Mohammed, A., (2014). The Challenges Facing Science Education in Developing Countries and the Way Forward. International Journal of Scientific Engineering and Research (IJSER) (pp. 84–89).
13. Judith, Gal-Ezer, & Chris, S., (2014). A Tale of Two Countries: Successes and Challenges in K-12 Computer Science Education in Israel and the United States. ACM Transactions on Computing Education, 14(2), Article 8, pp. 1–18.
14. Lakshmi, M., (2009). Microteaching and Prospective Teachers (1–79). New Delhi: Discovery Publishing House.
15. Marilyn, L., & John, M., (2000). Teaching and Learning with ICT in the Primary School (pp. 1–81). London: Psychology Press.
16. Masafumi, N., John, M. R., & Marcelita, C. M., (2007). Mathematics and Science Education in Developing Countries: Issues, Experiences, and Cooperation Prospects (pp. 61–68). New Delhi: UP Press.
17. Movaghar, A., (2012). Performance evaluation of computer systems. Semantic Scholar (pp. 1–51).
18. Odera, F. Y., (2011). Computer education policy and its implementation in Kenyan secondary schools. International Journal of Information and Communication Technology Research (pp. 221–229).
19. Orit, H., Tami, L., & Noa R., (2015). Guide to Teaching Computer Science: An Activity-Based Approach (pp. 1–94). Berlin: Springer.
20. Pradeep, K. S., Bijaya, K. P., Nagender, K. S., Sudhir, K. S., & Amit, P. S., (2019). Proceedings of ICETIT 2019: Emerging Trends in Information Technology (pp. 3–95). Berlin: Springer Nature.
21. Sara, H., Brown, O., David, H., Enos Kiforo Ang'ondi, Susan, N., Azra, N., & Leonard, W., (2010). Developing the Use of Information and Communication Technology to Enhance Teaching and Learning in

East African Schools. Nairobi: Centre for Commonwealth Education & Aga Khan University Institute for Educational Development – Eastern Africa Research report No. 1.

22. Seendani, A., (2014). Teaching Computer Science Without Computer (pp. 6–48). Teaching computer science in Afghan secondary schools.
23. Singh, (2008). Teaching of Computer Science (pp. 21–87). New Delhi: APH Publishing.
24. UNESCO, (2011). Transforming Education: The Power of ICT Policies (p. 237). London: UNESCO.
25. Woollard, J., (2007). Learning and Teaching Using ICT in Secondary Schools (pp. 7–98). New York: Learning Matters.

INDEX